Procuring Successful Mega-Projects

For my parents, Ben and Doris Hart
In celebration of the 50th anniversary of their decision to move to Australia.
Good call.

Procuring Successful Mega-Projects

How to Establish Major Government Contracts Without Ending up in Court

LOUISE HART

Routledge
Taylor & Francis Group
LONDON AND NEW YORK

First published in paperback 2024

First published 2015 by Gower Publishing

Published 2016 by Routledge
4 Park Square, Milton Park, Abingdon, Oxon OX14 4RN

and by Routledge
605 Third Avenue, New York, NY 10158

Routledge is an imprint of the Taylor & Francis Group, an informa business

Publisher's Note
The publisher has gone to great lengths to ensure the quality of this reprint but points out that some imperfections in the original copies may be apparent.

British Library Cataloguing in Publication Data
A catalogue record for this book is available from the British Library.

Library of Congress Cataloging-in-Publication Data
The Library of Congress Cataloging-in-Publication Data has been applied for.

ISBN: 978-1-4724-5508-6 (hbk)
ISBN: 978-1-03-283724-6 (pbk)
ISBN: 978-1-315-60229-5 (ebk)

DOI: 10.4324/9781315602295

Contents

List of Figures

Preface

This book represents a distillation of 30 years' experience in the public and private sectors dealing with extremely large contracts. Practically everyone I have encountered professionally in that period has contributed to its development, although most of them are entirely unaware of it. Some contributed more directly by agreeing to be interviewed, reviewing text or sending me information about specific issues or projects: my thanks go to John Alexander, Mike Blanchard, John Brooks, Alan Cameron, Susan Carter, Howard Collins, Adam de Fries, David Enever, Ron Finlay, Danny Graham, Vince Graham, David Harding, Owen Hayford, Matt Hinchcliffe, Doug Jones, Brendan Kavanagh, Clare Kitcher, Simon Linnett, Chris Lock, John Nuttall, Heather Oswald, Fred Paton, Gary Pedersen, Tony Poulter, Juliet Reingold, Kerry Schott and Peter Shepherd.

Special thanks to Anthony Alexander, John Dawes, Pamela Freeman, Sallie Mason, Helen Murray and Dominique Tubier, all of whom read the entire first draft and made comments which enabled me to improve it considerably.

Thanks also to the excellent team at Gower Publishing, especially Jonathan Norman, my commissioning editor. He not only accepted my book proposal more or less by return email, which was immensely encouraging, he also told me to bin the sample chapter I had sent him, which was less encouraging but very good advice.

Notwithstanding all the help I have been so freely given, this remains a very personal account. Except where I have specifically quoted others, the opinions I express and the advice I give are my own. They should not be taken as representing the views of my former employers nor of any other person.

This is a practical book for project directors, written by a former project director who now spends her time as a speaker and independent consultant on major projects and procurement. Although one of my qualifications is a law degree, I have not held a practising certificate as a lawyer in any jurisdiction for 15 years. This book does not constitute legal advice. It refers to various laws, guidelines and law reports, but only by way of illustration, and I do not represent that they are necessarily either current law or applicable to your particular circumstances. If you want legal advice, get a lawyer. If you want advice on how to get a lawyer, read Chapter 10.

Establishing a major Government contract is a tough gig, with long hours and stress an inevitable part of the package. It makes a big difference if you have a spouse who understands what you do for a living and provides unfailing encouragement and support. I can vouch for this. I have one.

Louise Hart

PART I
Introduction

Chapter 1

Introduction

The world changes when Government establishes a contract worth billions. One minute before signature, there is nothing. Just tired people hanging around a table in the lawyers' offices. Sixty seconds later, Government and the contractor have each acquired huge rights and obligations. A little private law has been enacted: the parties are now entitled to the full majesty and protection of the law courts to enforce their bargain. The bridge will be built. The submarines will be delivered. The hospital will provide medical services. The IT system will streamline operations. And if it doesn't happen according to plan, there is a judge out there somewhere whose job it could become to find out who is to blame. The world is now different.

It is not necessarily better. Government projects descend into spectacular failure in embarrassing numbers.

Over the last 30 years there have been many public inquiries into failed Government projects. The specifics of failure are always different, following the *Anna Karenina* principle that every unhappy family is unhappy in its own way, but the inquiries invariably find the roots of failure in the procurement phase. This gives the failures another thing in common. They were unnecessary. Expensive, often appallingly expensive, but unnecessary. If the establishment of the contracts had been better done, every one of those spectacular failures could have been avoided.

> *If the establishment of the contracts had been better done, every one of those spectacular failures could have been avoided.*

Sometimes the contract hasn't even been awarded before the problems trigger a court case. Sometimes the catastrophe takes a few years to manifest itself. But time after time, the failure is caused by something the project director could have identified and sorted out in the procurement phase.

Easily said. A project director who has been charged with establishing the contract for delivery of an extremely large Government project, one where the overall budget is calculated in billions, is working in an extremely difficult environment. I've been there. The pressures are close to overwhelming.

The political stakes are high. The economic stakes are high. The media are all over it. The players in the market are yanking every string they can pull to position themselves to win the tender. The would-be advisers are in your ear and the already-appointed advisers are cluttering your office. The stakeholders are demanding incompatible requirements, the latest public sector hiring freeze has left you with half a team and the Minister wants everything delivered yesterday.

If you are in this position, this book is for you. This is the book I wish someone else had written years ago, so that I could have had the benefit of it when I was establishing major Government contracts. It would have given me some reassurance that yes, the job can be done – with effort, but without rocket science. I could have asked my team to read it, so they would know how to help me. I could have asked my bosses to read it, so they would know how to support me. I could have asked my stakeholders to read it and hoped they might realise theirs was not the only point of view in the universe. You can do all of these things, but what I hope you will do is read the book yourself.

It is not a student textbook. The occasional sentences highlighted along the way may help you notice and remember some of the things I have found particularly important or interesting, but there are no checklists to extract and tick the boxes on, no bullet point summaries at the end of each chapter that save you the bother of reading the chapter at all, no practice exam questions. The only examination you face is cross-examination in the witness box if your project joins the long list of Government fiascos. That isn't an examination you can pass, because if things get that far you have already failed. Reading this book will help keep your project off the fiasco list and you out of the witness box.

> *The only examination you face is cross-examination in the witness box if your project joins the long list of Government fiascos.*

One caveat. If you are an employee of a Government agency and you have just been charged with establishing the contract for delivery of an extremely large Government project, but you also have a day job like Infrastructure Director or General Counsel or Head of Procurement, you are *not* the project director. You may still find this book very useful, but the most important thing it will tell you is that setting up a contract on this scale is a full time job. You cannot do it and run a department at the same time. Either ditch the day job for the duration or appoint a dedicated project director.

Your Project

Your task is to establish a contract. Not just any old contract. You want to deliver a binding agreement for the contractor to deliver your mega-project in a way that meets Government's objectives, on terms that represent value for money to Government. Your task is a project in itself, separate from and additional to the mega-project which forms the subject matter of the contact, and quite unlike the examples normally found in project management textbooks. The application of project management principles is always a good idea, but you need to think about things differently when your deliverable is as long as a piece of string and commits the Government to staggering amounts of expenditure. Establishing a contract for someone else to deliver a project is qualitatively different from managing the delivery of a project.

Establishing a contract for someone else to deliver a project is qualitatively different from managing the delivery of a project.

To help you make sense of your project, the book is divided into parts:

- The Contract
- The People
- The Procurement Process
- Finishing in Style.

THE CONTRACT

People seem happy to accept that there will be significant design and development required for a fleet of trains, or a bridge, or whatever the underlying project is, but somehow expect that a contract will miraculously spring into being fully formed. The truth is, contracts also need a design and development phase, which requires just as much thought as the design and development of the underlying project.

There is also a tendency to think that since the final detail of the contract will have to be negotiated with the selected tenderer, it does not matter if the contract issued with the Request for Tenders is an early draft. It matters a lot. You won't enter the delivery phase with a litigation-proof contract if you don't enter the procurement phase with one. The terms of the contract will dictate the pricing put forward: a poorly-developed contract means the successful tenderer cannot be held to the bid price. Time pressure is no excuse. Concluding negotiations on a poorly-drafted contract is likely to take longer than the time it would have taken to develop the contract properly in the first place, and the longer negotiations go on, the more Government will concede.

You need to understand where the limits are, so you don't allow Government to be sucked into accepting the unacceptable.

The chapters in this Part follow the process for contract development. The first step, examined in Chapter 3, is to understand what Government wants to achieve and the scope of work required to deliver that. From this a choice can be made of the type of contract to be developed. At this time, too, you need to understand where the limits are, so you don't allow Government to be sucked into accepting the unacceptable.

Chapter 4 builds on this to examine what, precisely, you want the contractor to do and how you are going to incorporate it in the contract. The division of obligations between Government and the contractor needs to be made on a sensible basis and without ambiguity. Most contract disputes relate to the specification: make the investment to get it right.

Chapter 5 examines how to use the contract as a tool for risk management, through the appropriate allocation of risk and the inclusion of obligations to undertake activities that have the effect of reducing risk. It also examines some risks specific to mega-projects that need to be dealt with in the contract.

Chapter 6 takes risk management a stage further, looking at contract performance incentives as a way to improve the chances of success of the underlying project. Some incentives are inherent in the contract structure, while others need to be specially developed to ensure the incentives drive the outcomes you want, not the outcomes you don't want. Contractors will not hesitate to 'game' the incentives if you make it possible for them to do so.

Chapter 7 looks at the contract 'boilerplate', a derogatory term for the clauses nobody wants to read. Many clauses, such as those covering default and termination, are only of use in situations you hope will never happen, but they can have a profound impact on Government's ability to manage the contract you deliver, and therefore on the success of the project overall.

THE PEOPLE

You don't set up a contract for a mega-project in isolation. The range of stakeholders is on a par with the scale of the project itself, and public sector stakeholders are in a class of their own. If you are new to the public sector, pay particular attention to the first two chapters in this Part. The differences between the private sector and the public sector can be exaggerated, but they are real and you need to tailor your approach accordingly.

Chapter 8 examines the role of the Minister and how your dealings with other stakeholders are affected by the Ministerial relationship. This is rarely relevant for small projects, but when the contract value is denominated in billions, political involvement is a given.

When the contract value is denominated in billions, political involvement is a given.

Chapter 9 looks at the Government agency that will be entering into the contract, focusing on how to find and train your team. I have assumed you will be directly employed by the Agency, which may not always be the case, but if you are working in some other part of Government (perhaps on a cross-Government shared services project) very similar considerations will apply.

The next two chapters are there to help you engage and get the best value from the advisers you will need to assist you. Since your deliverable is a contract, your key advisers are the lawyers, and they have the whole of Chapter 10 to themselves. Because this is a Government contract, you may need to deal with parliamentary counsel, and uncover the mysteries of how to identify sources of authority in the public sector organisations. Chapter 11 looks principally at financial and technical advisers, but also considers other advisers you may need or have foisted upon you.

Chapter 12 is about how to make governance work to support you rather than hinder you. It looks at how to establish functional governance frameworks for the project and for the evaluation of the tenders. It also looks at the use of Gateway reviews and other independent checks to provide you and others with the assurance you need to keep the project on track.

THE PROCUREMENT PROCESS

Having and following a good procurement process is critical for success. It doesn't just save you from being sued for process failures: if you get it right it also means you will select a contractor who is capable of doing the job. A failing contractor may sue you in the delivery phase out of desperation; a successful contractor won't need to.

One of the problems with a mega-project is that the Agency's standard form procurement process will not be appropriate. Many of the techniques used on small procurements are actively counter-productive when applied to large scale projects, and public sector procurement processes are cluttered with myths about what probity does and does not require.

Chapter 13 examines how to establish a process that is fair to bidders but still enables you achieve good outcomes for Government without tying yourself in knots.

Chapter 14 looks at how to put out your communications to the market effectively, from the market sounding through to the issue of a Request for Tenders, so as to command the best quality bids the market has to offer.

Once the bids are received you have to evaluate them. This is the subject of Chapter 15, which examines the evaluation methodology: establishing evaluation criteria, structuring the evaluation process and scoring system and selecting a preferred bidder.

When the contract is for something on the scale of a mega-project, no bid will be capable of simple acceptance. Chapter 16 is about the negotiation required to bridge the gap between the draft contract you issued with the Request for Tenders and the final contract you will sign with your chosen bidder.

Chapter 17 looks at how to ensure your procurement process will withstand challenge, and how to discourage any challenge from being made.

FINISHING IN STYLE

Your carefully-crafted contract will not work effectively unless people understand what is in it and their own role in its delivery.

With the contract established, the final hurdle is the transition from contract establishment to contract management, examined in Chapter 18. Whether you will stay to manage the contract yourself, or hand it over to a dedicated contract manager, this transition needs to be managed well. Your carefully-crafted contract will not work effectively unless people understand what is in it and their own role in its delivery.

Chapter 19 attempts to capture the main themes in this book into a 'Top Ten' list of things to remember. Number 11 is that there are more things in this book than can be captured in a Top Ten.

The Witness Box

You may wonder about my determination to keep you out of the witness box. Why should this book focus on not ending up in court? Surely the objective is not to avoid litigation, but to ensure the mega-project is successfully delivered?

Good question. Let me take a little time to answer it before we delve into the specifics of your contract.

Chapter 2
Ending Up In Court

> *A reputation for settling claims rather than going to court will attract even more lawsuits.*

Litigaphobia, sometimes rendered liticaphobia, is a real word, although not one frequently encountered outside the United States of America. It means fear of lawsuits. Sufferers can experience symptoms such as sweating, nausea, trembling and an overwhelming desire to run away. Litigaphobia is irrational. Throwing up will not improve your chances of success in the litigation. Running away may result in summary judgment against you in a case you should have won. A reputation for settling claims rather than going to court will attract even more lawsuits.

Litigaphobia may be irrational, but it is not irrational to want to avoid lawsuits in connection with major Government contracts. The UK National Audit Office found the Department for Transport spent £1.9 million on the tender process for the InterCity West Coast passenger rail franchise in 2012. It then had to spend a further £2.7 million on professional fees when the losing bidder brought the action for judicial review that led to the competition being cancelled. Plus more than £40 million on compensation costs. Litigation is expensive. It soaks up management time and effort. It attracts negative media attention. It is, in short, a pain in the neck.

That is perhaps reason enough to avoid litigation. But the more serious problem is the negative consequences caused by doing the sort of thing people sue you for, up to and including the spectacular failures that generate public inquiries. Those consequences follow whether or not people actually sue you. You want to stop Government awarding a contract to an incompetent company not because the losing (competent) bidder may sue you for running an unfair process, but because the incompetent company will make a horrible mess of the job.

This book focuses on how to establish a major Government contract without ending up in court, not because litigation is evil (although it feels pretty evil to be on the receiving end) but because the actions that protect you against being sued also protect you against the project itself going wrong. When the project in question costs billions even when things go right, it is worth making a bit of an effort.

The arithmetic of not ending up in court is simple. Cause of action plus motivation equals litigation. Subtract the cause of action. Subtract the motivation. Litigation equals zero.

Causes of Action

When you establish a contract for a mega-project, you are more likely to be sued by the winning bidder than a losing one.

The procurement process itself may give rise to lawsuits by a losing bidder, but you have not necessarily evaded litigation even if the process is not challenged. It may seem counter-intuitive, but when you establish a contract for a mega-project, you are more likely to be sued by the winning bidder than a losing one. Losing bidders can only sue in relation to the procurement process itself. Winning bidders are still there when the procurement process is over and they sign up to a tableful of contractual documentation which opens up a whole new range of opportunities to go to court.

JUDICIAL REVIEW

The usual form of legal action in relation to the procurement process is a request for judicial review, and the essence of the action is a claim that Government has acted unfairly. Governments have an obligation of good faith and fair dealing. Any attempt to argue otherwise, even if a there is a remote chance a case could be made in particular legal circumstances, is a sign that you and your lawyer have lost the plot. Quite apart from the reputational risk associated with fronting up to a judge and claiming it is okay to be unfair and act in bad faith, this is about procuring a successful project. Being unfair not only gives rise to legal claims, it doesn't do the project any good.

Governments do have leeway to do things that in some contexts could be regarded as unfair. For instance, it used to be common in a procurement of large manufactured items (say, submarines) for Governments to give higher scores in the evaluation if manufacture took place locally. (This is now less common, since treaty obligations often require 'local' to be defined so broadly it defeats the purpose of the exercise.) Local preference could result in a foreign tenderer losing out, even if their submarine was in every way better than everybody else's submarine. Unfair? No. Governments are entitled to buy jobs as well as submarines. It may be economically inefficient to procure jobs and submarines in a single tender and there is a risk the jobs will be unsustainable or the submarine won't be as good, but it is not unfair.

At least, it is not unfair if Government tells the bidders in advance that this is how the bids will be evaluated.

Unfairness can manifest itself in many different ways. Things you need to be on the lookout for are:

- Telling bidders you are going to use one set of evaluation criteria or weightings, but then using a different set.

- One bidder getting access to material Government information that the other bidders don't have (particularly difficult where there is an incumbent supplier).

- Administrative decisions, such as granting an extension of time for submissions, that have materially different impacts on different bidders. (Some difference in impact is more or less inevitable, unfairness is a matter of degree.)

- Not giving proper consideration to material factors because of bias for or against one of the bidders.

There are other possible ways to run an unfair tender process, a subject discussed in Part IV. There is no fixed list. Iniquity will not evade judicial review merely by being innovative.

Iniquity will not evade judicial review merely by being innovative.

BREACH OF PROCESS CONTRACT

Sometimes legal action in relation to the procurement process may be couched as an action for breach of the 'process contract' between Government and the bidders. That is, the bidders will say that by going to tender Government has created a contractual relationship with them under which Government has binding obligations to do certain things, such as evaluate bids in accordance with published criteria. Because the nature and extent of the process contract is not always clear, your draft contract and specifications will be accompanied by a document setting out the terms and conditions of the tender. At least they will if you have any sense. One of the early signs of trouble in the Queensland Health Payroll System debacle was the project director sending out a proposals request consisting of one brief email with no technical requirements and no conditions of tender.

The terms and conditions of tender often do not get the attention they deserve in the preparation of the tender documents, possibly because they are seen as a standard form document. The rule of thumb for a mega-project is that the standard form of anything is not going to be adequate. Loose drafting may allow bidders to allege that other terms and conditions are included by implication, with results you did not intend. Do not, for instance, include a provision saying the tender will be carried out in accordance with some code unless you have actually read the code and are satisfied every word of it is appropriate.

In the New South Wales Integrated Ticketing case, the judge was scathing about the terms and conditions contained in the call for tenders, saying 'logic and consistency of expression do not seem to have been regarded by the draftsperson as important'. He went on to say: 'Aspirational statements may provide a warm inner glow but they are no substitute for unambiguous language targeted at actual risks with clearly stated consequences. Had such a call been issued in this case, this litigation may well not have ensued'.

'Aspirational statements may provide a warm inner glow but they are no substitute for unambiguous language targeted at actual risks with clearly stated consequences'.

Sometimes these documents include statements saying they do not give rise to contractual obligations, presumably on the basis that if it isn't a contract, Government can't be sued for breach of it. By all means include whatever disclaimers your lawyers advise are appropriate for your jurisdiction. My own view is you are likely to be better off if you acknowledge the existence of a process contract and make sure it is on favourable terms than if you try to prevent a process contract arising at all. (Prevention will fail. There will be a process contract, but its terms may not be what you want.)

The fact remains that if you say to bidders you are going to do one thing and then do another, you are at risk whether you say it in a document labelled 'contract' or say it in an informal communication.

CAUSES OF ACTION AFTER AWARD OF CONTRACT

Once you have signed up your contract with the winning bidder, and the losing bidders are no longer in the picture, the form of an action brought against you will almost invariably be a suit for breach of contract. Most commonly the contractor will allege that Government has not paid amounts owing to the contractor under the contract. Often the allegation will be that the amount is payable because Government has directed the contractor to do something the contract did not require, so it is entitled to additional payment for the variation. If Government has terminated the contract, the contractor may also allege wrongful termination. Government will of course claim the contractor has failed to meet its obligations under the contract: the alleged variation was not a variation at all but something already required by the contract. Sometimes Government will get its writ in first, so the lawsuit by the contractor will be brought by way of counterclaim. But it is all about breach of contract.

The subject matter of disputes that can arise is as broad as the contract itself. In practice, two categories of dispute swamp all others:

1. What did the specification or scope of work actually require the contractor to do?

2. Who pays to fix the problem if something unexpected happens?

These questions can get a bit tangled: if works are damaged in a flood, the essential problem is whether the contractor pays to fix it, but that may be down to either the scope of works or the risk allocation, or possibly a combination of both. The outcomes may be slightly different.

If the specification required the works to be able to withstand the flood, the fix is to rebuild to a standard capable of resisting such a flood, so that the problem does not recur. If the risk allocation gave the risk of flood damage to the contractor, the fix is to rebuild, but the contractor decides whether to build to a higher standard or take the risk of having to pay again if flooding recurs. If the specification and risk allocation are ambiguous, there will be a dispute.

If the specification and risk allocation are ambiguous, there will be a dispute.

Either way, the action is for breach of contract, so the courts will decide these cases on the basis of what the contract says. The ability of the contractor to bring an action, the ability of Government to defend the action, who wins, who loses, it's all down to the contract.

No matter when the action is brought, even if you are long gone, it is the words you negotiated, the words you recommended to Government that will determine the outcome. If the scope is ambiguous or inadequate, if the contractor has taken on work it is not capable of doing, if Government has taken on obligations it is unable to deliver, disputes will follow. It is not enough to avoid actions for procurement process failure, you need a contract that is fit for purpose. You have to do the deal right, but you also have to do the right deal.

PERSONAL LIABILITY

The good news is that it is very unlikely you will be sued personally. The legal action will normally be brought against the Agency running the tender process

Every form of action which can be brought against the Agency involves the project director having to give evidence.

or entering the contract. The bad news is that every form of action which can be brought against the Agency involves the project director having to give evidence. In the New South Wales Integrated Ticketing case, where the losing tenderer alleged various process failures, the project director was in the witness box for nine whole days, eight of them under gruelling cross-examination. From your point of view, this will feel very much as if you *are* the one being sued.

Why Do They Sue?

In the commercial world, the reason for bringing a lawsuit is to achieve commercial advantage.

PROCUREMENT PHASE

In the context of actions for failure of the procurement process, the most obvious commercial advantages will be:

- securing the contract (having it awarded to the claimant instead of to the winning bidder); or
- securing another opportunity to win the contract (having the competition cancelled and rerun).

These are by no means the only opportunities for commercial advantage. When Virgin Trains brought an action for judicial review of the decision of the UK Department for Transport to award the InterCity West Coast franchise to someone else, the effect was not only to cancel the competition, but also to secure a two-year contract for Virgin Trains to continue as franchisee until a fresh competition could be completed.

The commercial advantage to an incumbent of prolonging the award process can apply even if the incumbent is not eligible to bid at all. The competition for the award of a third television licence in Perth commenced in April 1984. The two existing stations were excluded from bidding on competition grounds, but had no wish to see their lucrative advertising market share diluted. The Australian Broadcasting Tribunal was taken to court by one or both of the two incumbent stations on process grounds not once but multiple times. The new station didn't make it to air until May 1988.

A losing bidder may still see commercial advantage in bringing legal action even if they have no hope of ever being awarded the contract themselves. If a competition is cancelled as a result of a legal challenge, Government may be obliged to compensate all bidders for their lost bid costs, not just the one who might have won. And there is always the possibility that Government will choose to pay the claimant to go away rather than defend court proceedings.

Another reason for bringing proceedings is to get Government's attention. Few bidders will choose litigation as a first option. They will instead call to discuss a problem, or write a letter asking for consideration to be given to their position. If they receive no reply, or only polite nothings, there may come a point when they stop writing letters and serve a writ instead. Court proceedings are not amenable to the brush-off treatment. Virgin Trains had no new cause for complaint when it lodged an application for judicial review of the InterCity West Coast franchise decision. It just hadn't been able to persuade anyone to pay enough attention to Richard Branson's letters of protest.

DELIVERY PHASE

Once the contract has been signed, the tenderer bent on winning the contract becomes the contractor bent on making money from it. Despite the reassuring rhetoric of partnership and cooperation, contractors are in business to make money. This is neither sinister nor immoral. It can, however, be disconcerting when the first employee appointed to the contractor's project team is a claims manager.

Once the contract has been signed, the tenderer bent on winning the contract becomes the contractor bent on making money from it.

Even when all is going well, a contractor can make more money if it can demonstrate that what Government wants is a variation rather an existing contractual requirement. When things are going badly, the range of claims broadens: delay to the project, for instance, brings a risk of claims that the delay is caused by the actions of Government rather than of the contractor.

Worse, when things are going badly, people are more motivated to sue. Psychologically, human beings tend to expend more effort to limit losses than to increase gains. They also dislike accepting responsibility for failure: the contractor's project team may choose to protect their self-respect (not to mention their jobs and bonuses) by blaming their own inadequacies on Government.

Increased motivation can apply at a corporate level. Companies capable of carrying out contracts on the scale of a mega-project are often publicly listed. This means they have an interest in maintaining their share price and an industry of investment analysts anatomising their financial results. A black hole in the accounts caused by the project being late and over budget is a serious issue. If the hole can be plugged by an optimistic estimate of how much it will be possible to recover from a lawsuit against the Government, there is an incentive to maintain both the optimism and the lawsuit for as long as the auditors will allow.

A contractor in really deep trouble may commence lawsuits of even the most tenuous merit in order to achieve some semblance of a bargaining position. When the contractor has managed to drag a project down into the mire, firing them is not necessarily the right answer (although it is probably the right answer more often than Government chooses to do it). A fired contractor may still have legal obligations under the contract, but will have little incentive to clean up worksites, provide as-built drawings, secure Government title to assets or indeed do anything at all. Sometimes the easiest way to get the project delivered is to pay the failed contractor even more money in order to finish the job. From the contractor's point of view, this is better than being fired. From the Government's point of view, it is a public relations nightmare. Being able to characterise payments as a settlement of litigation rather than a reward to the incompetent may make a bad situation somewhat more palatable for Government. Contractors know this. It is a variation on the theme of commencing litigation in the hope of being paid to go away.

Sometimes the easiest way to get the project delivered is to pay the failed contractor even more money in order to finish the job.

PERSONAL GRIEVANCE

Commercial litigation is not always about commercial advantage. The final reason for suing Government, which can apply equally in cases of procurement process failure or post-contract disputes, is a sense of personal grievance. 'How dare they treat us like that?' 'They shouldn't be allowed to get away with this.' 'This is outrageous.' 'They've done this once too often.' 'They promised me.' Feelings such as this can drive behaviour to places where commercial advantage will not go. Exposing Government's perceived iniquity in court can take on an importance that may not be diverted by an offer of settlement or even by an objective view of the chance of success in the litigation. People in advanced stages of outrage are not very good at being objective.

Public Inquiries

Although the thrust of this book is about not ending up in court, being in the public sector means you are not only at risk of being taken to court, you are also at risk of being the subject of a public inquiry. This is like being sued, only worse.

I mentioned earlier that the UK National Audit Office found the Department for Transport spent £1.9 million on the tender process for letting the InterCity West Coast franchise in 2012 and £2.7 million on professional fees when the losing bidder brought the action for judicial review that led to the competition being cancelled. What I didn't mention was that it also found the Department spent a further £4.3 million on the various public inquiries associated with the fiasco.

It isn't just the cost and the time and the stress of being cross-examined in the witness box. At least if you're being sued you can hope to win. Government doesn't initiate a public inquiry unless you've already lost. Most public inquiries are set up by Government specifically to investigate some particularly spectacular failure that has induced a media feeding frenzy.

At least if you're being sued you can hope to win. Government doesn't initiate a public inquiry unless you've already lost.

There are a number of different types of public inquiry. The Laidlaw Inquiry into the InterCity West Coast franchise, for instance, was initiated internally by the UK Department for Transport: Sam Laidlaw was the lead non-executive director of the Department's advisory Board. Although the report was tabled in parliament, Laidlaw had no special powers of investigation in conducting his inquiry.

The Queensland Health Payroll System debacle, in contrast, was investigated by a Commission of Inquiry pursuant to an Order in Council under the Queensland *Commissions of Inquiry Act 1950*, with coercive powers to require the attendance of witnesses, the production of documents and so on (although powers in relation to the use of listening devices were excluded by the terms of the Order in Council).

There will generally be a standing parliamentary Select Committee with responsibilities in relation to whichever Agency has covered itself in something other than glory: even if there is no separate inquiry established, the matter is bound to be raised in the Committee's ordinary proceedings. Hansard will record the awkward questions and pathetic answers, to the discomfiture of all involved.

Some jurisdictions have standing anti-corruption bodies, such as the New South Wales Independent Commission Against Corruption. These bodies generally have independent choice of what matters to investigate and extensive powers with which to conduct the investigation. Their inquiries may be carried out privately, so a notification that the body is about to hold a public inquiry is often not the start of an investigation but the announcement of when the dramatic denouement will be played out for the media.

Whatever the type of public inquiry, you don't want it. The only sure way not to have a public inquiry into a Government fiasco is not to have the fiasco. The good news is, the steps you take to avoid a fiasco are the same ones you take to avoid ending up in court.

The place to start is with the contract.

PART II
The Contract

Chapter 3
The Project

Establishing a major Government contract is a project in itself. You, as project director, have been charged with bringing the contract into existence. Your job is to deliver the best contract you can: the right parties, the right terms, the right price. But the contract is being brought into existence not for its own sake but as a means to an end. It is the subject matter of the contract – the bridge, the submarines, the hospital, the IT system – that Government really wants.

Ask why.

If you have just secured a prestigious and (by public sector standards) highly-paid job as project director, you may feel this would be looking a gift horse in the mouth. The Minister has made the decision – who are you to challenge it?

Asking for reasons is not a challenge, you just need to know. When you are setting up a contract for something on the scale of a mega-project, the contract documents will take up all of the available space on a boardroom table. Every clause and sub-clause in the contract, every clause and sub-clause in the subsidiary agreements, every paragraph and sub-paragraph in the specifications, each and every one represents a choice to be made. The contract is delivered when you put together all of those thousands of choices and add the requisite number of signatures, but the people whose signatures appear on the documents do not make those choices, at least not clause by clause. They sign up to the final package. As project director, you are responsible for putting that package together. If you don't know why Government made the decision to proceed, it will be the wrong package.

If you don't know why Government made the decision to proceed, it will be the wrong package.

The world changes when the contract is signed. Make sure you know what the new world is supposed to look like.

Strategic Alignment

Asking why is not a challenge, but sometimes you need to challenge the reasons you are given. Otherwise you will end up not just with the wrong package, but the wrong project.

Anything big enough to be labelled a mega-project is strategic more or less by definition. It should therefore be undertaken for strategic reasons. If it is a health project, such as building a new hospital, it should align with Government's overarching strategy for the provision of health services over the next 20-plus years. It is not enough that its location in a marginal electorate aligns with Government's strategy for being re-elected.

It does occasionally happen that a Minister in pre-election mode will announce a stupendously large project without adequate consideration of whether the project is deliverable, fundable or provides a benefit in excess of the costs to be incurred. A mere announcement can be withdrawn after the election at the cost of a broken promise: cheap as chips, judging by the breakage rate. But if Government goes through a full tender process, the costs of deciding not to proceed with the project will be measured not just in millions but in tens or even hundreds of millions. The cancellation of the $2 billion Sydney CBD Metro project in 2010, 16 months after the original announcement, reportedly cost the NSW Government around half a billion dollars, much of it in compensation to bidders. A decision by the incoming Government in Victoria in late 2014 to cancel the recently-awarded East West Link toll road contract met the added complication of having to unwind a $3.5 billion debt facility syndicated across some 20 banks and other financial institutions.

> *The public sector rarely pushes back very hard when the politicians make a decision.*

The public sector rarely pushes back very hard when the politicians make a decision. If what Government is doing will deliver benefits and is not manifestly stupid, then civil servants mostly take the view that their own preference for other benefits is just one of those things. Governments are elected to make choices about how taxpayers' money is spent, let them get on with it. The usual approach in the public sector is to support your preferred outcome until the Government has made its decision on the way forward, then shut up and get on with implementing Government's choice.

Unfortunately, every now and again a Government will go with an option that *is* manifestly stupid. Ideally you will have spotted this in time to avoid accepting the job in the first place. Virulent opposition from intelligent commentators is a useful clue, as is a non-existent business case. Once you have accepted the job, you are in a very difficult position indeed if you become convinced the project itself is a seriously bad idea. Should you try to make it over into something less toxic, or tell the Minister to pull the plug? That one has to go to a conscience vote. Just remember, the longer you leave it, the more expensive it will be to cancel the project.

Hidden Objectives

Blatant electioneering is deplorable, but it is unreasonable to expect a politician to pay no attention to politics. Any mega-project will have negative side effects. The light rail system of tomorrow is the traffic-jam-generating construction site of today. Local businesses serving the old hospital lose custom that is not replaced when the new hospital opens elsewhere. When the bridge opens, the ferry crew lose their jobs. This will not be highlighted in the media release. Ministers know you can't make omelettes without breaking eggs, but they don't want bits of eggshell and goo all over their faces.

Ministers know you can't make omelettes without breaking eggs, but they don't want bits of eggshell and goo all over their faces.

Suppose Government wants to buy fighters for the air force. The procurement will, whether Government likes it or not, create or preserve jobs in aeroplane manufacturing. If the local industry currently only survives through taxpayer-funded protectionism, Government may be delighted if the contact is awarded elsewhere and the subsidy-eating factory closes. It is likely to be political suicide to say so. The aeroplane procurement will also create or preserve jobs in aeroplane maintenance. The physical location of the maintenance will be driven by the deployment of the aeroplanes, but the jobs could go to defence forces personnel or to external contractors. If current aeroplane maintenance is riddled with expensive inefficiencies, Government will be pleased to see a change and triggering this outcome may even have been the primary driver for the aeroplane procurement. But it is not an objective your Minister will necessarily admit to in public.

In crafting the media release for the announcement of the project, outcomes which play well in the political arena (lots of shiny new aeroplanes!) will have been represented as objectives. Outcomes which do not play well in the political arena (the people who maintain the old aeroplanes will lose their jobs!) will not appear. If pushed, the Minister will have represented these outcomes not as objectives but as regrettable consequences that must not be allowed to stand in the way of the great and glorious mega-project. This, in a public relations context, is all perfectly normal and you do not need to get excited about it.

You do need to understand the reality behind the media release. If there is a hidden purpose of the project, perhaps to stop paying subsidies or to transfer workers to the private sector, the package you put forward for signature will need to deliver that.

Identifying the Showstoppers

> *Any project develops its own momentum. The momentum of a mega-project is correspondingly large.*

Knowing what you want is fundamental, but you also need to know what you don't want. Any project develops its own momentum. The momentum of a mega-project is correspondingly large. Unless you have clear grounds for deciding *not* to enter the contract, there is a very real danger of becoming gradually committed to a deal that would never have been considered acceptable if it had been offered at the start. Mega-projects are particularly at risk because it takes months, sometimes many months, to complete the tender process. It is 100 per cent certain that before you can get to the point of executing the contracts, unexpected things will have happened. Unless you have absolute clarity of purpose, you will deal with these things in whatever way seems expedient at the time. When the time comes for hindsight, you may wish you hadn't.

In 1998 the UK National Audit Office produced a report into the £1.7 billion 1996 flotation of Railtrack, part of the highly complex and politically charged privatisation of British Rail. The situation was loaded with hidden agendas, but the National Audit Office determined that 'Government's policy was to secure the sale of Railtrack within the lifetime of the then current parliament' and the 'main objective for the flotation of Railtrack ... was to secure the flotation as soon as reasonably practicable'. The only possible showstopper was the fall of the Government before the flotation could be accomplished.

Nothing was allowed to stand in the way of the flotation. Performance regimes not fully tested in circumstances of disruption? Make the train companies pay £75 million a year in access charge supplements to compensate. Shaky balance sheet? Write off £869 million of debt. Not sure if employees and the general public will buy shares? Add £47 million of incentives. Institutional investors don't see growth opportunities? Include the Thameslink 2000 project, reducing flotation proceeds by around £125 million. Directors still edgy about signing the prospectus? Promise the chairman a knighthood.

Measured against its simple objective, the privatisation was a resounding success. Given the subsequent history (multi-fatality train crashes, multi-billion pound cost overruns and a complete breakdown in the relationship with Government that saw Railtrack put into administration), one may speculate that better outcomes might have been secured if the show had been stopped.

Where the overriding purpose of a major contract is to raise money by selling a business or asset, it is relatively easy to determine what should constitute a showstopper. In July 2013 the NSW Government embarked on the sale of Macquarie Generation, a state-owned electricity generator, with the announced objective 'to unlock funds for critically needed infrastructure across NSW'. (Translation: 'raise money'.) The agreed showstopper was that the sale would not go ahead if the sale proceeds did not exceed the retention value of the asset. This amount, although not made public, was calculated before assessing any tender.

Where the overriding purpose of a major contract is to raise money by selling a business or asset, it is relatively easy to determine what should constitute a showstopper.

Of the three bids received, only one exceeded the retention value, and that one required clearance from the Australian Competition and Consumer Commission (ACCC). In the media release announcing the decision in early 2014 to accept the $1.7 billion bid, subject to clearance by the ACCC, the NSW Treasurer was able to state unequivocally, 'Should the ACCC not provide clearance … the Government will not proceed with the sale of Macquarie Generation at this time.' Absolute clarity. We're doing this to raise money. If we don't raise enough money, we won't do it. Clearance was refused by the ACCC (something unexpected *always* happens before you can sign the contract), but the bidder appealed to the Australian Competition Tribunal, which allowed the deal to go ahead, and the sale was eventually completed in September 2014.

When the contract being established is a procurement rather than a sale, things get more difficult. Typically you will be procuring something complicated: submarines or a railway line or a hospital, which need to be specially manufactured or constructed; the development and implementation of major IT systems; or the provision of complex services over a number of years. It is rarely obvious in advance what will constitute a genuine showstopper. These things tend to be matters of degree and of balancing a range of outcomes. One or two slices of salami aren't important, particularly if offset by other benefits. On the other hand, if you keep slicing you will run out of sausage.

Don't set absolute exit points, but work out trigger points for project reviews: define circumstances where Government should step back and take a good look at whether the project should proceed.

Guidance for Contract Development

You are responsible for putting together the contract package, but you won't be personally drafting the contract and specifications or the Request for Tenders.

Take that clarity of purpose and turn it into a formal set of objectives for your project team.

Dozens of people, perhaps even hundreds, will be providing inputs. They need guidance on what is acceptable and desirable. You now know why Government wants the project, and you have at least an idea of what might constitute a showstopper. Take that clarity of purpose and turn it into a formal set of objectives for your project team.

In theory, those objectives should have been set before a project director is appointed. In practice, you may need to invent them, or at least tweak them a bit. The NSW Government decided in the autumn of 2004, after a sweltering summer, to replace some 500 carriages of old non-air-conditioned passenger rolling stock with new trains that would become known as Waratahs. A Treasury official correctly pointed out that if the new trains were also not air-conditioned, the replacement would be significantly cheaper. He did leave the room alive, but it was touch and go for a minute there. To ensure the procurement team would not be swayed by helpful advice of this nature, a requirement that the new trains be air-conditioned was promptly added to the formal objectives.

Sometimes you will be handed an objective that is undeliverable. Public relations puffery such as 'secure the future of the industry' can be ignored, or even regarded as deliverable if you take a sufficiently short term view of the future, but substantive objectives need to be achievable.

Schedule objectives are frequently both wildly optimistic and unnecessarily specific, because Ministers have a distressing tendency to announce a schedule before the scope has been established. Fantasy produces brilliant fiction but horrible project outcomes. Scope is what you put into the schedule – if you don't know what the scope is, you don't know what the schedule is either. If the unrealistic objective is retained, then either the deadline will be met by sacrificing something important or the deadline will be missed, making the Minister look foolish.

Sacrificing the important in an attempt to gratify the egos of politicians is a classic way to end up in court, but equally, the procurement team is not there to make the Minister look foolish. You can sometimes skate round the media relations problem by pretending the Minister was talking about when project delivery would start rather than when it would finish (I have done that and more or less got away with it), but a better option is to negotiate a more realistic objective before any overly specific public announcement has been made.

If you can't be realistic, be vague. The pressure to move faster than is consistent with good project outcomes will be quite bad enough without setting up undeliverable expectations. But keep the vagueness over there in public relations. Your own team needs specific objectives if you are to manage the project effectively.

The pressure to move faster than is consistent with good project outcomes will be quite bad enough without setting up undeliverable expectations.

DISSEMINATING THE OBJECTIVES

It is no use having objectives if people working on the project don't know what they are. Put the objectives into any document that will be used for reference purposes – project plans, requests for expressions of interest or for tenders, approval requests and so on.

Bear in mind that objectives may change on the sometimes tortuous route between bright idea and Cabinet approval. People involved with development of a project during the embryonic phases may never have been informed that the world has moved on. Since they are already convinced they know what the objectives are, they are likely to skip over the introductory paragraphs in documents and fail to notice that the one headed 'Objectives' is not in accordance with their view of the world. Point it out to them.

When the objectives have been settled, be systematic about making sure the entire project team knows what they are and keep them front and centre, especially when decisions are being made.

Scope

Once you have your objectives, you know what you are trying to achieve. This is not the same thing as knowing what you are going to do.

Establishing a contract is an unusual project in that it finishes in the middle. The moment when your contract is signed will be the culmination of months of effort, but that effort is only part of the larger project to deliver whatever it is your contract is for. You may be 'successful' in establishing the contract, but no one will regard this as a success if the underlying project is then a disaster. This means you need to go beyond the traditional project manager's scoping exercise, which looks only at what the project manager needs in

You may be 'successful' in establishing the contract, but no one will regard this as a success if the underlying project is then a disaster.

order to produce their deliverable. It is not enough for you to ask what you need to do to deliver a signed contract. You also have to discover the scope of work for the underlying project. The whole scope, not just what the contractor will be doing.

When South West Trains in the UK ordered a new fleet of 'Desiro' trains in 2001, the trains being replaced were so old they had 'non-retention' toilets that dropped waste straight onto the tracks. The new trains had modern toilets designed to retain waste on board until it could be pumped out into the sewer system. The South West Trains depots had no pumping facilities, because they had never been needed. Fortunately, upgrading the depots was recognised as a critical part of the project scope. If the focus of scope capture had been only on what needed to go into the contract with the train manufacturer, the project would have been an extremely embarrassing failure instead of the success that it was.

When you are first appointed, someone will probably tell you what the scope is. Do not believe them. Large public sector projects have usually been around for a long time before the Government finally commissions them. The Corinth Canal was first proposed in the seventh century BC but not completed until 1893, 26 centuries later. Trireme tonnage in the Aegean had fallen off a bit in the interim. Albert Mathieu put forward a proposal to build a tunnel between France and England more than 180 years before Eurotunnel was incorporated, and it wasn't an original idea even then. By the time the project comes to the point of going to tender, things will have moved on from the original proposal. Even when the gap between bright idea and commencement of the tender process is measured merely in decades there is a fair chance the user requirements are no longer what they were.

At the opposite end of the scale is the newly-hatched bright idea that leaps straight from the back of an envelope to a Minister's media release without passing through anyone's brain in the intervening period. While such extreme situations are fortunately rare, it is fairly common for there to be significant gaps in the identified user requirements.

Whether the problem you face is outdated requirements or insufficient preparation, the scope of the project will not be what is initially represented to you.

Whether the problem you face is outdated requirements or insufficient preparation, the scope of the project will not be what is initially represented to you. It will be bigger. Find out how much bigger before you settle the contract, or the variation costs will kill the project.

SCOPE CAPTURE

It is worth undertaking a workshop or two early on to scope out the full extent of the requirements. At this stage you want fairly senior people who understand the business, not just their technical specialisation. Once you get into the details of the specification you will need to get input from all levels, but to start with you want a broader brush approach.

Think about what parts of the business could be affected by the contract and make sure they are all represented. Managers at Railtrack once did a review of inherited British Rail projects to discover why they always had cost overruns. Curiously, it turned out British Rail had actually been quite good at estimating costs. What they were terrible at was estimating scope. The projects cost more because the estimates left out chunks of activity. I suspect it was a combination of a silo organisation and poor process: the silo organisation meant engineers would produce estimates that just said 'plus property costs', rather than venturing over to the property department to find someone who could work out what the property requirements were; and poor process allowed projects to go forward when the estimates still said 'plus property costs'. If you want your project to be a success, you need to get all of the scope onto the table.

South West Trains, for instance, had to do more than just upgrade its depots to make the train procurement a success. There were infrastructure modifications to be made, which required negotiation with the network owner; there were around 950 drivers to be trained, which was facilitated by the procurement of simulators; and the trains had to be brought into service without disrupting operations, which required extensive timetable planning. This list is by no means exhaustive, but the message is clear. The basic premise of your contract – buy trains – may be simple, but before you can go out to tender you need to think about a lot more than just trains.

Equivalent questions will arise in other types of project. The Corinth Canal, when finally built, suffered scope problems. The plans had not included retaining walls, despite the canal being cut through heavily faulted sedimentary rock in an earthquake zone: retaining walls had to be added later, at considerable expense. Try to pick these things up before you go to tender so you and the contractor don't have to sue one another to find out who's going to pay for them.

> *Think not only about what needs to be done, but also about what people need to stop doing.*

Think not only about what needs to be done, but also about what people need to *stop* doing. If a new computer system is supposed to replace a paper-based system, how do you kill off the paper-based system? (Trust me, it won't die unless you kill it.) What happens to the people who manage the paper-based system and should you sell the filing cabinets? By definition, the business of an Agency that has signed a billion dollar contract is a billion dollars' worth of different – or will be by the time the contract is fully delivered. There may be a significant change programme ahead for the Agency, one that will have to continue well beyond the point of contract signature.

If the project has been around for a while, check the scale is still appropriate. Demand forecasts are sufficiently dodgy without starting from an out-of-date baseline. The stabling yard associated with the $1.8 billion South West Rail Link in Sydney was originally planned to be built for 12 trains with provision for later expansion to accommodate 20 trains. By the time the contract went to tender it was thought advisable to request pricing for a contract option to build the additional accommodation and the contract when awarded included not an option but an immediate requirement for the stabling yard to accommodate the full 20 trains.

Also consider things that may be required for the success of the procurement process rather than the underlying project. For instance, if the contract you are letting is a replacement for an existing services contract, it may be prudent to negotiate options for the extension of the existing contract at an early stage so that, if your tender process is delayed beyond the expiry date of the current contract, the existing service provider is not in a position to hold you to ransom.

You need to capture all of the scope necessary to make the project a success. Run the scope workshops in the brainstorming spirit: no criticism of ideas until they have all been captured. It is extraordinary what can be missed. A London lawyer whose client had just made a major acquisition in the UK received a complaint from the client: 'You didn't tell us we were going to have to manage the company once we'd bought it.' Unfair to blame that one on the lawyer: it isn't a legal issue and the client should have spotted it for themselves. It was staggeringly obvious … wasn't it? Yet missing the obvious is easy. The famous video by Daniel Simons on selective attention has demonstrated to millions of people that it is perfectly possible not to spot the gorilla in the room. (If you haven't seen it, check it out at https://www.youtube.com/watch?v=vJG698U2Mvo.) You see the things you focus on. Spread the focus wide. It's the gorillas you don't find up front that cause the problems later.

Spread the focus wide. It's the gorillas you don't find up front that cause the problems later.

EXCLUDED SCOPE

There will sometimes be activities that really ought to form part of the project but which Government does not want to undertake either at this time or at all. Omitting them may not be a good idea. After the new Queensland Health Payroll

System went live in March 2010, the event was described by the subsequent Commission of Inquiry as a 'catastrophic failure'. Thousands of staff received the wrong amount, or nothing at all. It took months to develop a functioning payroll system, with more than 400 additional payroll staff engaged to enable Queensland Health to pay its employees.

A report by KPMG noted that the 85,000 staff of Queensland Health were employed under two different pieces of legislation, covered by 12 industrial awards and impacted by six different industrial agreements. The effect was to create over 200 allowances and up to 24,000 combinations of pay. It is plain to the least IT-savvy observer that this state of affairs is a terrible starting point from which to implement a centralised payroll system. An enormous amount of risk and cost could be eliminated from the project by first reducing the complexity of the terms of employment. What did KPMG have to say about this? They weren't asked. To quote their report, written in impeccable Government-speak: 'Simplification of the current awards structure would require a Whole of Government approach. An assessment of the feasibility of this is beyond the scope of the current review.' In other words, it's in the too-hard basket.

It is a persistent issue in Government that some problems remain unsolved because they are just too difficult.

It is a persistent issue in Government that some problems remain unsolved because they are just too difficult. No one can summon up the will or the capability to deal with the management and industrial relations challenges of fundamental change. You may have to accept this. You have, after all, quite a lot on your plate already. But where you have been obliged to omit scope that the project really needs, you will need to put additional safeguards into the contract when you come to think about risk management.

Your more immediate problem is likely to be not the scope you can't include, but the scope that should never be included at all. People with pet projects will leap out of the woodwork at the mere suggestion that a billion dollars is about to make an appearance in their vicinity. Identifying and including all necessary scope is essential. Excluding *un*necessary scope is equally important. Cabinet, in approving the procurement of a new hospital, may or may not have envisaged a private operating theatre for every surgeon, a subsidised cinema and spa complex for hospital staff or an on-site zoo to encourage small children to visit sick relatives. One can be fairly confident that, if Cabinet had in fact envisaged one or more of these exciting options, the Minister's media release would have mentioned it. Alas, the absence of such mention is no barrier to an enthusiast who has just sighted a large pot of money. Be firm. It doesn't matter if a pet project is a genuinely worthwhile initiative. That is not a good enough reason to take it on. If you need it to make the procurement a success, do it.

If you don't, bin it. Contracts for mega-projects are quite complicated enough without the optional extras.

Dealing with the Budget Crisis

Congratulations. Now you have discovered just how big your project really is, you have also discovered that even without the pet projects the budget is totally inadequate. Welcome to the public sector. Time to sit down with the chief financial officer and decide what you are going to do about it.

The traditional public sector funding strategy is to tell Treasury the smallest plausible number and fail to admit the rest until the project is too far advanced to cancel. I do not recommend this approach. If you adopt it, the sequence of events will probably go: allocate virtually all the budget to the work the contractor has to do, so the headline number in the contract matches the number previously announced by Government; fail to carry out Government's obligations under the contract because of not having any budget to do it with; get sued by the contractor; watch delays and costs escalate; finally get bailed out by Treasury in a hail of media attention for between two and four times the amount it would have cost to do the thing properly in the first place. Don't go there.

Treasury does not hate Government agencies spending money. Treasury hates Government agencies spending more money than they have been allocated.

The good news is that the period before you go out to tender is probably the easiest time to negotiate with Treasury on funding issues. Despite its reputation, Treasury does not hate Government agencies spending money. Treasury hates Government agencies spending more money than they have been allocated. It would far rather have the right amount allocated in the first place, even if the number is a big one. Treasury is not fazed by zeros. Present it carefully, and you will even be commended for having done your homework properly. Deciding what to spend the money on is by and large not Treasury's problem, they just have to provide the cash.

Your Minister is in a slightly different position. Ministers do decide what money is spent on. If your Minister has already made unrealistic promises to Cabinet about how much the project will cost, things could get a bit awkward. That is, however, no reason for wimping out on breaking the bad news: it won't get any better for waiting and the Minister will definitely prefer to hear it from you than from the media. Sorting things out in the pre-tender phase means Government at least has the benefit of presenting the increased scope as deliberate policy ('Wow! We're going to build a new submarine maintenance facility!' rather than 'Oops! We forgot we were going to have to maintain the submarines!')

Structuring the Contract

Uncovering the broad scope of the project enables you to make decisions about the structure of the contract. These decisions are largely driven by what it is you want the contractor to do, which explains most of the strange acronyms for contract structures. BOOT stands for Build Own Operate Transfer. DBOM is Design Build Operate Maintain. DCMF is Design Construct Maintain Finance. BLT is not Bacon Lettuce and Tomato but Build Lease Transfer. Some contract acronyms have other origins. PFI, Private Finance Initiative, was a UK Government programme. PPP stands for Public Private Partnership, which is not in law a partnership at all: the term is used for contracts where the contractor finances, designs, constructs, operates and maintains the asset. Do not get hung up on acronyms. There is no 'right' form. Contracts are capable of almost infinite variety and the categories shade into one another.

The choice of contract structure can make or break a project. Take particular care if the contract model you are going to adopt is new to the Agency. A PPP, for instance, is typically a very rigid structure. One of its advantages is that the difficulty of amending the contract discourages people from trying: there are fewer variations, which are the things that lead to cost and delay and dispute. The disadvantage is that if the Agency instead manages a PPP contract as if it were a standard design and build contract, costs and delays will go through the roof. To make it work, you not only have to create the PPP, you have to create an equally rigid PPP-shaped hole in the Agency management structure to plug it into.

You not only have to create the PPP, you have to create an equally rigid PPP-shaped hole in the Agency management structure to plug it into.

There is no single right answer to structuring a contract. The South West Trains procurement of Desiro trains in the UK and the Waratah train procurement in Sydney both required maintenance facility works and simulators as part of the project. South West Trains chose to award separate contracts for trains, facility works and simulators, while in Sydney all three types of works were wrapped into a single contract structured as a PPP. Both approaches are valid. A key difference was that South West Trains retained the responsibility of ensuring that the timing of the delivery of the simulators and the facility works meshed with the train delivery, whereas in the Waratah train procurement that responsibility was passed to the contractor.

The capacity of the Agency to manage both the contract and the retained responsibilities should be a major factor in determining the form of contract you use. The Holyrood Inquiry into the construction of a new Scottish Parliament building, investigating how the project went from a January 1998 estimate of £90 million for completion in July 2001 to a final £431 million completing in August 2004, found that rather than set up a single contract for delivery of the entire project, a 'construction management' approach had been adopted. That is, the project team appointed a designer and a construction manager in two separate competitions and with the assistance of the construction manager then awarded individual contracts for some 60 construction work packages, an approach which essentially left the design and construction risks with a client not well placed to manage them. The Inquiry concluded the adoption of this contracting structure was 'the single factor to which most of the misfortunes that have befallen the Project can be attributed'.

There is no form of contract which does not require active management by the Agency.

There is no form of contract which does not require active management by the Agency. If there is no existing capability within the Agency to manage the contract, building that capability should be top of the list on the scope of work for Government.

Creating the New World

The work you have done so far should have given you a vision of how you want the world to change on the day the contract is signed. If the contract is poorly designed, the world will still change, but the result you see will not match the vision you had. The succeeding chapters examine how you design the contract so that what the contractor delivers will match Government's objectives.

Chapter 4

The Specification

The overwhelming majority of contract disputes relate to the specification. What, precisely, are you paying the contractor to do? If that is clear to both parties, the chances of ending up in court are very greatly reduced.

> *If the expectations are wrong, the words of the specification will never be right.*

The essence of a dispute about specification is that it happens when Government discovers it is not getting what it thought it was going to get. If the expectations are wrong, the words of the specification will never be right. Even if the expectations are right, you may still have trouble with the words, but the single most important thing you can do is bring your stakeholders to complete agreement on what you are supposed to be procuring. If your stakeholders all have an input into the specification and they all want mutually incompatible things, then (surprise!) the specification will be inconsistent and disputes will follow. Your work on objectives and scope should have been effective in securing agreement among your stakeholders, but don't take it for granted: things can look different when you drill down into the detail.

What you need is a specification that contains everything necessary and nothing unnecessary, a specification that is accurate and unambiguous. The reasons are obvious:

- Failure to specify something that *is* necessary will result in the contractor having to be paid more money to deliver something you thought was included in the price.

- Specifying something that is *not* necessary creates a constraint on the contractor that may add cost, add risk and stifle innovation. The Sydney Opera House would be a very boring building if the specification had required construction in brick.

- Inclusion of an *inaccurate* specification may result in the contractor making a shedload of money for delivering something useless.

A bypass won't take big trucks off the road through the village if the bridge is only built to take the weight of small trucks. Give the wrong dimensions for the rail network and the trains will be too wide to fit next to the platforms.

- Inclusion of an *ambiguous* specification will lead to disputes with the contractor, particularly where the different interpretations have widely different cost implications. Is the size of the intensive care unit related to the number of hospital beds or the number of surgical beds? If it isn't clear, you will get the smaller unit.

Incorporation into the Contract

One of the main reasons for ambiguities and inconsistencies in specifications is that the document attached to the contract and labelled 'Technical Specification' or 'Statement of Works' rarely contains the complete set of obligations for the contractor. Commonly, the covering deed sets out the overall purpose of the project and the terms and conditions contain some relevant provisions, including warranties about fitness for purpose. These would be drafted by the lawyers. The Statement of Works contains Government's description of what it wanted, as issued with the Request for Tenders, possibly including a reference design. This is prepared by the project engineers or subject matter experts. The tenderer's response to the Statement of Works, which will also be attached to the contract, sets out its offering to Government, perhaps in the form of a high level design and a series of project plans. This, of course, would be prepared by the tenderer. With the contract incorporating inter-related and complex documents prepared by three different parties, the chances of ambiguity and inconsistency are alarmingly high.

With the contract incorporating inter-related and complex documents prepared by three different parties, the chances of ambiguity and inconsistency are alarmingly high.

The 'cure' for this is normally a clause included in the terms and conditions which specifies which document will take precedence over which if an inconsistency is discovered. I dislike these clauses, because my view is always that the documents should not be included in the contract unless they *are* consistent. Any inconsistency is by definition an error, and who can say at the start which document will include the error? Unfortunately, on very large contracts it is not always practicable to expend the time and effort required to make the documentation fully consistent. Some 'priority' clause is likely to be necessary, but try for something a little more sophisticated than just 'this prevails over that'. The effect you are seeking is that the contractor's product is required to be in accordance with both the Government specification and the tender submission, but if compliance with both is not possible, the contractor still has to meet the specification and must produce something at least as good as the tender submission.

INCORPORATING MATERIAL FROM THE TENDERERS

You will be selecting your preferred tenderer on the basis of a number of criteria, but one or more of those criteria will relate to what the tenderer proposes to deliver for you: their vision for what and how to deliver something that will meet your requirements. You want to be sure the things you select them for are actually delivered, so the tenderer's vision needs to be incorporated in the contract. Unfortunately, you can't put this material in the contract up front because you don't know what it is.

You can, however, plan its inclusion in advance by designing the contract and the Request for Tenders in tandem. If you get it right, the material supplied by the tenderer will be in form and content ready to drag and drop into a schedule to the contract. You will never get it completely right, except perhaps with easy ones like a schedule of key personnel, but a bit of forethought does wonders. Where you know that forethought can't help you much, because you are deliberately being as open as possible with your initial specification in order to generate innovative solutions, build some extra time into the schedule to capture those solutions in a proper specification. Open-ended requests are good for encouraging innovation but terrible for pinning down what is supposed to be delivered.

Open-ended requests are good for encouraging innovation but terrible for pinning down what is supposed to be delivered.

The tender evaluation and negotiation process will lead to a number of changes both in the specification and in the material originally supplied by the preferred tenderer. Incorporate these changes in the relevant document before incorporating the document into the contract. Do not under any circumstances try to deal with it by including both the original document and the subsequent exchange of correspondence identifying the change. The contract is going to be quite complicated enough as it is. And be really, really wary of the phrase 'for the avoidance of doubt', which normally precedes a passage that casts more doubt than it avoids. If the material is properly drafted in the first place, there will *be* no doubt, which is a much better outcome.

Dividing the Project

The specification must include the whole scope of works to be completed by the contractor. Your investigation of what scope is necessary to make the project a success will have left you with a long list. Your first task is to work out which things on the list will be done by the Agency and which by the contractor. (This is not the same thing as allocating the risk: deciding who pays if the activity turns out to be more expensive than anticipated is a separate issue, dealt with in Chapter 5.) In dividing up works between the Agency and the contractor, do what suits your situation rather than clinging to a particular format.

There may sometimes be pressure to unload every possible activity onto the contractor. This is likely to happen where the track record of the Agency on projects is so abysmal that the Minister is reluctant to allow the Agency to do anything at all. That tells you something about how you are going to have to manage your key stakeholders. It should not be the definitive answer to who does what. Having the contractor do everything may not be the least-risk option.

Having the contractor do everything may not be the least-risk option.

There will be a lot of factors jostling for consideration in how the work is divided up, but some deserve special mention:

- critical path
- interfaces
- tender process delays
- third party works.

CRITICAL PATH

'Critical path' is a term used by schedulers. It represents the shortest possible route through to completion. If any task on the critical path is delayed, the completion of the project is delayed by a corresponding amount. A task that isn't on the critical path has 'float' available – it can be a bit late without causing problems – but if the float is used up the task joins the critical path. In joint project meetings you will occasionally hear one project manager screaming to another, 'Get off my critical path!'

If activities allocated to the Agency are on the contractor's critical path, then any delay by the Agency in completing those activities causes a delay to the contractor. This becomes a source of dispute, particularly if the contractor is subject to very strong time incentives. To the extent you can manage it, keep the Agency off the contractor's critical path. It makes it much harder for a contractor to blame project delays on the Agency.

On the Waratah train procurement, necessary construction works included refurbishment of an existing stretch of rail to use as a dedicated test track for the trains and track extensions in rail yards to enable the new trains to be stabled there. (In railway jargon, trains are 'stabled', not 'parked'.) Although both sets of construction work were necessary to the overall success of the project, the work in the stabling yards was not on the critical path for the delivery of the trains whereas the test track was, so the stabling yard work was allocated to the Agency and the test track work was allocated to the contractor.

Take special note of anything Government has to do that *will* be on the critical path: when it comes time to hand the newly minted contract over to someone else to manage through the delivery phase, your successor will need to know.

INTERFACES

Every interface between Government and the contractor is a potential cause of dispute.

Collaboration is a beautiful thing, but not always easy to achieve. Every interface between Government and the contractor is a potential cause of dispute. If you can ring-fence the project away from the Agency's day-to-day operations, you eliminate the risk of Agency people in the delivery phase treating day-to-day operations as more important than the project, without regard to the impact on the contractor.

This was another reason for the division of construction works in the Waratah train procurement: works in a busy stabling yard have a direct impact on the operational railway, so the Agency was best placed to manage the risks associated with those works. Works for the test track could literally be carried out on the far side of a fence.

Do not go overboard with eliminating interfaces. Too much segregation can be counter-productive. It is one thing to prevent the Agency interfering with the contractor, but quite another to prevent the contractor from getting enough access to Agency staff to ensure the user requirements are properly met. Just remember that every interface that is not eliminated must be managed.

TENDER PROCESS DELAYS

Setting up a contract on this scale takes time. Sometimes, it may be worthwhile for the Agency to carry out some work packages during the tender process in order to bring forward final completion of the overall project. If a designated construction site is not completely vacant, for instance, it may be sensible to allocate clearance works to the Agency, particularly if the works could be completed before the conclusion of the tender process.

If the better answer is to allocate the work to the contractor, this is also possible. Although the contractor is normally not going to do any work until they have a contract, once you have a preferred bidder, a side deal can be done. On Stage 1 of the Channel Tunnel Rail Link project ('Stage 1' represented a restructure of the project after the original contractor had run into difficulties), negotiations on the main contract were prolonged perilously close to the start of the badger mating season. The contractor agreed to dig up some badger setts while negotiations were still continuing, as environmental regulation would otherwise have required construction to wait upon the *amours* of the local badger population. The works were paid for under the main contract, but by arrangement, the contractor would have been able to claim separately had the negotiations fallen through.

Environmental regulation would otherwise have required construction to wait upon the amours *of the local badger population.*

THIRD PARTY WORKS

Some works may need to be carried out by a party other than the Agency or the contractor, most commonly because the third party has some special expertise or intellectual property right: perhaps you want your new frigate to have the same type of communications equipment as the rest of the fleet. Although the work will have to be carried out by the third party, you still need to allocate responsibility for the work to either the contractor or the Agency. Either you require the contractor to engage the third party, in which case the works are in the contractor's scope, or the Agency engages the third party directly and provides the output to the contractor, in which case the works are in the Agency's scope.

The difference is critical in the delivery phase. When the works are in the Agency's scope, it may still be convenient for the contractor to liaise directly with the third party, but if problems arise, that doesn't stop the Agency being on the hook.

Introducing Constraints

In addition to specifying the characteristics of the asset or service, you may need to specify some constraints around how and when the individual elements can be delivered. This is a particular issue when project delivery has significant interfaces with Agency operations.

Accepting delivery of a train, for instance, means the Agency has to stable the train, incorporate it into the working timetable and operate it on the network. This is much more complex than it sounds, with all sorts of implications in areas such as crew training and rostering, maintenance scheduling and network power supply. If too many trains arrive at once, they are likely to disrupt service operations instead of enhancing them.

The Waratah train procurement included a restriction in the contract that a train could not be accepted onto the network until ten business days after the acceptance of the previous train (15 business days for the first six trains). This represented a rate about four times faster than the operator had had to cope with on previous procurements, but the procurement was so large that to accept them at the earlier rate would have meant a delivery period of around 13 years, which was politically unacceptable. It was nonetheless slower than the contractor would be capable of achieving, and therefore constituted a real constraint on delivery.

Schedule constraints should not be included lightly, because schedule is a powerful driver of cost. The implications of an apparently simple constraint may be far reaching. Done with forethought, this can work in Government's favour. In the Waratah case, the effects of the constraint were:

Schedule constraints should not be included lightly, because schedule is a powerful driver of cost.

- the bids were easier to evaluate, because all tenderers were able to offer the fastest permitted delivery rate;

- because tenderers were capable of faster delivery rates, the restriction enforced contingency in their schedules, reducing overall risk;

- it prevented any attempt by the contractor to 'game' the contract by delivering a large number of trains at once: had it been able to do so, it could have put Government in the position of either accepting trains without checking for unfixed defects or extending the acceptance period and paying delay costs to the contractor;

- it gave Government a bargaining chip that remained valuable throughout the delivery phase: if Government consented to faster delivery, the contractor's very significant interest costs would be reduced.

Benefits do not come without a cost. The bids received by the Agency would undoubtedly have contained lower prices in the absence of the schedule constraint. Do not include any constraint in the specification unless you are satisfied the benefit outweighs the cost.

Preparing the Specification

The need to involve multiple stakeholders in the preparation of a specification is no excuse for incoherence.

It is within your control to ensure any document going out from the Government side of the process is well-structured and internally consistent. Insist on it. It is regrettably common to see a specification document which has been prepared by lumping together the inputs from a variety of subject matter experts without any technical challenge or editorial input. The need to involve multiple stakeholders in the preparation of a specification is no excuse for incoherence. The structure should be a considered decision as to what will convey the Government's requirements most clearly, not an agglomeration of contributions from the functionally illiterate. Give editorial control to one individual who accepts responsibility for the document. And give it *before* contributors produce their bit of the drafting so that clear guidelines can be set.

Some common errors are:

- *Mixing specification of process with specification of works.* Keep them separate. For example, if there is to be a process for review of design submissions, set it out in one place and one place only, rather than keep repeating it each time you specify a different design submission. That way you know what the review period for submissions is. It will be findable under a single obvious heading instead of having (probably inconsistent) references scattered throughout the document, and if you negotiate a different period with the tenderer, the change is easy to capture.

- *'Hobby horse' specifications.* Any expert worthy of the name has decided views on the techniques, approaches or widgets applicable to their specialisation. This is commendable – in its place. Where the contractor is also an expert, and what is more, the expert taking the risk of the decision, then the contractor should be permitted the widget of their choice. It is not always easy to get it across to a subject matter expert, who is after all only seeking the best outcome for Government, that the contractor's choices of inputs may be none of their business.

- *Inconsistent levels of detail in the requirements.* The level of detail incorporated in specifications is often a reflection of the level of knowledge of the individual writing it rather than of any considered decision as to how much is appropriate. When a document has many individual contributors and no effective editorial control the result can be threadbare in places and overly prescriptive in others. This leaves it open to a contractor to argue they need do virtually nothing in relation to the threadbare bits, because the level of detail elsewhere shows that if you had wanted more you would have said so.

When a document has many individual contributors and no effective editorial control the result can be threadbare in places and overly prescriptive in others.

- *Excluding the operators.* When your project is the construction of a very large asset, it is likely to be several years before the finished asset is handed over for operational use. If you wait until then to establish the needs of the operators, it is too late. If the specification did not identify that the ambulance bay should be next to the Accident and Emergency unit, the contractor building the hospital may have located it somewhere else.

- *Excluding the lawyers.* It is unlikely you will want a lawyer to draft the specification, because the technical content will be beyond them, but don't exclude them entirely. They need to know which matters are being dealt with in the terms and conditions and which in the specification, so you don't get duplication or omissions. It is also a good idea to have them review the specification before it is issued to tenderers. The nature of lawyers' training and experience means they are good at spotting discrepancies. Some of them have trouble seeing the wood for the trees, but they are all *really* good at seeing trees. Don't knock it, use it. It is true they will occasionally amuse your engineers with their unfamiliarity with technical jargon. One lawyer, seeing a reference to installing a 'leaky feeder' in the Severn Tunnel, queried whether it wouldn't be better to install something that didn't leak, not realising this was jargon for a radiating cable used in communications systems. Despite this, their input is usually valuable. If the lawyers, as intelligent laypeople, can't understand what your technical experts are writing, there is a fair chance the tenderers won't either.

- *Not having a 'cold read' of the specification.* Arrange for someone who hasn't worked on the specification to read the final draft 'cold'. The fresh eye will often pick up something the project team has missed. If your firm of technical consultants isn't big enough to provide a spare expert to do it, find one from somewhere else.

- *Not securing stakeholder sign off.* Variations kill projects. It is not enough to seek input from your stakeholders. You need to secure their agreement that the final specification meets their requirements. *All* their requirements. Do not be satisfied with anything less than the signatures of the senior technical expert and the executive line manager who is head of the relevant division. Preferably written in blood.

STANDARD PRODUCT

Some mega-projects involve manufactured product that will need to be specially produced: manufacturers do not keep helicopters and trains and trams and submarines and frigates sitting on a shelf somewhere in the hope someone will turn up and buy a few. There will, however, be standard designs already in existence. Similarly, major IT systems will come in standard configurations. For some reason, Government agencies appear constitutionally incapable of accepting them. This is unfortunate.

> *Customers are, not infrequently, complete idiots who don't know what's good for them.*

'The customer is always right' is one of the more dubious business propositions. Customers are, not infrequently, complete idiots who don't know what's good for them. Your tenderers will generally have a lot more experience and expertise than Government, probably across many different countries, and may have a much better feel than Government for what the end users would really like. One tram manufacturer politely, for a fee, modified its standard design for a public sector customer who demanded the removal of poles from the area near the doors. The company simultaneously prepared a quotation for installing the poles as a modification, knowing perfectly well that tram passengers are more concerned with being able to hang on to something than with the aesthetics of the vestibule. It didn't have to wait very long before the quotation was requested.

When you request modifications of a standard form product, you add cost. If the standard form tram comes with CCTV, for instance, it will be more expensive to buy the tram without CCTV. This is counter-intuitive but true. A CCTV-free tram might have been cheaper if the tram had been designed without CCTV originally, but that is not the situation you are in. If you change the design, you not only have the cost of the redesign, the manufacturer has to stop the production line to reprogramme the machines and stop it again to put the settings back to standard when your job is over. Plus, the fact the manufacturer decided to put CCTV into the standard model means most of its customers want it. Why should you be different?

This is the archetypal way of ruining a software project. Seek to minimise risk by procuring an off-the-shelf product already in commercial use, then send the risk level through the roof by demanding customisations. Consider the failure of the Queensland Health Payroll System: the software had to be customised to cope with over 200 allowances and up to 24,000 combinations of pay. While there were significant flaws in the tender process, which didn't help matters, the project was essentially too complicated to live.

If you are procuring a product that is already standard in the market, persuade your stakeholders that their choice is between one supplier's standard product and another supplier's standard product. There will be certain elements of the standard product that are genuinely configurable: the colour of the tram, the size of your logo, whether you want Version A with bench seating or Version B with individual seating. Apart from that, every modification required by your specification is a potential horror story. Especially in IT projects. Delete one field from a database? Thirty seconds to delete the field and somewhere between 30 seconds and 30 days to discover the automatic data transfers between all the databases linked to this one no longer function. No modifications. Repeat. No modifications.

No modifications. Repeat. No modifications.

The 'no modifications' mantra is not without risk. Accepting a standard product may well mean something in the existing organisation has to change to fit: perhaps new business processes to match new software. That change needs to be included in the scope of your project, possibly as something for the contractor to deal with, more likely something for Government. If it is in

Government's scope, the project plan should be reasonably well developed before you sign with the contractor. Otherwise, when the change management programme runs into trouble, someone will have the bright idea that their life would be easier if your contractor would just make a few modifications to the standard product – and the horror story you so carefully avoided will rise again.

Rarely, the standard product will be genuinely unsuitable for your situation. A vehicle designed to work in the tropics may seize up in sub-zero temperatures, for instance. Look at what is different about your operating environment and put into the contract enforceable assurances from the contractor that the standard product will be fit for purpose. If modifications are necessary, realise that your low risk procurement is not as low risk as originally intended and manage it accordingly. But don't accept *any* modification demanded by your stakeholders without understanding why it is worth the risk.

Generating Good Responses

Your specification has two iterations. The first is the specification you issue with the Request for Tenders. The second is the one that forms part of the contract. The extent of the change between the two depends on the bids you receive.

In preparing the first iteration of the specification, you should always be thinking in terms of how the bidders are likely to respond.

Very large projects often result in a structure that will dominate its immediate surroundings.

You may, for instance, be seeking to encourage innovation or iconic design. Very large projects often result in a structure that will dominate its immediate surroundings. If you are seeking to procure a bridge, you may want something that is functional and looks spectacular, but not be concerned whether the structure is of concrete or steel, or whether it is a suspension bridge or supported by arches. In this case you will need the specification to be clear about the functional characteristics of the bridge (load-bearing capacity, peak traffic capacity, required clearance over the waterway, which roads it must connect to, and so on) but exclude any unnecessary 'requirements' that might stifle design innovation.

Alternatively, you may already have a design – perhaps as the result of a separate competition – which you want constructed without alteration. In this case the existing design will form the basis of the specification for the tender phase, and you should specify that you do *not* want to receive innovative designs.

Think about the choices that the tenderers will have to make in responding to the specification. In the Waratah train procurement, the contractor's principal obligation was to make 72 trains available for service each day during the operations phase. This required more than 72 trains to be manufactured, to allow for some trains being out of service for regular maintenance. Pre-tender calculations by the Agency indicated the optimum number of spare trains was five and a bit. Since you can't have a bit of a train, tenderers would have to choose between offering only five spare trains, meaning their bid would be cheaper but they would struggle in the operational phase, or offering six, which would keep them well covered during the operational phase but would put up the cost of the bid so they might not win the contract at all. The Agency decided the risk of under-provision for maintenance was too great and took the decision out of the bidders' hands by specifying a minimum of six spare trains.

Planning for Evaluation

Keep in mind that you will have to evaluate the bids made in response to your specification. If the Agency does not have enough expertise at its disposal to understand and distinguish between the answers it is likely to receive, it probably also does not have enough expertise to be asking the right questions. Engage your technical experts early.

It is perfectly legitimate to issue a draft specification to the market before commencing the formal procurement process. Potential tenderers will of course put their interests ahead of yours – they are likely to encourage you to want the things they are most capable of providing – but their feedback is usually valuable.

Potential tenderers will of course put their interests ahead of yours ... but their feedback is usually valuable.

Some elements of your specification may be mandatory, while others may be described simply as desirable, offering bidders the chance to differentiate themselves by including desirable features. Review these with your technical advisers to understand the implications of what you ask for.

The Melbourne CityLink tollway, which opened in late 2000, included about five kilometres of elevated roadway supported by columns. Choices for construction of the roadway included the use of T-beams or match-cast concrete. Using T-beams, it would be possible to work all the way along the five-kilometre stretch of elevated road at the same time. Using match-cast concrete, construction would have to start at one end and work along to the other in precise sequence, with each concrete section fitted to the previous one. The second method was used. One of the sections broke during construction and the entire project was extensively delayed while a replacement section was cast and cured. The choice of construction method had not originally been specified by Government: it appears a subcontractor responded to an informally-expressed preference for the superior aesthetics of match-cast concrete. But it was definitely a case of be careful what you wish for.

Specification of Government Works

All of the work to be done by the contractor must be specified in the contract, for the simple reason that if it isn't, the contractor will not do it. Work to be done by the Government may not be in the contract at all.

Whether the work to be undertaken by Government should be included depends on whether the contractor needs Government to deliver that work in order to carry out their own obligations. On a project to procure tanks, for instance, the contractor may need the army to make soldiers available to test drive the tanks on manoeuvres before the tanks can be certified as ready for service: making those soldiers available should be an obligation on Government under the contract. However, while it may be essential for the success of the project overall that more soldiers be recruited and trained to operate the tanks, the contractor doesn't need those additional soldiers in order to make the delivery, so their availability should not be a contractual obligation on Government.

Do not allow Government to take on obligations to the contractor that it is not capable of delivering.

Do not allow Government to take on obligations to the contractor that it is not capable of delivering. Do not allow Government to take on *any* obligation to the contractor unless you can identify an individual who will accept responsibility for delivering it. Make sure that person has understood the nature and extent of the obligation and put their signature at the bottom of a document that says so. If Government needs to review design documents, for instance, an engineer might tell you the standard turnaround time is five working days. Do not take this as a green light to put an obligation on Government to review design documents in five working days. That 'standard' may well be optimistic at the best of times and it will reflect the current throughput of design documents. Resourcing may be wholly inadequate to deal with the volume generated by a mega-project. Get a realistic commitment from your engineer. In writing.

Bear in mind that making life easy for your engineer does not necessarily reduce cost or risk to Government. The cost to you of putting in place special arrangements to enable fast document turnaround may well be dramatically less than the cost of requiring the contractor to plan their project around lengthy review processes. And while you're at it, check whether the engineers should be reviewing the documents at all. What value is being added? Are they importing risk instead of reducing it? If your engineers don't have to be on the contractor's critical path, get them off it.

If there is uncertainty around whether the Government is able to deliver something the contractor needs, do not fall into the trap of thinking you can avoid liability by not putting the obligation into the contract. Silence is only golden from the point of view of litigation lawyers. If the failure of Government to do something only Government can do is preventing the contractor from completing their obligations under the contract, the absence of specific provision in the contract will not be the sole determinant of who pays whom for delay costs. Plus, the contractor will price the risk of Government not delivering into the contract, so you will pay more than you need to.

Silence is only golden from the point of view of litigation lawyers.

The other trap to avoid is the reverse: putting obligations on Government to carry out associated works when the contractor does not need them. This is a public sector budgeting thing. Government generally honours its contracts, but any activity not covered by a binding contract may have its budget slashed at any time. Putting the obligation into the contract may seem like a harmless way of protecting the budget. It isn't harmless.

You may avoid an argument with Treasury, but you have instead given a hostage to the contractor: any failure of Government to deliver on its own contractual obligations makes it more difficult to enforce the contractor's obligations. Manage the delivery of associated works through your governance framework, not the contract.

Specification is Not Enough

Inclusion of the specification in the contract will give you a legal right to have something of the specified quality delivered to you at the specified time. That legal right does not of itself mean the something will happen as specified or at all. When any project is being delivered, things go wrong. When the project is a mega-project, there are more and bigger things and therefore more things to go more wrong. The contract needs to deal with these risks.

Chapter 5
Risk Management

In establishing your contract, you have three sets of risks to worry about:

1. risks to the procurement process;
2. risks to the underlying project;
3. risks to the business of the Agency arising from the project.

The contract you primarily use to manage procurement risk is not the contract you will enter for delivery of the mega-project, it is the 'process contract', the terms and conditions of tender discussed in Part IV. The delivery contract does have a role in managing your procurement process risk. If the draft you issue with the Request for Tenders makes the contractor's obligations clear, it is less likely that your tender process will be burdened with a tenderer who is not capable of delivering the obligations and more likely that the prices you receive will be realistic.

In this chapter, however, we are concerned with the use of the delivery contract as a tool for managing the risks to the project itself and of the risks associated with the impact of the project on the Agency. You do this in two ways.

Contracts have been allocating risk for centuries, but risk management became a profession and a buzzword only in the last 20 or 30 years.

First, the contract allocates risk between the parties. Curiously, it generally does this without mentioning the word 'risk' at all, probably because contracts have been allocating risk for centuries, but risk management became a profession and a buzzword only in the last 20 or 30 years. Contracts allocate risk by setting out the obligations on the parties and the circumstances in which each party is entitled to claim payment from the other. For instance, in a project where cables had to be laid, it was not known how much trenching for the cables would have to be cut through rock (expensive) rather than dug through soil (cheap). The contract provided for the Agency to pay a per-metre rate for trenching through rock: that is, the contractor did the work and took the risk that the rate would cover its costs per metre, but the Agency took the cost risk of how much rock there would be.

Second, the contract may specify activities in the contract that have the effect of managing risk. If the contractor has to submit designs for approval by the Agency, there is a risk the designs will not be in accordance with the specification. This risk is greatly reduced if the contract provides for all designs to be reviewed by an independent certifier before they may be submitted to the Agency.

To develop a contract that is effective as a risk management tool, you first have to understand the risks you are managing.

Risk Identification

The public sector appears infinitely capable of taking any business-enhancing process and ossifying it into mindless bureaucracy.

What could go wrong? What outcomes are uncertain? You need to find your risks and capture them in a register so you can deal with them systematically. Do not create your risk register by copying the one from the last project. The public sector appears infinitely capable of taking any business-enhancing process and ossifying it into mindless bureaucracy, but that is no reason for you to do the same. The value of a risk register is threefold: creating it makes you think about what can go wrong and how to make things go right instead; refreshing it regularly makes you think about what has changed and whether you need to start doing something different; and the register itself becomes a checklist for you to use in seeking regular assurance that the planned risk management is actually happening. You won't deliver any of these benefits by filing a photocopy.

Start with workshops to brainstorm the risks. If you are working with a new team, you will find the risk workshops a good team-building exercise that can give you real insights into how people think and how they are likely to react when things go wrong. The workshops can also be fun. I like putting forward bizarre risk events and challenging people to guess whether they actually happened on a previous project. (A bridge built out from each bank of the river and failing to meet in the middle? Yes, it was over the Rhine between Germany and Switzerland at Laufenburg. An error in calculating sea level meant the heights differed by 54 centimetres. Oops.)

If you have worked with the team previously on similar projects, you need to avoid the trap of assuming the risks will be the same. As the army puts it, generals are always very well equipped to fight the previous war.

Keep on asking, what is different about this one? How has the industry changed? How has the stakeholder environment shifted? The last time I led a train procurement in Sydney, there was a single company running the whole metropolitan passenger railway. Since then a reorganisation of the railway has split ownership from operation and regional services from metropolitan services: new interfaces mean future train procurements will have new risks to consider.

If your Agency does not have its own risk team, you may find it helpful to engage a risk consultant as a facilitator. Finalising the documentation can be a bit tedious and it speeds the process up if workshops are facilitated by someone who is practised in capturing and recording material for the register.

Extra speed is helpful because the process of creating a risk register does take time. You not only have to identify the risks, you have to identify the potential causes of risk events, and the potential consequences if they occur: not just financial ones, but also other consequences which may be operational, safety-related or reputational. You need to identify the probability of the risk event and form a view, based on the probability and the consequences, on whether each risk is acceptable.

If it isn't, you need to identify controls that reduce the probability of the risk event occurring or reduce the severity of its consequences, and you need to identify the people who will take ownership of each risk and be responsible for implementing each control. You need to form a view on whether the existing controls are effective. Done badly, this is all a bureaucratic waste of time. Done well, it saves projects.

Done badly, this is all a bureaucratic waste of time. Done well, it saves projects.

Do it well. If you do not understand the risks, you cannot manage them effectively. The contract is one of the most powerful tools you have for managing risk and you sign the contract only once. Some risk management controls can be introduced or eliminated at any time, but controls in the contract are either there on day one or not there at all. If you haven't understood the risk, you won't put the right provisions into the contract.

Some common failures in putting together the risk register are:

- *Focusing only on what went wrong last time.* Human beings are not very well wired to calculate probabilities accurately. It is not just a matter of optimism bias. Something that happened to you or someone you know appears more probable than something that happened to a total stranger. Something that has happened recently appears more probable than something that hasn't. (On the day in 2014 the media reported SNCF had procured trains which were too wide for many

Don't ignore all the other things that could go wrong, even if they went right last time.

of the regional platforms in France, every project director of every train procurement project on the planet would have been contacted by their steering committee seeking reassurance it wasn't going to happen to them.) You should certainly not ignore risk events that have happened to the Agency recently, if only because you will make your chief executive look a complete prat if it happens again, which is career-limiting. But don't ignore all the other things that could go wrong, even if they went right last time.

- *Over-enthusiastic introduction of risk controls.* For some reason the public sector is particularly prone to introduce controls that have more onerous consequences than the risk the control is supposed to mitigate. It took years for Government agencies to realise the traditional method of managing stationery needs, namely issuing stationery to employees from a single storeroom staffed by a dragon who will not release so much as a pencil without a requisition form, was far more costly than the petty pilfering the system was intended to prevent.

- *Poor ownership of risks and controls.* The owner is the person who agrees to take responsibility for the management of the risk or the implementation of the control. Note the word 'agrees'. Writing someone's name down in a risk register as an owner without their knowledge or consent achieves nothing except an entirely false sense of security. You need informed agreement accompanied by a genuine sense of ownership and responsibility. On a project of this scale, the risk owners should not be people too low down in the organisation. If things go badly wrong, parliament will expect a senior executive to front up to the Select Committee and grovel. As project director, yours is the default name for every entry in the owner columns, whether it is appropriate or not. At least this should give you an excellent incentive to find the correct owners.

- *Wishful thinking.* Part of the process of creating the risk register involves plotting onto a risk matrix the consequences of the risk event and the probability of it coming to pass (see Figure 5.1). The introduction of controls reduces consequences and reduces the probability of occurrence, moving the risks from the red zone on the matrix towards the green zone, transforming risks that were unacceptable when uncontrolled into risks that can be accepted by the Agency. Sometimes the available controls still leave you with a risk sitting in the unacceptable corner of the risk matrix. Be very, very wary of solving this problem by deciding you must have over-estimated the probability of the unacceptable outcome. Seek independent advice.

Sometimes the available controls still leave you with a risk sitting in the unacceptable corner of the risk matrix.

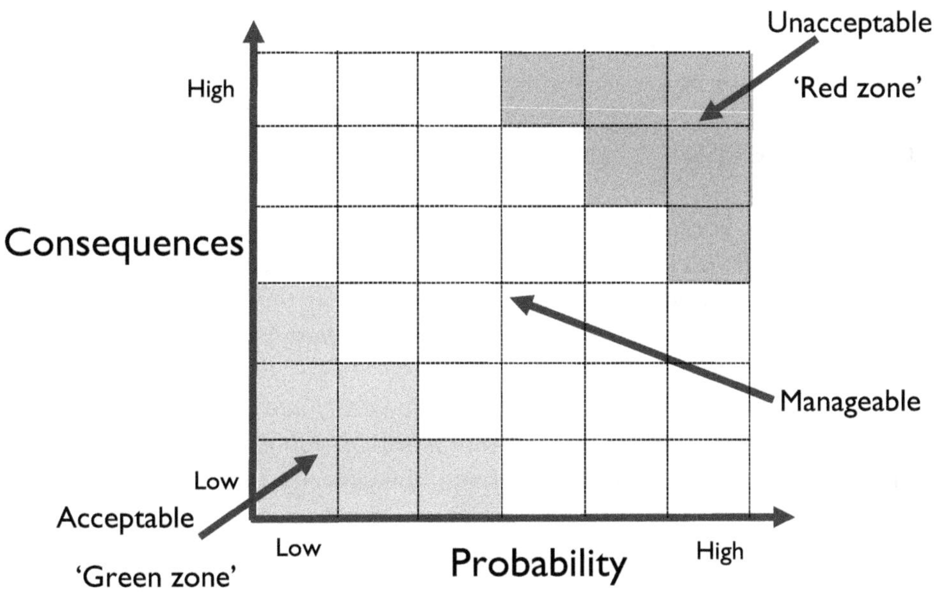

Figure 5.1 The risk matrix

- *Failing to follow through.* Documents don't manage risks. People manage risks. Controls written into a risk register achieve nothing unless they are implemented and continue in place. Set up a monthly review process to support your risk management plan, and don't skip it when things get busy. Include a contract check from time to time. The draft contract you issue with the Request for Tenders will change before final signature as you progress negotiations: don't lose sight of the impact on your risk assessments.

Special Risks

Some risks are easy to miss or underestimate because the risk event won't come to pass until well after you have signed the contract. These include:

- acceptance risk
- transition risk
- strategic risk.

Depending on the nature of the contract it may be two, five or even ten years before the catastrophe manifests itself. The fact that you may not be around when it happens is no excuse for not sorting things out up front.

ACCEPTANCE RISK

You have to ask yourself the question: when the contractor has delivered the project, how will you know? On first hearing, the question sounds silly. You're hiring the contractor to build a bridge: you will know they've finished because there will be a thumping great bridge over the waterway that wasn't there before. Next question.

It's not as simple as that. Your specification will have said rather more than just 'build a bridge'. You don't just want a bridge, you want one with specific characteristics: the right number of lanes, the capacity to take the load, high enough above the water not to obstruct shipping and so on. When the contractor sends in the invoice for the completion payment, how will you know whether you should pay it?

Acceptance risk is particularly acute in construction contracts where the contractor is providing the finance and will be remunerated not with progress payments on construction but with payments related to the use of the asset once completed. At the point when the asset is about to come into service, the contractor's debt will be at its highest and the available time and cost contingency at its lowest. This is not the moment to discover you don't know how to tell whether you should be accepting the asset or not. Depending on the way the contract is written, either Government will be held to ransom by the contractor or the contractor will go bust while you trail around your stakeholders trying to figure it out. Cue the sound of lawyers sharpening pencils.

This is not the moment to discover you don't know how to tell whether you should be accepting the asset or not.

The time to work out how you will deal with this risk is now, not at the time. Not only will it save you a lawsuit later, it will also save you money. If tenderers cannot see in the contract a clear process for signing off completion of the delivery, they will price the risk of delay into the tender.

Bear in mind that you will only get one chance at this bridge. That is the nature of mega-projects. In the two cases I know of where the contractor delivered trains too wide for the platforms, the fix was to shave a bit off the platforms, not scrap the trains. If a contractor gets the alignment of your new garden fence wrong, you can tell them to take it down and start again, but nobody is going to take down a billion dollar bridge just because the specification said the contractor should have built it 50 metres further west. If the 50 metres is important to you, develop an acceptance process that picks up the error before anyone starts pouring concrete. Set out the process in the contract to limit the risk of disputes.

TRANSITION RISK

You have not one but two critical transitions to worry about, both of them bristling with risk. The one that will hit you first is the project transition from the tender process to the delivery phase, from contract set-up to contract management: once the contract is signed, will the project team hit the ground running or just hit the ground? The second is the business transition when the asset or service delivered by the contractor becomes available for the Agency to use. If the contract you are letting is purely for services, rather than the development and delivery of an IT system or physical asset, the business transition may occur simultaneously with the project transition.

It would be nice to think of the business transition as the business's problem. They tell you what they want, the project team delivers it, let them worry about the rest. That is a perfectly reasonable approach for a project manager. It won't do for a project director. When you are responsible for procuring something that will make a billion dollars' worth of difference to the business, you also need to take responsibility for ensuring the business can cope. That doesn't mean your project team has to do the work. If there is a risk new trains will sit unused because there aren't enough drivers, it is the person in the business with responsibility for train crew who should initiate the driver recruitment and be the risk owner. But the risk sits on your project risk register, because if your project is to procure trains, no one will regard it as a success until the trains are out there on the network carrying passengers. People also won't regard it as a success if the

That is a perfectly reasonable approach for a project manager. It won't do for a project director.

new drivers are being paid for twiddling their thumbs because the trains aren't ready. Most risks have an equal and opposite risk caused by going overboard in trying to manage the first one. Cultivate a sense of balance.

Recruitment and training of new drivers at the optimum time is unlikely to be a risk you should allocate to the contractor. But there may be obligations you can put into the contract that will reduce the risk to the Agency, such as requiring the contractor to provide regular forecasts of the delivery dates for the trains. In the Waratah train procurement, where the contractor was providing simulators to be used for training the crew in readiness for the arrival of the trains, the contractor was not entitled to start presenting trains for acceptance until a specified period after delivery of the simulators.

STRATEGIC RISK

Things can become a little fraught if there is an imminent election, a Government trailing in the polls and an Opposition that prefers the highway.

When an Agency decides to embark on a mega-project, Government is making a strategic choice. If you build a hospital on a block of land, you are choosing not to put a six-lane highway through the same location. This choice is made when the go-ahead for the procurement of the hospital is given. Things can become a little fraught if there is an imminent election, a Government trailing in the polls and an Opposition that prefers the highway. The obvious way to manage the risk of excessive cancellation costs is to put the project off until after the election, but this may not be politically acceptable. An alternative is to include a provision in the contract allowing for a no-fault termination for agreed compensation: compensation agreed as part of a competitive tender process is likely to be less than compensation argued about after the event. There remains the possibility that Government is so determined the project will proceed that you may instead be instructed to make it as difficult as possible for any future Government to unwind the contract. Although the issue was not canvassed in the National Audit Office report, a key reason for the Conservative Government's determination to proceed with the UK flotation of Railtrack in 1996 against all opposition was to make it impracticable for an incoming Labour Government to stick British Rail back together again.

These situations, although regrettably by no means unknown, are unusual. The risk that Government will later decide to build the highway after all and knock down your hospital before the business case benefits have been earned is normally not one that needs to appear on your risk register. It is nonetheless quite possible that in the conduct of your procurement you may be called upon to make decisions with strategic impacts that have not been assessed.

Design choices

Your politicians and policy makers, while undoubtedly aware that parliament has no power to repeal the laws of physics, may not be fully cognisant of the implications. MPs with engineering qualifications are rare. The details of line and level for a new railway, for instance, will normally be left to the project team and (within limits) to the contractor. Yet engineering choices made now may prevent or permit the addition of a connecting link to another line later. That is a strategic decision. Your Minister will be upset if you make it without letting anyone know. Worse, when your decision is discovered it may be overruled, leading to major design changes when the project is already underway. This is a recipe for project failure. Unless you have evidence to support it, do not assume decisions have been made with any understanding of the engineering challenges involved in the project or the potential consequences. If you aren't sure whether decision-makers understood the effect of their decision, now is the time to explain it to them. Once you have locked strategic design choices into the contract, changing the choice puts the whole project at risk.

Hidden game-changers

Make sure you understand what the project and the contract terms will do to the existing business of the Agency. One of the key factors in the demise of Railtrack was that it entered into a fixed price contract to allow Virgin Trains to run additional services on the West Coast Main Line. The price for the infrastructure works required to provide capacity for the new services assumed that £2 billion of upgrade works on the same line would be funded by Government through regulated access charges. Railtrack couldn't provide the capacity for the new services without the upgrade, but there was no provision in the contract for what would happen if the cost of the upgrade went up. As the forecast cost went from £2 billion to £4 billion and kept on climbing, Government decided not to fund the extra cost and the black hole opening up in the Railtrack accounts just got bigger. The company was eventually forced into administration.

Risk Allocation

The theory of risk allocation is that you should allocate risk to the party best able to manage it. Too often, Government allocates risk by dumping every risk possible onto the contractor.

> *Too often, Government allocates risk by dumping every risk possible onto the contractor.*

This practice appears to derive from a misguided belief that a risk which has been allocated to the contractor ceases to exist.

It is certainly possible to eliminate risks, and it is often a very good thing to do. Every one you eliminate is one less you have to worry about, and you have quite enough to worry about as it is. You do have to remember that elimination of one set of risks generally gives rise to a different set. For instance, you can eliminate risks associated with converting an old maintenance dock to service new ships by building a new maintenance dock instead. You then have to deal with the risks associated with the new build. When you think about eliminating a risk, check that any new risks or costs being introduced won't leave you worse off than you were before.

But risk allocation is just that – allocation. No matter where the risk is allocated, it still exists. Allocation of a risk to the contractor does *not* eliminate it. It just means you are now managing the risk by managing the contract, instead of managing it directly. If you have loaded so much risk into the contract that the contractor goes bust, all those risks come bouncing straight back to Government again.

If you put out a draft contract with an unreasonable risk allocation, you will simply have made the negotiating phase of the procurement more difficult for Government.

You will also have done yourself no favours on the procurement front. If the tenderers accept they will be loaded with risk, the pricing they submit will reflect the amount of risk they are being asked to take on. The less able they are to manage a risk, the higher they will price it. Perhaps more to the point, they may simply refuse to take the risk at all. Just because you issue a draft contract with the Request for Tenders doesn't mean the tenderers will be willing to sign up to it without amendment. If you put out a draft contract with an unreasonable risk allocation, you will simply have made the negotiating phase of the procurement more difficult for Government.

In areas where a particular risk allocation is standard industry practice, you should not depart from it without good reason. Governments have made commendable efforts in recent years to increase the standardisation in major contracts. Some jurisdictions have issued Treasury guidance on the allocation of risk in privately-financed contracts, for instance. Such guidance is helpful and should be followed unless there is reason not to, but never take the guidance as conclusive without thinking whether it really is appropriate for your particular situation. The standard form of anything will never be entirely applicable to a really large contract. It is also the case that some guidance represents what Government would like to see happen rather than what is acceptable in the market.

In tailoring the risk allocation to your situation, do not feel constrained by the type of contract you have selected or by past practice. It is perfectly possible, for instance, to include in an otherwise fixed price contract a package of work remunerated on a cost plus basis, thereby allocating the cost risk of that package to the Agency, even though all other works are done for a fixed price, allocating the cost risk to the contractor.

Risk Management Activities

In addition to allocating risks, the contract can place obligations on the contractor to do things that have the effect of controlling or mitigating risk. The activities may relate to risks allocated to the contractor or risks allocated to the Agency. Constraints introduced into the specification may also have the effect of reducing risk, as we saw in Chapter 4. Do not go overboard on individual risks. You may have come across the Swiss cheese model of risk management. (If not, you can find it in James Reason's book *Managing the Risks of Organisational Accidents*, Ashgate, 1997. It was developed in a safety context but applies equally to commercial risks.)

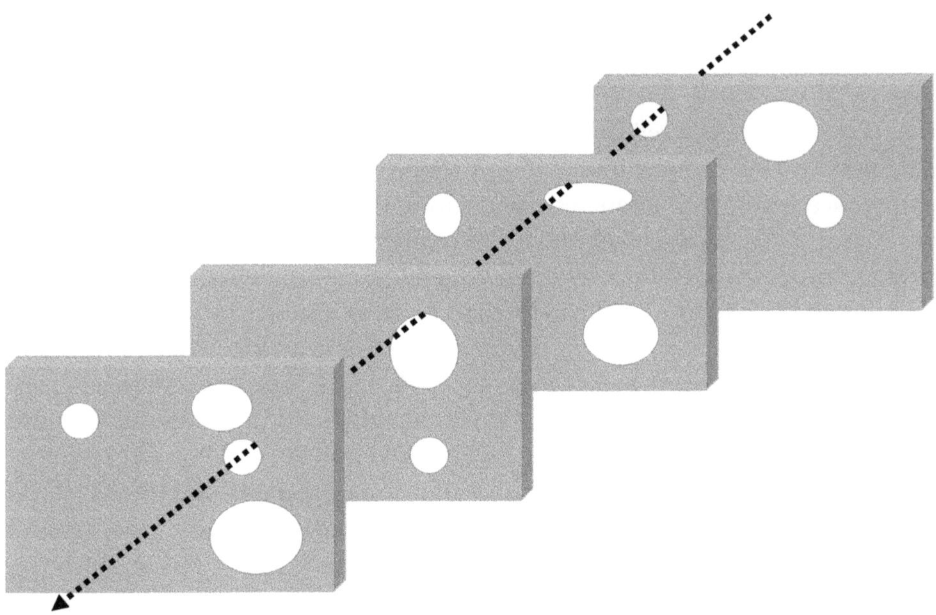

Figure 5.2 The Swiss cheese model

The controls you put in place are like defensive walls against loss. Multiple controls give you defence in depth. The walls are not perfect, but have holes in them like Swiss cheese, as in Figure 5.2. If you don't pay attention, the holes will get bigger. People stop bothering to follow procedures, don't fix broken alarm bells and generally slacken off. Sooner or later, the holes line up and the bullet with your name on it goes straight through the lot.

Don't let this encourage you to add more and more defensive layers. The lesson of the Swiss cheese model is that you need fewer and smaller holes, not that you need more cheese. Risk controls come with costs: they cost money, they cost effort and they may have negative impacts, whether reputational or physical, that make it harder for the Agency to conduct its normal business. Plus, the more defensive layers you have, the less people think the layer they are responsible for is important and the more likely they are to let holes grow unchecked. One person signing off something is correct will pay attention. Two people will probably each assume the other has done the work of checking. Ten people signing off the same document may not even bother to notice what they just approved.

Be particularly careful when you require the contractor to do things to mitigate their own risk. Their risk is, after all, their responsibility, which is what risk allocation is all about. There was a time when many contractors were behind the curve on risk management. It made sense for Government to mandate things like the production of project plans and risk registers because contractors were apt to charge ahead in the general direction of trouble without even relatively basic risk controls. It is now more likely to be the case that the contractors have well-developed risk management systems of their own. Attempts by Government to mandate specific risk management activities may in practice result in bureaucratic accretions with more nuisance value than assurance value. On the other hand, Government does need assurance that that bridge isn't going up 50 metres from where it ought to be. Work it through in detail with your advisers to find the right balance for your project.

If important scope is excluded because some sacred cow must remain unslaughtered ... you are likely to need more risk controls to give the project a chance of success.

There will be times when you need to put risk management activities into the contract because Government can't or won't get its act together. If important scope is excluded because some sacred cow must remain unslaughtered – perhaps you aren't allowed to simplify the industrial awards before embarking on centralising the payroll system, to use the Queensland Health example – you are likely to need more risk controls to give the project a chance of success.

This may give you problems with your stakeholders. Building a dedicated test environment for an IT system or a physical asset can be expensive and time consuming. Piloting systems in a sheltered area of the business for long enough to eliminate the bugs will delay the final roll out. Allowing local exceptions to a project to consolidate activities centrally may reduce the benefits of the centralisation. The better you can communicate the risk, the easier it will be to get authority to implement the controls you need to manage it. If you are having particular difficulty hauling heads out of the sand, engage outside assistance: either a skilled communicator who can help you get the message across, or an independent consultant to tell you what you already know with a level of authority sufficient to convince the stakeholders.

Incentives

The theoretical allocation of risk in a contract does not necessarily reflect where the risk lies in practice. This is the bridge-in-the-wrong-place issue. Under the contract, Government may not be obliged to accept or pay for a bridge that does not meet the specification: the contractor has taken that risk. In practice, there are two problems. The first is the usual uncertainty surrounding litigation: the contractor will seek to push the risk back onto Government by arguing that Government knew and acquiesced in the non-compliance, or that the specification was ambiguous, or whatever. But the real problem is that if what the contractor has delivered is broadly fit for purpose, Government will be under enormous pressure to accept it. The public simply cannot be asked to endure another billion dollars' worth of disruption while the contractor takes down the bridge and puts up another one in the right place.

If what the contractor has delivered is broadly fit for purpose, Government will be under enormous pressure to accept it.

Including obligations in the contract to carry out risk management activities, such as implementing design assurance processes, goes some way towards limiting the risk to Government. It may not be enough to counterbalance the pressures on the contractor to cut costs and save time. The greater the contract value, the greater the pressure.

There is another contract measure you can use to counteract this: performance incentives, to align the interests of Government and the contractor.

Chapter 6

Performance Incentives

Government and contractors approach projects from opposite viewpoints. Contractors are in business to make money. The project is the means by which they make it. For Government, it's the other way round. The project is what Government is there to do and money is the way to make it happen. A well-drafted contract puts the two together so Government ends up with a completed project and the contractor ends up with the money. With a badly-drafted contract, they both end up in court.

> *If contractors can't make money on the contract, they will try to make it on the claims.*

To produce a contract that will not end up in court, you need to think like a contractor. Where are the opportunities for the contractor to make money? If contractors can't make money on the contract, they will try to make it on the claims, so give them the opportunity to make money on the contract (but not so much that it will be embarrassing to Government when the media find out). If they can make money on the claims, they will make the claims even if they are also making money on the contract, so don't give them the opportunity to make money on claims. Badly-drafted contracts are lawsuits waiting to happen.

You *want* contractors to make money by:

- Doing the work you want them to carry out.

- Taking on risks that Government does not want to take. (People can get a bit resentful of this when the risk doesn't eventuate, but it's like insurance premiums. The contractor has to make money when risk events don't occur, in order to have money to pay up when they do. If yours is the accident that never happens, be grateful.)

You *do not* want them to make money by:

- Delivering delayed or substandard product.

- Getting extra money for doing things you thought were already included in the price.
- Being evil. (Child slavery, dangerous work practices and environmental pillage, for example.)

If there is anything you don't want the contractor to do, make sure they don't make money by doing it.

Remember, contractors are in there to make money. Good ones will refrain from evil of their own volition, but apart from that, money is what it is all about. If there is anything you need the contractor to do, make sure they get paid for doing it. If there is anything you don't want the contractor to do, make sure they don't make money by doing it.

Building incentives into the contract increases the probability that the contractor will deliver the contract obligations without the need for intervention by Government.

There is a car repair yard near where I live which has a sign outside saying 'Good, Quick, Cheap' in very large letters. When you go closer you can read the words underneath: 'You can have any two out of three.' Ideally you want all three, but inevitably there will be trade-offs and many of those trade-offs will be made by the contractor, not by Government. You cannot prevent this. What you can do is structure the contract incentives so as to align the contractor's choices with Government's preferences.

Structural Incentives

Some incentives are inherent in the contract structure you choose for the procurement. This should influence your choice of structure. It is almost inconceivable, for instance, that you would choose to deliver a mega-project through a 'cost plus' contract. The contractor, paid more if the costs incurred are higher, is encouraged to push costs as high as possible. Mega-project costs will already be sufficiently stratospheric without creating an incentive to increase them.

If the contract is 'design and build', where the contractor receives a fixed price for delivering the asset, the inherent incentive is to build the asset as cheaply as possible. There is also at least some time incentive, because delays increase costs. There is no inherent quality incentive, which is a problem. When you procure a major asset, you want value for money on a whole of life cost basis, not just on construction. A cheap structure may require more maintenance or more frequent replacement, so that overall it may cost Government more.

An alliance contract is often used where there is significant uncertainty on costs. Initial work is done to establish a reasonable target cost, with overs and unders then shared with the contractor. (Getting this target cost right is key – one that is way out will not provide the right incentives.) In alliance contracts, once the target has been set, the more profit made by the contractor, the lower the cost to Government. This is counter-intuitive, so you need to make sure it is understood, because Agency staff tend to be reluctant to put themselves out just so a contractor can make more profit. The contractor's agreed profit is made when costs come in exactly on the target cost. To make a greater profit, the contractor must bring the job in *below* the target cost: since Government takes a share of the savings, the overall cost to Government is lower. The sharing of cost risk only provides an incentive for the parties to collaborate if the parties understand the benefits that collaboration brings to *both* parties.

The payments are fixed, which clearly provides an incentive to reduce costs. Less obviously, there is a very strong time incentive.

A common model for very large projects is the Public Private Partnership, or PPP. In a PPP, the contractor is remunerated with 'availability payments' or 'access payments'. They build the bridge or the hospital or whatever at their own expense, then when the asset is built receive payments for allowing people to use it: the payments are sufficient over the life of the asset to pay off the loans raised to finance construction. The payments are fixed, which clearly provides an incentive to reduce costs. Less obviously, there is a very strong time incentive. Since the contractor provides the construction finance for an asset costing a billion or two, and access payments only kick in when the asset is delivered and the money has been spent, the financing costs associated with delay are huge. There is also an inherent quality incentive in a PPP, but it is much less robust. In theory, the contractor makes money by keeping down the whole of life costs. It is not in their interests to deliver a poor quality asset, because they will lose all the money saved on construction through increased repair and maintenance costs and lost access payments when the asset is out of service for maintenance. In practice, if things start to go wrong, contractors come under so much financial pressure from the time incentive they are likely to cut corners on construction anyway, regardless of the impact in future years. They will then struggle financially for the whole period of the contract, which always increases the likelihood of claims and disputes, and may even go bust, leaving Government with a poorly constructed asset.

The imperatives for each project will be different. Recognise the incentives that are inherent in the contract structure you have adopted, and include additional focused incentives where you need to change the balance.

The contract for a project on this scale will last for a long time ... you have only this one chance to get it right.

It is worth investing time and thought in this with the best advisers you have access to. The contract for a project on this scale will last for a long time, possibly 30 years or more, and you have only this one chance to get it right.

Delivery Incentives

Delivery of an asset and ongoing provision of services require different approaches to structuring incentives. If your contract includes both, commonly the delivery of an asset followed by the services of operating and maintaining the asset, you need separate incentive regimes for the two phases of the contract.

The simplest form of delivery incentive is the milestone payment, a lump sum payable on delivery of part of the contract works. Because the money is not paid until the works are delivered, Government cannot be put in the undesirable position of having paid for something it then never receives. Most contracts will benefit from milestone payments providing at least part of the contractor's remuneration. They are a useful cross-check on whether the contractor is managing their schedule effectively: a report that a task has moved from 20 per cent complete to 40 per cent complete can be fudged but meeting the conditions for a milestone payment has to be verified. They are also useful where subsidiary obligations are important to Government but are not on the contractor's critical path for the main deliverable: for instance, releasing land used for a temporary worksite. If Government is waiting to use the site for something else, a milestone payment on release of the site will encourage the contractor to hand it over sooner rather than later.

Some incentives are negative rather than positive, creating a cost to the contractor for failure, rather than offering a payment for success. Many contracts provide for liquidated damages (LDs) if the delivery is late, that is, require the contractor to make fixed payments, or have fixed amounts deducted from other monies owing to the contractor, for every day (or week or month) that delivery goes beyond the due date. These can be very effective as incentives, but there are downsides.

One is that Government has to be able to demonstrate that the amounts to be paid or deducted are a genuine pre-estimate of the loss Government will suffer in the event of delay, otherwise the LDs will be unenforceable. Estimation is not always straightforward and it can even be the case that delays *reduce* the cost to Government, because a new asset offering new benefits may result in increased operating costs that are not incurred if delivery of the asset is delayed.

Another issue is that if there is provision for LDs, there must be a provision allowing for extensions of time if the delay is not attributable to the contractor: this can be a nuisance to administer and is a fertile source of disputes. A less obvious problem is that the imposition of LDs has to be a decision by Government at the relevant time. Political will may balk at enforcing a contract against a major local employer who cries poor and threatens job losses in marginal constituencies.

Political will may balk at enforcing a contract against a major local employer who cries poor and threatens job losses in marginal constituencies.

Delivery incentives may relate to quality rather than time. This was a particularly critical issue on the Waratah train procurement. The delivery of trains on an earlier, much smaller, train procurement by the Agency had been an operational and public relations nightmare. The trains had been rushed into service and were initially unreliable. One breakdown occurred on the Sydney Harbour Bridge in peak hour, catastrophic both in the extent of the disruption and in the excellence of the photo opportunity afforded to journalists reporting on the misery being suffered by commuters. This time around, more than four times as many trains were being procured and equivalent levels of initial unreliability would paralyse the network.

The reliability incentives introduced involved both carrot and stick. The carrot was a payment for the achievement of a certain level of reliability in service. At 'Practical Completion' trains entered passenger service, triggering the 'availability payments' associated with that train. As each train demonstrated a specified level of reliability in service, it achieved 'Final Completion' and the contractor became entitled to a one-off payment of $2 million: with 78 trains, a total of $156 million. This was intended to encourage the contractor to deal with the inevitable 'infancy' issues quickly.

The stick was a very big stick indeed. Acceptance of the seventh and subsequent trains was made conditional on the first six trains achieving a certain level of reliability: lower than the level required for the 'Final Completion' payment, but high enough to ensure the operator would still be able to run the timetable even if the trains never did any better. Failure to meet the hurdle would not only give the contractor just six trains' worth of availability payments to service 78 trains' worth of debt, but would also leave them with a production line churning out trains with nowhere to go.

The quality incentives were effective. Since the project did not run perfectly, there was a trade-off with cost and time, but that trade-off was acceptable to Government, because most of the extra cost was borne by the contractor or its subcontractors and the delay could be managed by retaining older trains in service.

Service Incentives

Delivery of services rather than assets requires different incentives, because you are looking to maintain standards or drive continuous improvement over an extended period rather than complete a one-off construction. One common approach during the UK wave of privatisations in the 1990s was to limit price increases by the privatised companies to something less than the increases in the retail price index (the 'RPI-X' formula), while requiring them to deliver the same or better levels of service. That is, the companies had to achieve real price reductions year on year if they were to maintain their profitability, forcing them to deliver services more efficiently.

> *One of the most important things in designing service incentives is to understand how you are going to measure them.*

One of the most important things in designing service incentives is to understand how you are going to measure them. If you want fast response times, do you start the clock when an incident occurs or when it is logged by the service provider? What if the service provider is only expected to work office hours and a request for service is lodged in the middle of the night? Is the response time when the service provider arrives on site or when the problem is fixed? What if the service provider thinks it is fixed but the Agency doesn't? What if a delayed response time was the fault of the Agency? Measures that are ambiguous, not adequately defined or just plain difficult to quantify are easy to have a dispute about.

Many service incentives are tied to service failures: the more service failures, the less the contractor receives. This is not always useful. Some critical systems require 100 per cent service availability, so that any interruption in service is a full-blown crisis that should in theory never happen. In these situations it may be better to measure 'precursor' events, that is, events which do not directly cause service failure but which establish conditions where service failure is more probable. If you have a system and a back-up system, for instance, failure of the system brings the back-up system into use, meaning that until the original system is restored, there is no back-up. This does not result in service downtime, but because there is now no back-up, the risk of downtime is increased. Linking the incentive to the frequency or duration of system failures is likely to be more useful than linking it to a service failure.

Some behaviours that you wish to encourage may not be capable of measurement at all. You may want service providers to greet customers with a smile, for instance, but it is not practicable to check up on each and every customer interaction. For such behaviours you need to find 'proxy' measures, things that are highly correlated with the behaviour although they do not measure it directly. Examples might be measures of customer complaints or regular customer satisfaction surveys.

Something easy to measure won't necessarily provide a sound basis for a service incentive. Too little thought and you will saddle yourself with *perverse* incentives, that is, incentives which have a negative rather than positive impact on contractor behaviour. The number of people on a waiting list for service is easy to measure. If the service is provided more quickly, which is the behaviour you want to encourage, the number of people on the waiting list will fall. Unfortunately, the number of people on the waiting list will also fall if the contractor instead makes it difficult for people to be put on the waiting list in the first place. Do not be optimistic about a contractor's ability to resist the temptation to make money by gaming the system.

Do not be optimistic about a contractor's ability to resist the temptation to make money by gaming the system.

One of the major criticisms of the performance regimes introduced after the privatisation of British Rail was that, although they were intended to create incentives for the privatised companies to reduce delays to rail passengers, their most visible effect was to generate a small army of rail employees whose only job was not to reduce delay but to argue about who was responsible for it. In some cases, if a train company took steps to minimise a delay caused by someone else, it would actually be worse off, because it both bore the cost of minimising the delay and reduced the compensation payments it would receive.

Having only a single incentive is particularly likely to lead to unhelpfully skewed behaviour by the contractor: you will probably need an integrated package of incentives to generate the outcomes you need. But keep the administration as simple as possible or the costs will outweigh the benefits.

Calibration of Incentives

If an incentive is too small, it will have no impact on behaviour: a negative incentive will be treated as a cost of doing business and a positive one will be ignored as not worth the effort. If the incentive is too large, it will drive perverse behaviour. Offering a price per tail for killing rats may be intended to eradicate rats, but pay enough and people set up rat farms. (Yes, really. It happened in Hanoi.) If the incentive is extremely large and also negative, it may put the contractor out of business.

Offering a price per tail for killing rats may be intended to eradicate rats, but pay enough and people set up rat farms.

Bear in mind that you have no unilateral right to impose an incentive regime. There are some legal constraints around unenforceable penalties, although lawyers can usually draft their way round this. More importantly, the contractor has to agree to the regime in the first place. While the excitement of winning what is probably the biggest deal in the industry may lure the contractor into signing up to something where the balance is tipped too far against them, this is not necessarily a plus. A contractor losing a bit of money merely adds tension to the relationship. A contractor losing a lot of money is a court case in the making.

For service incentives, it can be useful to calibrate your incentives by reference to the contractor's anticipated profit. Poor performance eats up the monthly profit but only bad performance pushes the contractor into loss.

Another issue with calibration is that if there is a cap, whether on a positive or negative incentive, the incentive ceases to have any impact as soon as the cap is reached. Removing the cap is not necessarily the answer, since the contractor may be unwilling or unable to enter the contract without one. Sharing mechanisms can be used to prolong the effect of the incentive. Some scenarios for sharing cost overruns are shown in Figure 6.1.

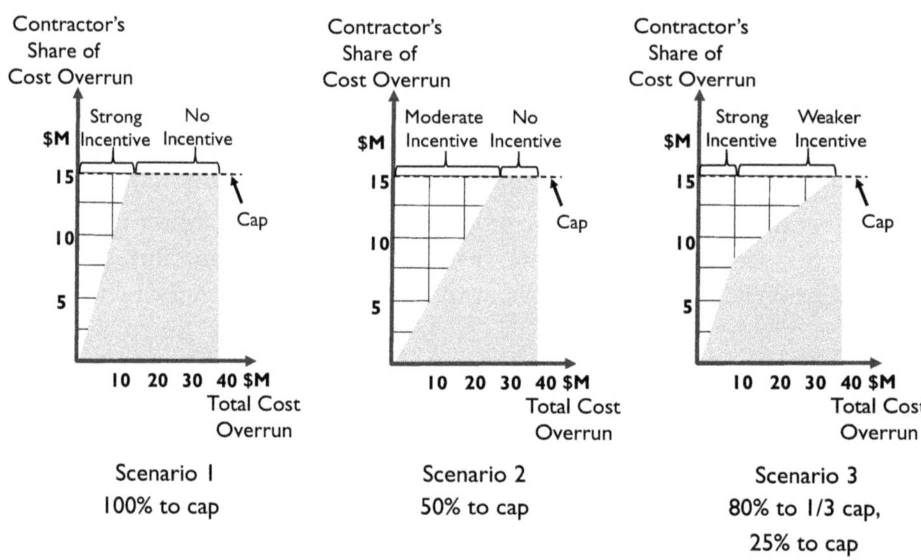

Figure 6.1 Risk sharing scenarios

Scenario 1 has the contractor taking 100 per cent of cost overruns, a strong incentive to reduce costs, until the cap is reached. In Scenario 2 the contractor shares the overruns on a 50/50 basis, a moderate incentive, but the cap is not reached until the overrun is twice that in Scenario 1. In Scenario 3 the contractor takes 80 per cent of the overrun up to one-third of the cap, but only 25 per cent thereafter: the incentive continues for longer than in Scenarios 1 or 2, but the incentive against an initial cost overrun is almost as strong as Scenario 1.

Review Time

The point at which you settle your preferred incentive regime is a good time for a review of your project objectives. Performance incentives are critical in driving contractor behaviour. The details are vital, because the details make the difference between an effective incentive and a perverse one, but it is easy to get bogged down in the detail and lose sight of what you are really trying to achieve.

A mega-project is, by definition, huge. It is not practicable to incentivise every possible aspect of contractor behaviour and a very bad idea to try. This contract will bind the parties for years. If you have a nit-picking performance regime you will have a nit-picking relationship, which is not a productive way to run a contract as big as this one. Incentives should drive the fundamentals, not drive the parties insane.

It is not practicable to incentivise every possible aspect of contractor behaviour and a very bad idea to try.

Consulting with the market before issuing the Request for Tenders is often a useful way to obtain some good feedback on how the regime is likely to work in practice – and how likely the successful tenderer is to sign up to it. An independent review is also a good idea, because you have to get this one right. Contractors will follow the money. Make sure it leads them in the right direction.

Chapter 7
Boilerplate Clauses

Decisions around scope, specification, risk management and incentives will have enabled you to give instructions to your lawyers to produce the draft contract. When the draft arrives at your desk, it will contain more clauses than the ones you specifically asked for. Contracts generally contain a lot of clauses that pop out of the lawyers' precedent bank and are slotted into every contract they produce in virtually identical terms. These clauses are known as 'boilerplate' and many clients don't bother to read them. Sometimes even the lawyers don't bother to read them. This is a mistake.

These clauses are known as 'boilerplate' ... Sometimes even the lawyers don't bother to read them. This is a mistake.

The issue is not about proofreading. Not that a bit of proofreading hurts – typographical errors are usually harmless, but computers have been known to corrupt clauses into total gibberish. The issue is, as always, that the standard form of anything is never entirely appropriate for a mega-project. All clauses are worthy of your attention, but some clauses you should specifically examine are:

- definitions
- conditions precedent
- confidentiality
- contract management
- force majeure
- variations
- dispute resolution
- default and termination.

Definitions

There will inevitably be a large section at the front of the contract containing definitions. Do not ignore it as irrelevant lawyer-fodder: there are traps for the unwary.

The use of defined terms is a handy way of shortening the length of contracts. Being able to refer to 'the Principal' rather than 'The Council of the Municipality of Hunters Hill' or 'The Centre for Environment, Fisheries and Aquaculture Science' saves a surprising number of pages. It also enables lawyers to recycle contracts more easily. If the terms in the body of the contract are anonymous words like 'Principal', 'Contractor' and 'Works', the contract clauses can be picked up and used in a different contract without amendment. This is good, since you don't want to be paying lawyers to reinvent wheels. The downside is that if the lawyer lifted the clause without thinking hard enough about it, the error is less likely to be picked up. Be alert to the fact your contract is not drafted from scratch but is based on a precedent. Don't be shy about asking what a definition or clause is for and why it was included. It may be in there because the lawyer forgot to take it out.

Don't be shy about asking what a definition or clause is for and why it was included.

It is usual to choose defined terms that are descriptive of the thing being defined. If you are buying trams, for instance, you may need to refer to a package of works for the construction of an associated maintenance facility. Your definition of this would be called something like 'Maintenance Facility Works'. There is no reason in law why you couldn't call it 'Taj Mahal' instead, and the relevant clause would require the contractor to deliver the Taj Mahal before delivering the trams. The legal effect would be identical. Your lawyers are unlikely to proffer anything quite so off the wall, but they may be unaware of common Agency usage. I once had a conversation with a railway colleague about the procedure for changing PSRs, which went on for a surprisingly long time before we discovered I was talking about Passenger Service Requirements and he was talking about Permanent Speed Restrictions. If the name of the defined term is likely to give rise to confusion, or gives a misleading impression of what the thing defined is really about, change it.

It is bad practice for lawyers to include substantive obligations in the definitions section of a contract. Obligations should be out there and obvious in the appropriate clause under a useful heading. Good practice is not always followed, so check the definitions section for hidden obligations. If the contractor is required to deliver a series of plans, for instance, the named plans may be identified in the definitions section, but obligations around time of delivery or the applicable review period should be clearly set out in substantive clauses.

Many definitions are standard. That doesn't mean they are right for you to use, but it does mean that if you change them, you should make sure people are aware you have done so. Take the definition of 'Business Day'. In Australia, Christmas comes in summer. The entire country is more or less closed for non-tourist business from Christmas Eve to New Years' Day and the school holidays continue until after the Australia Day public holiday on 26 January. Cunning contractors have been known to deliver large quantities of documents or product just before 5pm on Christmas Eve, hoping the review period specified in the contract will have expired before anyone notices. To prevent this happening on the Waratah train procurement, the definition of Business Day excluded the entire period from the Monday before Christmas to the Friday after New Year, so the clock stopped ticking during the break. Which was fine on that contract, because everyone knew about it. When a similar definition went into a later contract, the contractor failed to notice and was badly caught out on their scheduling through not allowing for the longer design review period.

Conditions Precedent

Sometimes you don't want to sign a contract unless something else happens first, but the something else can't happen until you sign a contract. Occasionally a tenderer will be unable to secure a vital subcontractor without first having a firm agreement with you. Required guarantees may not be available. A licence may not be granted. You can't have a contract without it, but you can't have it without a contract. In ordinary life this is called a Catch 22, after the book by Joseph Heller.

> *Sometimes you don't want to sign a contract unless something else happens first, but the something else can't happen until you sign a contract.*

Little things like a Catch 22 cannot be allowed to get in the way of a mega-project. The legal technique used to square the circle is called a condition precedent. Suppose the problem is the need for the tenderer to get a licence that they cannot get without a confirmed contract. You enter into a contract which is immediately binding, but it contains a clause saying most of the provisions in it are only triggered if a 'condition precedent' is fulfilled. In this case, the granting of the licence within a specified time period is the condition precedent. (Always specify a time period. There is only so long you should be prepared to wait.) If the licence is granted, you are committed to go ahead – the contract is binding, you can't change your mind. If the licence is not granted within the period, the contract terminates and you are free to do something else.

Don't use conditions precedent unless you have to. It is rarely a good idea to enter into a binding contract when you aren't sure of the outcome. But when you are faced with a genuine Catch 22, it is a really useful tool.

Confidentiality

The rhetoric of openness and transparency in public affairs is in most jurisdictions now backed by legislation requiring Government agencies to make information available on request and in some cases to publish it whether or not anyone has any interest in it at all. To avoid disputes with the contractor over whether Government is or is not entitled to release information in relation to the contract, it is usually helpful to agree specifically which information is genuinely commercially confidential. The structure of a performance regime would normally not be confidential, for instance, but the quantum of payments to be made under it may or may not be.

> *Government traditionally works on a perversion of the need-to-know principle: if you need to know, they don't tell you.*

The openness prescribed by the legislation has had only a limited impact on the natural tendency of the public sector to conceal absolutely everything, even from other people in the same Agency. Government traditionally works on a perversion of the need-to-know principle: if you need to know, they don't tell you. Even with the legislation in place, the first reaction of some Government agencies when confronted with a request for information is to see if there are any plausible grounds for withholding it. Government's tendency to secrecy and paranoia can sometimes lead it into wholly inappropriate attempts to control communications. The contract for the Victorian Desalination Plant project, signed in 2009, not only included a very restrictive confidentiality provision, the performance regime provided for a financial 'abatement' for any breach. Whether the 'abatement' would actually be enforceable against the contractor or whether it would be struck out as a penalty has never been tested, but the purpose of a performance regime is not to pander to Government paranoia. Some matters do need to be kept confidential, but ask yourself whether your clause can be regarded as consistent with transparency and fairness.

Contract Management

One of the most important things a contract does is govern the relationship between the parties. Project managers will always have their own ways of making things happen, and you should never underestimate the importance of personalities and personal relationships. Saying 'please' and 'thank you' takes you a long way. But on a mega-project the stakes are high, and businesses do not spend millions just because someone smiles and says 'please'. Project managers do not always last the course, but the project needs to keep right on going. (Turnover in project managers is highly correlated with project failure – we may, with Lady Bracknell, regard losing one as a misfortune and losing two as carelessness, but the departure of a third should mean press the panic button.) To ensure the relationship can survive a change of personalities, you need to make provision in the contract.

Relationships are all about communication. You need the contract to make provision for three things:

1. a channel exclusively used for formal contract communications;
2. one or more forums for resolving day-to-day issues;
3. regular reports.

FORMAL COMMUNICATION CHANNEL

It is hard to get your head around the realisation that the whole thing can be completely undermined by an idiot sending an email.

Your contract may come with a public signing ceremony, involving VIPs and a press conference, or it may be signed quietly in the small hours of the morning after crunchy negotiations. However it happens, it will be the culmination of an enormous amount of effort. It is hard to get your head around the realisation that the whole thing can be completely undermined by an idiot sending an email.

In days gone by, sending a letter was a big deal. There was rigid control over who was entitled to use letterhead and being allowed to sign your own letters was a significant step up the ladder of promotion. This didn't entirely prevent people sending stupid letters, but it certainly limited the opportunities. Many a boss was saved from their own idiocy by an alert secretary, or by having second thoughts before the mail vanished from the out tray. These days, bosses do their own typing and there is nothing between them and the send button.

Emails count as 'writing'. Unless you do something special, all those clauses that say nobody does anything different without written authority, all those clauses that say the design can't be changed or time periods can't be extended or obligations can't be waived, all the protective value of those clauses can be overturned with one click of a send button. So do something special.

Do not attempt to avoid the problem by telling the project team they aren't allowed to send emails. The world has gone beyond that. You need to make specific provision in the contract for a formal communication channel, which says that no emails or other communications can be relied upon unless they are confirmed through the formal channel. The formal channel must not be something you can do by accident, but it doesn't have to be complicated. A signed letter on letterhead, scanned and attached to an email as a pdf file will do. Having one route for formal communications, and one route only, cuts down the risk of disputes and inadvertent changes to the contract.

Note that you have not eliminated the rogue email risk entirely. There will remain circumstances where idiot emails may still have legal effect – in particular if you get lazy and make a practice of expecting the contractor to act on communications not sent through the formal channel – but the risk control is a useful one.

COMMUNICATION FORUMS

> *The first thing many contractor project directors do when things start to go wrong is hide from the customer.*

It is far from best practice, but the first thing many contractor project directors do when things start to go wrong is hide from the customer. The second thing they do is hide from their boss. On one project I was involved in, the boss at the contractor kept insisting all was well, which was probably what the project director kept telling him. By the time we had an independent schedule audit done, which was many months into the project, completion was further away than it had been when we signed the contract. Don't allow the contractor project director to hide. You will need a mandated regular forum, which will probably be called something like the Senior Project Group, where the two project directors and their immediate bosses get together to review how the project is doing. The more open and honest this forum can be, the greater the chances of project success.

You can write behavioural aspirations into the contract: they are most commonly seen in alliance type contracts, which often talk about the Senior Project Group having a responsibility to model the sort of collaborative behaviours that make alliance projects successful. You don't have to limit this to alliance contracts, since collaborative behaviours are also useful in other project structures (uncollaborative behaviours such as lying, bullying and shooting messengers have adverse impacts in pretty much any context) but don't be under any illusions that writing the words into the contract will of itself have much impact. While there are things you can do to get off to a good start with the contractor, the behaviours most likely to emerge from the contractor are those driven by the money. If there are behaviours you don't want to see from the contractor, don't give them a financial incentive to indulge in them.

Most communication on the project will be handled at least one level below the Senior Project Group. Depending on the amount of interaction between your team and the contractor's team that will be necessary to deliver the project, you may need to build a level of formality into the contract around how this will occur. You may need to have a design forum, or a safety forum, or other specialist groups that meet regularly and cover a set agenda. This doesn't prevent people talking outside those forums, but it provides a minimum level of interaction. It is not really a matter of being able to enforce the interaction (although you can: the obligation to attend meetings is just as much a legal obligation as any other in the contract). The point is that if the meetings don't happen, or the contractor starts dodging some of the agenda items, you know there's trouble. The sooner you know, the sooner you can do something about it.

The obligation to attend meetings is just as much a legal obligation as any other in the contract.

If you reach mutual agreement that a forum is no longer necessary, that is fine, but both the Senior Project Group and your Government steering committee need to know. Contract forums are part of the project governance structure and their continued existence should not be within the discretion of the project director unless the steering committee has expressly agreed to that.

REPORTS

Managing a contract requires knowledge. Since the contractor is the one doing the work, not you, you won't know what is happening unless the contractor tells you. What do you want to know? What do you *need* to know? How are you going to find out?

Some of this depends on the type of contract. An alliance contract is predicated on everybody knowing everything, with Government being entitled to see all of the contractor's financial information about the project. In a fixed price contract, the contractor does not expect to hand over any financial information at all. Work out what is appropriate and include minimum reporting requirements. In practice, reporting formats are normally agreed fairly amicably, but a minimum requirement gives you some protection if the contractor starts hiding.

You may sometimes wish to go behind the reports to provide assurance the information the contractor is giving you is accurate. Government typically demands very intrusive audit rights then either gets in the contractor's way by exercising them without due thought or (far more commonly) fails to exercise them at all. Think about what you really need and set the contract management team to prepare an audit plan that provides assurance without interference.

Scheduling software these days is capable of providing unparalleled information.

One thing you should consider seeking is unfettered read-only access to the contractor's project schedule. Scheduling software these days is capable of providing unparalleled information. If the contractor is using the full functionality of the software, and you have someone capable of understanding what the software is telling you (neither of these are givens) then it is a very reliable guide to the current state of the project. When the time comes, use your access privileges tactfully to develop trust between the parties: unfettered access will be counter-productive if it discourages the contractor from putting information into the schedule at all.

When Things Go Wrong

Most of the contract provisions discussed to this point are about trying to ensure the project goes well. A clear specification, so you don't have disputes about what the contractor is supposed to do. Risk allocation, so the parties know what risks they have to manage. Prescribed activities to reduce the risk of things going wrong. Clear channels of communication to prevent misunderstandings. In risk management terms, this is all aimed at the left hand side of the risk bowtie (see Figure 7.1: no prizes for guessing where the name comes from) by introducing controls to block the causes of risk events.

Much of the boilerplate in a contract is instead directed at the right hand side of the bowtie, at coping with the consequences of something going wrong. The risk event has occurred despite everyone's best efforts at controlling the causes. What can now be done to limit the severity of the consequences? One of the most important functions of the contract is to set out the rights and obligations of the parties when things don't happen in accordance with Plan A.

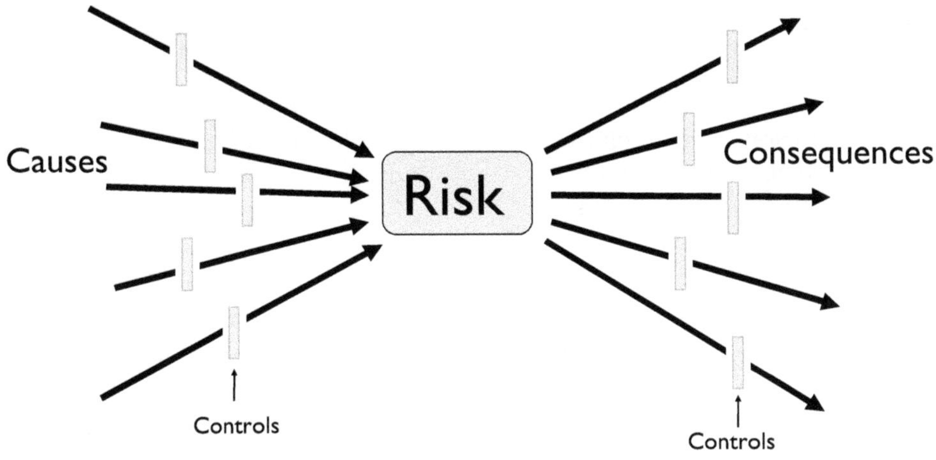

Figure 7.1 The risk bowtie

Force Majeure

The 'Force Majeure' clause will come straight from the precedent bank of your lawyers and it will definitely need attention. These clauses deal with natural disasters and other circumstances where it is considered unreasonable for the normal risk allocation to apply. The risk of these 'Acts of God' is always with Government. You can interpret this as meaning that God is never on Government's side, or alternatively that Government *is* God, depending on how cheerful you are feeling at the time.

The reason the clause will need attention is that what would be an Act of God in a small procurement may well be business as usual for you. I haven't seen the Thames Barrier contract, for instance, but you can be sure it didn't let the contractor off the hook for high tides and 20-year storm surges, because the whole purpose of the Thames Barrier is to protect London against such events. Electrical storms in Sydney are a regular feature of summer weather: a contractor building a communications tower needs to build in protection against lightning strikes, not to be held harmless when a strike occurs. Adjust the standard formulation as necessary to meet your circumstances.

What would be an Act of God in a small procurement may well be business as usual for you.

Variations

However carefully you draft the specification, however viciously you subdue the ambitions of your stakeholders, something will come up.

You will not make it through to completion of a mega-project without any contract variations. However carefully you draft the specification, however viciously you subdue the ambitions of your stakeholders, something will come up. Make sure there is a variations process that allows you to identify all the costs and consequences before you press the go button.

While it is probably essential to retain a power to allow Government to direct variations without waiting for the outcome of such a process, this is a nuclear option that in practice should be avoided if at all possible. Once you give a direction, the cost of the consequences will fall on Government. This is not something to risk lightly. Mega-projects have mega-consequences.

That does not mean you can afford a process which takes up a lot of time. Simplicity and speed pay dividends here. Costs of variations are often very strictly time bound. There may be a short window when you can make a minor variation with very little difficulty – do you want it this material or that material? This wide or that wide? This functionality or that functionality? Once the window is closed, the cost of change becomes totally disproportionate to the difference between the choices. You cannot keep a low cost window open just by writing a longer time period into the contract: yes, you can force the window to stay open, but no, it won't be low cost.

The trick is to match the contract variation process with your internal governance framework. You need the commitment of your stakeholders to a structured approvals process that will enable you to make clear decisions on variations, whether initiated by Government or the contractor, in the shortest practicable time.

Do not let the beauty of the process you devise distract you from the main game. Variations are bad news for projects. Put the investment into the specification up front to keep variations to a minimum.

Dispute Resolution

The best way not to end up in court is to sort out any problems before you get there. A well-run Senior Project Group can deal with most issues, and it is customary also to include in the contract a provision requiring a head-to-head session between chief executives before the parties are entitled to proceed to litigation. Sometimes this is not enough.

You don't have to make litigation the next step. There is now a range of alternative dispute resolution procedures available. Mediation is great when it works, but can usually only bridge a relatively narrow gap between the parties. Arbitration is effectively litigation with your own private judge. An increasingly common approach is the use of Dispute Resolution Boards. These come in various formats. Common to all is that the Board (usually three experienced independents) is appointed at the very start of the contract and meets regularly throughout, regardless of whether any disputes are happening at any given time. Although such Boards have a good track record in resolving disputes, their real value is in heading off disputes in the first place. Since Board members are both experienced and independent, they can often spot potential trouble before the parties and will encourage them to deal with issues before the cost of resolving them has risen to the point where amicable settlement is impossible.

Mediation is great when it works, but can usually only bridge a relatively narrow gap between the parties.

All approaches to dispute resolution have their advantages and disadvantages. Form a view on the nature and extent of the risk and make provision in the contract accordingly.

Default and Termination

The contract will have a number of clauses useful only when the project is in dying cockroach mode, flat on its back with its little legs waving feebly in the hope of attracting a miracle. No one goes into a tender process in the expectation of project failure. It is hard to pay much attention to clauses that you confidently believe will never have any relevance at all. Do not neglect them. If the project does do a dying cockroach on you, you will be extremely grateful to have workable provisions about step in rights, termination and the like available.

The main thing to focus on with these clauses is clarity. While that is a useful attribute of any contract provision, it is particularly important here because the idea of these clauses is to impose a simple defined solution onto a situation which will be a horrible suppurating mess. This will not be something that is sorted out by one chief executive calling another and saying,

The idea of these clauses is to impose a simple defined solution onto a situation which will be a horrible suppurating mess.

'It's about time you guys got your act together.' You do not invoke default and termination provisions unless matters have deteriorated well beyond that point. Work through some horror story scenarios and check that you will be able to trigger the provisions while there is still something left to salvage.

Then go back and work on the other side of the risk bowtie. Limiting adverse consequences is essential risk management, but a gram of prevention is worth a kilogram of cure. The horror stories with the least bad outcomes are the ones that don't happen at all.

Stakeholder Management

From your point of view, dealing with the boilerplate clauses may come as something of a relief. Since the clauses are insufficiently sexy to interest the bulk of your stakeholders, they are likely to be developed primarily between you and the lawyers. Practically everything else will find you attempting to reconcile the irreconcilable demands and opinions of an extraordinarily diverse range of civil servants, advisers, technical experts, politicians and all of the others who become caught up in the project.

How you manage these people is critical to your success. Since this is a public sector project, let's start with the Minister.

PART III
The People

Chapter 8
The Minister

If your background is in the private sector, you may not immediately comprehend the public sector obsession with politicians. The Minister, after all, is not God. (This may not always be apparent from the behaviour of the people in the immediate vicinity, or indeed the behaviour of the Minister.) But Ministers are empowered by law to give directions to their departments that must be obeyed. Government agencies are only too well aware they may spend many years and much of their budget developing a strategic project, only for an incoming Government to decide it is the wrong project and bin it. The Minister's power and influence over your project is real.

This means you have to divide your stakeholders into two categories: the ones who complain to the Minister and the ones who don't. The staffers who work in the Minister's office think *everybody* complains to the Minister. This is a mild exaggeration.

Divide your stakeholders into two categories: the ones who complain to the Minister and the ones who don't.

Agency employees, for instance, will freely *blame* the Minister for disrupting their lives with restructurings and cost savings programmes, but generally prefer to express their complaints within Agency walls, to their manager, union representative or anyone willing to have their ear bent at the coffee point.

Agency advisers will also normally refrain from complaining to the Minister: they know the Agency would perceive this as betrayal, which is bad for future fee-earning opportunities. If concerned, advisers will seek a quiet word with the Agency chief executive or a senior line manager, but the Minister is normally regarded as off limits.

Agency employees and advisers apart, the rest of the world will complain to the Minister, whether directly or through an intermediary such as another MP, a lobbyist or the media. This means you have to manage most of your stakeholders not only for their own sake, but for the sake of what they may say to the Minister. There are four categories of complainants you have to worry about:

1. *the community*, particularly those directly affected by whatever your project is delivering: the commuters who will catch your trains, the residents who will suffer the environmental impacts of your bridge construction, the criminals who will be locked up in your prison;

2. *the media*, who are always interested in anything costing as much money as a mega-project, especially when they can put the word 'fiasco' into the headline;

3. *the unions*, who will be quick to perceive threats to themselves and their members; and

4. *the bidders*, without whose cooperation you will never manage to set up a contract at all.

The Community

The extent to which you need to deal directly with the people affected by your project (it is disrespectful to call them the 'punters', although the term is not uncommon) depends very much on the type of project.

By the time an Agency has reached the stage of appointing a project director to set up a contract, the time for focus groups has usually passed. In finalising the specification you need to take into account community input that has already been gathered but you don't normally have to set up a focus group yourself. If your project does require it, you will probably need professional assistance to find some genuinely representative groups and generate meaningful responses. If that expertise is not available within the Agency, obtain it through a proper procurement process rather than grabbing the first company to show up. Professionals in the marketing business apply their skills to marketing their own businesses: the first marketer you meet will seem like the greatest thing since sliced bread, but so will every other marketer you meet.

If that expertise is not available within the Agency, obtain it through a proper procurement process rather than grabbing the first company to show up.

One area where community consultation is often required is in relation to planning permissions. You will need to align the procurement process with the planning process. Will you obtain all permissions before going to tender? This may delay your approach to market but will give more certainty for (and therefore probably better pricing from) the contractor. Or will you require the contractor to obtain some or all of those permissions and pass the risk to them? If sections of the community are likely to have strong objections, do you want the consultation managed by the contractor, to keep it at arm's length from the Agency, or does the Agency want to run the consultation, to maintain its existing relationships with the community? How will you handle community groups that already meet regularly with the Agency, or are formed in response to the project?

Whichever route you adopt, do not take the community lightly. Public resistance can bring down a project before it gets off the ground. The advent of social media has changed the balance of power in public debate, but the community has always been capable of making itself heard at the highest level. In the Air Traffic Control System case, the Australian Civil Aviation Authority was procuring civil engineering works as well as the electronic system. Approvals for the works were required from the Public Works Committee of the Parliament, but because of various procurement process failures, no preferred bidder had been selected by the time the Public Works Committee proceedings commenced. The works proposals of both remaining bidders had to be presented, helping to ignite public controversy. The preferred bidder decision made in the face of this controversy was overturned after the Minister called for an inquiry and the procurement process had to be rerun with the two bidders.

Public resistance can bring down a project before it gets off the ground.

Very large projects often cross electoral boundaries. Where the community in question is not in the Minister's own constituency, disgruntled voters will trundle off to their own MPs rather than to your Minister. This does not let you off the hook, it just means the protests landing in the Minister's office will come from the MPs rather than direct from the voters.

You will win brownie points from the Minister and save yourself a lot of time responding to questions from their office (usually referred to as 'Ministerials') if you put together an information pack for each affected MP setting out the impact of the project within their electorate. Unless specifically requested by the Minister's office, do not send these direct to the MPs in question. The provision of the information is a personal favour from the Minister to the MP: you won't get the brownie points from the Minister unless the Minister gets the brownie points from the MPs.

Community impacts can be highly controversial. A freight terminal that brings business to one port will take business away from another port. A hospital that is not in one resident's back yard will be in some other resident's back yard. Choosing between alternatives means choosing which set of winners and losers you end up with, but there will inevitably be losers. You cannot please all of the people all of the time. You can always show them respect. The community is composed of taxpayers and people supported by taxpayers. Demonstrate your respect by procuring the project properly and setting it up to be delivered with no disputes, no delays and no cost overruns. If your project is an expensive failure, *everybody* loses.

The Media

Once a project has been announced, it is now taken for granted that there will be a dedicated website, or at least a page on the Agency website. This is officially for the purpose of providing the community with information about the project, but in practice it tends to form part of an overall media strategy which goes beyond your project and beyond your control. While you are unlikely to be directly responsible for the website itself – the Agency media team will handle that – you do need to make yourself responsible for the content relating to the project. Keep it simple and factual. The contract hasn't even been set up yet, so don't commit the Agency to things it may not be able to deliver and don't include anything that might compromise the integrity of the procurement process.

It is possible to view the media's chief role in the project as that of nuisance.

It is possible to view the media's chief role in the project as that of nuisance. They provide no assistance, take up your valuable time and report on the things you would rather they didn't. If this is your approach, you need to develop a little more sophistication. Mega-projects are news. Journalists and bloggers decide whether they are reported as good news or bad news, and if your project is being reported as bad news your life will be miserable. Favourable media coverage is a morale booster for the team, facilitates public consultations and encourages your public and your employers to regard the project as a success.

Anyone who has been savaged by the media will be wary forever, but relatively few journalists have rottweiler instincts. Many of the traditional media have so thoroughly downsized their professional staff that a substantial proportion of the content comes from media releases that barely get edited, never mind investigated. Journalists need stories and if you have something even mildly interesting to report they will often just take what you give them and be genuinely grateful.

The bigger problem is that news about a mega-project is news about Government, which often attracts the rottweilers for reasons that have nothing to do with your project. Minor issues that would ordinarily pass unnoticed may suddenly become front page news. Your media team will no doubt provide you with advice on how to deal with the media, and you may want to take some specific training if you are regularly being interviewed, but the number one rule is: do not lie. Ever. If the truth is not for publication, things can get a bit awkward when 'No comment' is insufficient to hold the rottweilers at bay, but resist any temptation to lie. A lying Government official is news. For you, bad news.

A lying Government official is news. For you, bad news.

Your project can also suffer severely if your Minister's personal standards do not accord with public morality and through misfortune or misjudgement this is uncovered by the media. A Minister who has just been caught molesting small children, charging brothel visits to the public purse, or accepting cash-filled brown envelopes to do favours for property developers is not going to be a Minister much longer. The media coverage will be explosive. If your project happens to be due for a Cabinet decision, you will probably be bumped off the agenda and it may take some time to achieve enough traction with the replacement Minister to be put back on it again. If the staffers are caught in the fallout, you will have to educate a whole new Ministerial team, not just the new Minister.

It is even more awkward if the Minister's misdemeanours relate directly to the project. The Jasper Inquiry by the New South Wales Independent Commission Against Corruption, which concerned tenders for coal exploration licences, found the Minister had requested an extension of the period for submission of expressions of interest to allow additional bids, even though the period had already expired. There was a probity auditor in place, an '*experienced public servant*'. He drafted a recommendation against the extension, but, as public servants tend to do, withdrew the objection on being advised the Minister had already made up his mind on the issue. In due course the Inquiry found the Minister had made the decision corruptly in order to favour a third party. Oops.

Even in circumstances when the media coverage is not running riot, the protocol within the project should provide for all media enquiries to be referred to the Agency's media team. Be firm about this. Your project people are perfectly capable of answering questions about the project, but will not necessarily appreciate the wider implications. (The media team won't necessarily appreciate them either, so make sure you are kept in the loop.) When the media team calls you up for input in dealing with a query they have received, make a point of responding quickly.

You may be managing a five- to 30-year mega-project but your Minister is managing a 24-hour news cycle.

You may be managing a five- to 30-year mega-project but your Minister is managing a 24-hour news cycle. I know which one you probably think is more important for the future of the national economy, but the Minister and the media are both stakeholders who can make your life difficult. Prompt responses and regular photo opportunities go a long way to keeping them off your back.

The symbiotic relationship between the media and the politicians has some interesting side effects. You can be reasonably sure that any company capable of tendering for a mega-project is aware when one is coming and will take less than 24 hours after you issue your request for expressions of interest, possibly less than 24 seconds, to download it from the Government e-tender website. You will nonetheless probably find the Minister's office is encouraging you to advertise the start of the procurement process in every national newspaper and perhaps some prestigious international journals as well. This has very little to do with the need to give fair notice to potential bidders and rather a lot to do with the Minister's wish to generate news stories favourable to the Government.

If an election is approaching, check out electoral restrictions on advertising so you don't inadvertently land the Minister in trouble, but it doesn't hurt to be helpful to the media. Journalists have a tendency to equate secrecy with scandal (scandal always energises the rottweilers) and don't necessarily appreciate that during the procurement phase a lot of information must be kept confidential to protect the integrity of the procurement process. Be generous while you can and bank some favourable publicity.

The Unions

The nature and extent of the interest shown by labour unions will vary significantly depending on the type of project. If it involves job losses or outsourcing, they will be at the Agency's door in no time. If it involves work that would not have been done by Government employees anyway, they may focus more of their attention on the bidders.

The area of industrial relations has become, on the whole, one that you need to leave to the experts, or at any rate approach only with their assistance. The union agenda will invariably be wider than your particular project and unless you are attuned to the bargaining environment, you could find yourself in unexpected trouble. The tone of the relationship with the unions, whether conciliatory or confrontational, may be set by the Minister, although some Ministers prefer to keep their distance and maintain that all decisions are for the Agency. Depending on which side of politics is currently in Government, the Minister may owe or hope to owe the unions some favours, which is apt to colour the rhetoric even if it has no impact on the policy.

Do not make the mistake of thinking that because you are going to some trouble to treat employees fairly and to persuade Government to be generous to those who are adversely affected by your project – which is what you should be doing – the unions will therefore automatically regard you with favour. You may be seeking a *fair* outcome, but the unions will be seeking a *better* outcome, and who can blame them? Unfortunately, they may take the view that the way to do it is to demonise everything you are trying to achieve.

The other trap is that the interests of unions are not identical with the interests of union members. Unions have won many concessions from public sector organisations. These may include:

The interests of unions are not identical with the interests of union members.

- allowing union membership fees to be paid by way of automatic payroll deductions, thereby putting the administrative cost onto Government and reducing resistance to payment;
- granting rights of entry into the workplace for union officials, which assist them to recruit new members, inspect conditions and influence the workforce;
- paying public sector employees to spend what would otherwise be 'company time' undertaking union business.

The point is not whether such concessions are good or bad, but that they are often more extensive than those available to the unions from private sector employers. This is particularly the case where an outsourcing or privatisation project results in the workforce being divided among a number of smaller organisations rather than a single large one. Not only are smaller organisations less able to afford generous concessions, the overall influence of the unions is divided and diminished. Unions may therefore have a reason to oppose a project even in cases where individual union members are better off if the project goes ahead.

As with dealing with the media, do not tell lies. Always play a very straight bat when dealing with unions. And whatever the temptation, use the bat to hit the ball, not the union representative.

The Bidders

The Minister probably knows the bidders better than you do. Mega-projects rarely come out of the blue. Even the general public can usually see them coming, so you can be sure the potential bidders are on the alert and polishing their profiles. Big companies hoping to win projects make political donations to buy face time with Ministers. They employ lobbyists to gain access to Ministers. They attend industry association lunches where Ministers will address them, as the price of the excuse to shake their hands and congratulate them on their scintillating speeches.

This interaction is rarely sinister, although corrupt Ministers are regrettably not entirely unknown. While the potential bidders will take any opportunity to remind your Minister that they are a benign presence in the local market, creators of jobs, caring about the environment and so on and so on, their main objective is that the project should go ahead, in a form that allows them a chance to bid. And if they happen to pick up some information along the way to help them make their bids more attractive to Government, they won't mind that either. Preliminary skirmishing of this nature is harmless. But the rules change once the formal procurement process has begun. It's your job to make sure everyone understands that.

Preliminary skirmishing of this nature is harmless. But the rules change once the formal procurement process has begun.

You tell the bidders in two ways. The formal invitation to submit an expression of interest, or a full tender, should include terms and conditions that require bidders to refrain from approaching the project team or anyone at the Agency or Minister's office in relation to the procurement process. Of course you give them specified channels to ask questions or raise concerns, plus opportunities for more general discussion in programmed workshops and the like, but it should be clear that lobbying or digging for information may lead to being thrown out of the competition. (May, not will – always leave yourself a discretion on whether the offence merits disqualification.) You should also make a point of mentioning it when you give your presentation to potential bidders at the launch event for the procurement process.

> *Anyone who has made it to Ministerial rank has a highly-developed sense of self-preservation ... but Ministers often have young and inexperienced staffers.*

Tell the Minister as well. Anyone who has made it to Ministerial rank has a highly-developed sense of self-preservation that would normally keep them out of trouble, but Ministers often have young and inexperienced staffers. Youthful enthusiasm is charming, but potentially lethal. A large part of a staffer's job description involves dealing with lobbyists and the media. The last thing you need is confidential information being let slip by a naïve staffer trying to be helpful or make themselves seem important. The best approach is usually to put together a short protocol (don't expect anyone to read more than two sides of A4) that identifies the bidders and gives a few simple rules for both Minister and staff. The irreducible minimum is probably that they should:

- declare any conflict of interest: special arrangements will be necessary if, say, a staffer is married to someone in one of the bid teams;

- not meet bidders alone: have a witness to the conversation and to the absence of brown paper bags full of cash;

- not talk to or email the bidders about the procurement process: keep it off the agenda and politely decline any conversational gambits;

- secure confidential briefing material: don't leave it lying around where people might see it.

Ideally the staffers will also agree to check with you before the Minister makes any public statement about the project, but you probably won't get that one in writing. The main thing is to reach an understanding that management of the bidders in the procurement process is down to you, not the Minister's office.

Your management of the bidders during the procurement process is a key factor in whether they decide to sue you if they lose. While the risk of a lawsuit is real, it would be a mistake to think of the bidders as the enemy. The bidders that don't win the contract are just as important as the one that does, because they provide the competition that will deliver you value for Government's money. You need them. Treat them well. These companies are going to spend millions on the bid process and you are going to entrust one of them with stupendous amounts of Government money.

In the InterCity West Coast franchise case, the UK Department for Transport originally advised the market it planned to issue the invitation to tender in May 2011. On the very day the invitation was to have been issued, the Department said it wasn't ready and put off the tender process indefinitely, eventually going to market in January 2012. The bidders, who had taken on premises and bid teams ready to start work the instant the tender request was available, were not amused. While there was no direct link to the problems that subsequently caused the competition to be cancelled, the failure to give notice of the change put up bid costs and did nothing for anyone's confidence in the process.

Bidders are grown-ups, used to the rough and tumble of the market, and they are not going to curl up and cry if you mess them around or make their job unnecessarily difficult. Nor should you see yourself as a suppliant. The balance of power between you and the bidders will vary, but when you are setting up a contract worth billions your power will never be zero. Nonetheless, courtesy pays dividends at the negotiating table and will also help directors of future Government projects. Yours may be the biggest in the country right now, but there are more in the pipeline and the market for mega-projects goes beyond your national borders. Governments with a reputation for being straightforward and easy to deal with attract a better class of bidder and more competitive pricing.

The balance of power between you and the bidders will vary, but when you are setting up a contract worth billions your power will never be zero.

Do not let courtesy stop you from remembering at all times that bidders will pursue their own interests with vigour and have no brief to protect yours. When you consult with the market about potential structures for the contract, for instance, potential bidders will seek a structure that gives them the best opportunity to participate. Do not expect a banker to recommend against private finance. When you reveal information in conversation with one bidder, do not expect them to remind you that the same information should be given to the other bidders too.

Bidders are trying to sell you something. The face they show you is the one they think you want to see. A bidder who does not complain when you make a procedural error is not necessarily a happy bunny. They may just be avoiding antagonising you now and saving it up in case they want to try to overturn an unfavourable decision later. Go behind the mask. Whenever you meet with a bidder after the formal procurement process has commenced, reserve a slot at the end of the meeting to check whether they have any concerns about the process you are following. They may not tell you, but if they say they have no concerns, minute their answer in case you need to use it in evidence. If they say 'yes', deal with their concerns.

Always take bidder issues seriously, if only because the fact that you take it seriously will often be sufficient to satisfy the bidder doing the complaining.

Always take bidder issues seriously, if only because the fact that you take it seriously will often be sufficient to satisfy the bidder doing the complaining. They know you have to make a judgment on things, and that if your judgment is made in good faith and on reasonable grounds they have very little chance of mounting a successful challenge, even if they think your judgment is wrong. But if they feel their protests are being ignored, they may take them further. Whether the protests land on the desk of a journalist, your Minister or a judge, you have just lost control of the process, and that is not somewhere you want to be.

Occasionally the issues that arise will be between bidder and bidder rather than between the bidder and Government. Having the same adviser on opposing bid teams is just as much of a problem as having the same adviser on bid and evaluation teams: confidential information may be passed across when it shouldn't. This is where I like the Australian system of appointing an independent auditor, known as a probity auditor, to certify proper process has been followed. The existence of a probity auditor means bidders have someone other than you to call if there is a problem. Probity auditors will deal directly with the bidders, suggest appropriate solutions and certify that the agreed solution is actually implemented. Bidders have no incentive to manufacture minor problems to get more face time with you, and the auditor is by definition not an evaluator, so they can raise issues without being worried about being marked down for being difficult. Without a probity auditor, this stuff is one more administrative headache for you to deal with.

When a bidder does have a problem with your process, deal with it. There is normally something simple you can do to resolve the issue. Sometimes further explanation may be sufficient. Sometimes a workshop with the bidder on a particular subject may do the trick, or perhaps an extension of a time period. Just bear in mind that you don't want the solution to give rise to a complaint from another bidder: if you offer further clarification to one bidder, for instance, make sure you make it available to the others, even if they haven't asked.

Your objective is to reach a position where the bidder is willing to confirm that your action is sufficient to close the issue. If you can't get there, be really worried. While one can never entirely discount the possibility that the bidder is just being a pain in the neck, persisting with a complaint usually signifies a genuine problem. Always give serious consideration to the possibility that a complaint is justified. In the InterCity West Coast franchise case, Richard Branson wrote a series of letters in an attempt to escalate the problem, only to have the complaint dismissed by the Department without adequate review. A full investigation

Never put the bidders into a position where the only way they can attract your attention is by bringing an action for judicial review.

before the preferred bidder decision was announced could have enabled a less expensive and embarrassing solution to be found. Never put the bidders into a position where the only way they can attract your attention is by bringing an action for judicial review.

The Opposition

Her Majesty's Most Loyal Opposition is not on the list of stakeholders you have to deal with, because the Minister will be very annoyed if you try. Except in the special case discussed above, where the Opposition politician is the Member of Parliament for a constituency directly impacted by the project, leave the politicians to slug it out in parliament or the media.

That doesn't always quite work. One of the issues with really large projects is that the Government which signs a contract lasting for years may not remain in office for the duration of the contract. This can be a bit tricky if you are expecting to be around for longer than the Government. The UK privatisation of Railtrack in 1996 by a Conservative Government was a case in point. Privatisation in general, and of Railtrack in particular, was not the policy of the Labour Party and was absolute anathema to many of its members. Given the expected landslide election victory, Labour would shortly have the power to do practically anything, including renationalise the company, and quite possibly would. At the same time, it was reasonably likely a Labour Government would permit Railtrack to continue in existence, if only because its renationalisation would be both complicated and expensive.

Maintaining a good relationship with the Labour Government would be essential for the company, which would continue to rely on direct and indirect subsidy, but would be completely unachievable if the directors signed off a prospectus saying elements of the Labour Party were out to destroy the company. Yet it was a clear political risk and there was no doubt disclosure was required. Finally, someone had the bright idea of inviting the Opposition to write a letter explaining its intentions, for inclusion in the prospectus. Not only was the letter couched in such forceful language it expressed the risk to perfection, it could not possibly have given offence to the incoming Labour Government, since their own text was published in its entirety.

The Minister Wants …

One of the hazards of working in the public sector is the possibility of political interference in a tender process. Political interference is not the same thing as political involvement. On a mega-project, the decision will be made at the political level, so it is pointless to expect politicians to absent themselves from the process entirely. But Ministers are always under a lot of pressure to demonstrate results, not least from their colleagues around the Cabinet table.

The risk that politicians will try to manipulate the outcome of a tender is low. The risk that they will try to manipulate its timing is much greater. Politicians of unimpeachable integrity still need announceables, and what could be more announceable than the award of a contract for a mega-project? They are quite likely to press you to make decisions and recommendations early, particularly if you have foolishly failed to take into account the timing of elections and party conferences in your tender schedule, or if they need to distract public attention from some supervening crisis. This can be awkward. Despite the rhetoric about frank and fearless advice, the common public sector mindset is to regard the Minister as a quasi-deity whose every whim must be catered for.

The risk that they will try to manipulate its timing is much greater.

Not a good idea. If, in response to political pressure, you put out the call for tenders before you have settled your commercial terms, you may select a preferred tenderer sooner, but take much longer to conclude a contract. If you cut back the time the tenderers have to prepare their bids, the bid quality will be poor and you may not have a sound basis on which to make a selection. If you cut back the time for evaluating the bids, you may be unable either to give the bids fair consideration or to demonstrate that you have done so if the decision is challenged. You need to explain to the Minister that accelerating the process may accelerate it straight into a brick wall.

You need to explain to the Minister that accelerating the process may accelerate it straight into a brick wall.

If the contract involves a sale of business or outsourcing, you may also need to explain that things will work rather differently afterwards. In the early 1990s I was advising Eastern European Governments on the laws required to establish a market economy after the break-up of the Soviet Union. I was struck by the difficulty these Governments had with the concept that once they had sold a business to the private sector, they didn't own it any more. It was offensive to them that where the business managers had once leapt to do their bidding, their requests were suddenly ignored and their instructions were unenforceable. At the time, I thought these Governments had difficulty with the concept because they were communists. With the benefit of another 20 years of experience, I think it was because they were Governments.

Ministers are empowered by law to give directions to their departments that must be obeyed. The etiquette of the public sector is such that a Minister is rarely called upon to formalise directions in writing: this happens only when there is a specific legal requirement for a formal document of authority, which is not common, or where the department officials are so appalled by what the Minister is stubbornly insisting on that they refuse to proceed without a direction in writing, which is exceedingly rare. As a result, Ministers often think public sector employees fall in with their suggestions as a matter of divine right rather than legal obligation, and therefore assume private sector businesses will be similarly compliant. They won't. That does not mean you should attempt to replicate the public sector constraints in an outsourcing contract, since the whole point of an outsourcing is normally to shed the shackles of the public sector. Just make sure your Minister understands the basis of the new relationship established by the contract.

Frank and fearless advice will get a better reception if it is not also tactless.

Frank and fearless advice will get a better reception if it is not also tactless. Don't spring bad news on a Minister who isn't expecting it, don't embarrass the Minister in front of third parties and never imply the Minister is an idiot, even in the face of evidence to the contrary. (Such evidence is rarer than the media might have you believe. Although lambasting politicians is a national sport, people do not normally rise to become Ministers of the Crown unless they are capable and intelligent.)

It helps if the frank and fearless advice comes from someone the Minister trusts and respects. If you don't yet have that kind of relationship, concentrate on convincing someone who does (perhaps your chief executive, or someone on your external steering committee) and arrange for them to deliver the message. But build that trust and respect at every opportunity. While managing the Minister is easier if you are doing well with the Minister's stakeholders, the converse is also true. The Minister will be as keen as you are that your project should be seen to be a success and can bring a lot of influence to bear in your support. Building a good relationship with the Minister pays real dividends.

Chapter 9

The Agency

In developing and structuring the project, you have to think of the Agency as a legal entity with rights and obligations that will be governed by the contract. But the legal entity is full of living, breathing people who also have rights and obligations and will have a positive or negative impact on the project depending on your leadership and their own inclinations. Some of them will be working directly to you on the project, some will be contributing at one remove and some will have their working lives significantly affected by the project and what it delivers. When the project is a mega-project, very little of the Agency will be entirely unaffected.

The Project Team

You can't set up a major Government contract all by yourself. You need help. Having a really good team is one of the best protections you can have against being sued. Bright, motivated people with the experience to spot the problems coming, the competence to deal with them when they can and the self-knowledge and confidence to call for help when they can't. The skills of leading and managing a team are not project-specific, but if this is your first time as project director working for Government on something of this scale, there are some things you want to look out for.

Having a really good team is one of the best protections you can have against being sued.

DON'T DO YOUR OLD JOB

If you were appointed from within the Agency, don't make it easy for the Agency to delay recruiting someone into your former position by continuing to do the work. Project director for setting up a mega-project is a full time occupation. Close the door on your old job. And if your successor isn't as good as you were, tough. That bit of the organisation will just have to soldier on without you.

It isn't just your former position you have to give up. You have been appointed to your first gig as project director because you were successful at something. Project directors come from a lot of different directions. Perhaps you were really good at negotiating contracts, or running a project management office, or managing a team of engineers. If your former full time role is replicated on this project, give that project role to somebody else, preferably someone who does it better than you. If your team is too lightweight in that area, you will be unable to resist stepping in and doing things yourself. Time spent doing the job you used to do is time not spent doing the job you have now. The job you have now is what needs your attention.

RECRUIT YOUR SUCCESSOR

If the Agency waits until there is a contract before hiring a contract manager, the project is in trouble.

In setting up your project for success, look beyond the day you sign the contract. Skilful contract management during the delivery phase may not be enough to save a project if it was badly structured on day one, but poor contract management can bring down any project. If the Agency waits until there is a contract before hiring a contract manager, the project is in trouble. Managing a billion dollar contract is not a job for a junior account manager from the procurement department.

I use the description 'contract manager' because 'project director' is the term I'm using for you, but make no mistake, on a mega-project the contract manager job is a project director role. The title should be handed on when you leave. Your recruit should be someone who is not overawed by the scale of the potential liabilities involved and is capable of much more than just following standard procedures. The transition from procurement to delivery is one of the highest risk periods in the whole project: delays and misunderstandings quickly become unrecoverable and irreconcilable. A first class contract manager ready and running during the procurement phase is the best risk mitigation you can have.

It also makes for a better contract. Developing the contract is all about making trade-offs: cost against risk, time against cost, the needs of one stakeholder against the needs of another, economic risk against political risk, present cost against future cost. Having the person who will be responsible for managing the contract involved in the set-up makes an enormous difference to the dynamics of the debate. I always find there is a great creative tension between me, with my focus on getting the deal done, and my successor, who has a vested interest in getting the deal done right.

And as a further bonus of an early appointment, if you make a bad choice of contract manager, you should find out in time to get a replacement while you are still around to maintain the continuity.

Your future contract manager will need a team of people during the delivery phase. Since the skills required for the management of the contract have a lot of overlap with the skills required for the development of contract terms and specifications and the evaluation of tenders, it makes sense to plan both teams together. Involving in the procurement phase the people who will manage the contract in the delivery phase will give you a team that will resist putting undeliverable obligations on Government (because they know they are the ones who will be stuck with trying to deliver them) and will understand the deal that was done (because they helped to do it).

You may, of course, be intending to manage the contract yourself. My own preference is to set it up and move on. I enjoy fitting all the pieces together and drawing the stakeholders into that single moment of mutual optimism when the contract is signed and the order of things is instantaneously changed into something a billion dollars different. Managing a contract doesn't give me the same buzz. Your preference may be for taking the job all the way through to completion of the project, in which case your bigger issue may be how to generate the creative tension that pushes a contract to the next level. But whether you intend to manage the contract yourself, or hand it over to a successor, pick your team with the transition to contract management in mind. The project won't wait while you take that much-deserved break after setting up the contract.

Pick your team with the transition to contract management in mind.

DIVERSITY IS NOT JUST ABOUT MINORITIES

People think diversity just means including women and ethnic minorities. You would be foolish to overlook the skills of either, and equally foolish not to take action if poor Agency hiring practices are blinding you to talent. (Did you know the proportion of women in orchestras has increased significantly since recruiters were allowed only to hear and not see those auditioning?) There is real value in diversity. But it is not only about gender and skin colour.

A very common failing on a large project is to forget to include people who understand the day-to-day operation of the Agency. If people had paid attention to the civil servant who reportedly said: 'Try collecting that in Brixton', would Britain's wildly unsuccessful poll tax have gone ahead? Performance regimes that look good on paper but create perverse incentives in practice are classic creations of well-intentioned people who don't understand operations.

UK railway privatisation was initially marred by performance regimes that in some instances incentivised companies to sit back and collect penalties for delays caused by failures of others, rather than to take steps to minimise the delay.

> *The tender process for setting up a Government contract involves doing business with aliens.*

You also need a mix of public and private sector backgrounds. The tender process for setting up a Government contract involves doing business with aliens. The public sector is not the private sector and the private sector is grateful for it. So is the public sector. But if this project is ever going to be delivered, the two parties have to sign a contract they both understand and everybody has to deliver on what they sign up to. If you are to bring the public sector and private sector parties to the 'meeting of minds' the contract should represent, you will want to have both species represented on your project team.

USE SECONDMENTS

Where you need people only for a short period, a useful tactic is to second people from other parts of the organisation, leaving their bosses to backfill their positions for the duration of the project. This has a number of advantages: the people already know how the Agency operates; working on a major project is a great learning experience for them; and it imposes almost no administrative burden on you. Their line managers are the ones who have to backfill the position. It only works if the permanent position really is filled for the duration, whether with a single individual or by dividing up the work. Otherwise the people spend their time trying to do their old jobs as well as working on your project, which is not sustainable.

RECRUITMENT

You are unlikely to be able to fill your team with people already employed by the Agency, particularly given the extent to which many Government agencies have attempted to introduce 'lean' organisations:

- *Availability* – the in-house experts already have a day job, so they may be too busy to provide adequate assistance.
- *Expertise* – mega-project contracts generally cover a lot of ground and Agency staff may not command the full range of expertise.

- *Flexibility* – you will not need all of the people all of the time: what they are doing when they are not working for you will affect how easy it is for you to get hold of them when you need them.

Some external recruitment will therefore be necessary. This brings you into the ambit of public sector hiring restrictions, which vary from nuisance to nightmare. At any one time they may apply to employees, contractors, advisers or any combination of the three. The two main hazards are an accretion of bureaucratic process and a sudden freeze on recruitment mandated by parts of Government outside the control of the Agency. The former is often a direct by-product of the latter: the recruitment process becomes cluttered with forms and filters that were cunningly designed to circumvent the freeze-before-last but now merely waste time and administrative effort.

You do have some leverage at your disposal. Your Minister will not take kindly to lack of progress on a project with a high public profile (there are few mega-projects without such a profile) and a powerful Minister can generally override hiring restrictions. But avoid calling on the Minister except in emergencies. There is only so much political clout even the strongest Minister will be prepared to wield on behalf of your project. You probably don't want to use it up on sorting out your administrative problems. Apart from anything else, it annoys the Agency admin staff, who have ways of making your life difficult. And it can be a bit awkward if your Minister is the one mandating the hiring freeze.

There is only so much political clout even the strongest Minister will be prepared to wield on behalf of your project.

Apart from the occasional total freeze on bringing in anyone at all, the public sector normally swings between favouring taking on employees (cheaper, better continuity) and taking on contractors (quicker to hire and fire). If your Agency does not let these big contracts regularly, and often even if it does, you will need contractors in the mix in order to put the right combination of skills at your disposal. Consult with the human resources director on what is the current flavour of the month for your Agency and plan accordingly.

GETTING IN FIRST

When it comes to external recruitment, whether of individuals or of firms of advisers, you are in competition with the tenderers, who need similar skills. You have one enormous advantage over them. You *know* the Agency will become a party to the contract. The tenderers have to spend millions bidding for the contract, but they do it without any certainty they are going to win.

If they put forward as their team people they already employ, those people will either have to be robbed from some other project team or be paid just to keep them available for a project the company may or may not secure. People not currently employed by the company may permit their names to be put forward, but few people can put their careers on hold for extended periods. External advisers can often be persuaded to work for tenderers on a speculative basis, but are likely to push that potentially unpaid work down to cheaper staff who may not be as skilled. In short, tenderers do not have your advantage of bringing people on board with certainty that the job is there for them to do. Even though the large contractors are used to this juggling act, their task is more difficult than yours in this respect.

You also have the opportunity for first mover advantage. You should know the scope and timing of the contract before the tenderers do, so you can go out to the market first for recruits and advisers. Of course, some people prefer not to work for the Government at all, particularly where public sector pay scales are poor or (in the case of advisers) Government's local reputation is for onerous terms, poor instructions and late payment. (Do not reinforce this reputation if you can help it, it is a serious drag on achieving value for money.)

However, even in places where this is the case, there are many good people out there who prefer the certainty of Government work to advising bidders who may not pay them at all if the bid is unsuccessful. Go and sign up the best people before they have locked in agreements with a bidder. You only get first mover advantage if you move first.

Go and sign up the best people before they have locked in agreements with a bidder. You only get first mover advantage if you move first.

USE PROPER PROCESS

Whether you are engaging contractors or employees, do it properly through a documented and preferably competitive process. A major issue in the Queensland Health Payroll System case was the highly damaging role played by an individual contractor to CorpTech, a division of Treasury that was managing the project on behalf of Queensland Health. Originally engaged without any competitive process to conduct a review of the project, he recommended the creation of a powerful position to which he then contrived to be appointed. This appointment was again made without any competitive process, and was made notwithstanding that the firm which had previously engaged him explicitly refused, in writing, to provide any recommendation.

Failure to check references is very poor practice; ignoring negative references borders on the suicidal.

> ***Failure to check references is very poor practice; ignoring negative references borders on the suicidal.***

The contractor proceeded to exhibit, in the words of the subsequent Commission of Inquiry report, 'exuberant indiscretion'. He encouraged the adoption of a 'prime contractor' model for the project and assumed *de facto* control of the evaluation process to select the prime contractor. He then intervened improperly, triggering a reassessment of scores that enabled the contract to be awarded to a tenderer who should not have been appointed. The subsequent implementation of the new payroll system ended in a failure described by the Commission of Inquiry as 'catastrophic'.

That doesn't mean a negative reference is an automatic do-not-employ. I once employed someone even after a colleague took me on one side and warned me I was about to engage a 'troublemaker'. Further investigation revealed the 'trouble' took the form of insisting on dealing with things other people were keen to sweep under the carpet. Since this was exactly what I needed at the time, I hired the troublemaker anyway. It proved an excellent decision. But if you are given a negative reference, don't proceed unless you are satisfied you have good enough reasons to ignore it.

Where practicable, don't limit yourself to the referees provided by the candidate: if you can identify other people who have worked with them, see if you can arrange for a second opinion. There will be constraints around this: the candidate has applied on a confidential basis and you must respect that confidence.

MANAGE YOUR TEAM

If the contract you are establishing is worth a billion dollars, you can think of it as one dollar for every item on your To Do list. Mega-projects are mega. Project directors who can't delegate can't cope. The better your team, the more you can delegate and the easier your job, so recruit the best team you can and watch them do great things. Just remember that when delegation of responsibility slides into abnegation of responsibility you are in trouble.

The exuberantly indiscreet contractor in the Queensland Health Payroll System case was a problem because nobody managed his activity. The Executive Director to whom he reported received complaints about him exceeding his authority but, far from dealing with the matter, left him 'unchallenged and uncontrolled' and took no action even in relation to an allegation (upheld by the subsequent Commission of Inquiry) that he had improperly interfered with the evaluation process.

Delegate freely, but keep aware of what is happening and take action where you need to.

Contributors

Not everyone at the Agency who works on the project will be reporting to you. The finance department may do your economic analysis. The engineering department may undertake enabling works. The communications team may write your media releases.

People have an amazing capacity to ignore information which appears to be of no immediate relevance.

Where you have people in other parts of the organisation doing work related to the project, don't assume that because they work for the Agency and have been exposed to newsletters or other communications about the project, they must know all about it. People have an amazing capacity to ignore information which appears to be of no immediate relevance. When you want people in other departments to do things for you, you need both to agree the scope of work with them in writing and also to provide them with sufficient context to understand the interdependencies. If a project manager delivering enabling works has no idea that delay to these works could cause the Government to be liable in damages to your contractor, you have no grounds for complaint if the works are rescheduled at someone else's convenience.

In the Intercity West Coast franchise case, individuals from a rail analysis group assisted the project team with the financial model at the centre of the controversy: its misuse eventually resulted in the cancellation of the tender process. The Laidlaw Inquiry found these employees thought they were only responsible for providing modelling input and were not responsible for sense checking the outputs. Always give people absolute clarity about what you expect them to do and what reliance is being placed on their advice or work.

It is tempting to avoid this issue by bringing everything to do with the project under your direct control, but that is rarely the right answer. Where the daily business of the Agency will change significantly with the delivery of your project, you are likely to get better commitment and results if people in the affected departments do the change management work to their existing reporting lines, with you providing overall leadership, problem-solving and coordination across departments rather than directly delivering on their behalf. Involve the Agency executive in deciding how to divide and coordinate project responsibilities, so that people with a non-project day job know they have support from their managers to do work for you.

It is possible to run the whole contract set-up phase through people in other departments, with no direct reports at all. The first time I did it that way was for a private sector company in the late 1990s, on a major infrastructure project done as a negotiated contract rather than a public tender. At that time the concept of having a dedicated project manager for setting up big contracts was in its infancy, and the person in nominal charge was the chief financial officer. Since the company was publicly listed, with a turnover of more than a billion pounds, he was not in a position to devote very much time to the project, so I just started running it. Nobody else was doing it and it was more fun than working on the due diligence, which was what I was supposed to be doing. I had no formal delegations whatsoever, financial or otherwise, and had to operate entirely on the basis of influencing skills. The chief financial officer decided it was a wonderful idea and I was asked to do the same thing again when the next big contract came along.

It is possible to run the whole contract set-up phase through people in other departments, with no direct reports at all.

Now that it has become usual (essential) to appoint a dedicated project director for a major procurement, it has also become usual for project directors to gather their own teams. Most would feel embarrassed about not having the budgetary authority to stock the stationery cupboard and few could cope with not being anybody's boss. It certainly requires a different approach to leadership. Everyone in the team reports to somebody else, so if you want them to do something, you have to ask politely and make sure they understand why it's important. You can't just tell them and expect it to happen. If that sounds scary, bear in mind that just telling people doesn't always work very well even when they report directly to you. Agreed scopes of work and provision of adequate context is a plus in any organisation structure.

If you do adopt the 'no budget, no employees' approach (I still do for some projects) be aware this can give problems with public sector human resources departments when dealing with your employment contract, because they are accustomed to measuring job sizes using budget and direct reports. When they discover you don't have any of either, they will probably have trouble matching a public sector pay grade to the salary you have negotiated. This is not your problem. Just tell them how many billions your project will cost and let them use their imagination.

Tell them how many billions your project will cost and let them use their imagination.

Affected Employees

Many mega-projects have a significant impact on the business of the Agency that affects the daily work of the employees. The impact may be a move to new premises, or the need to deploy a new type of helicopter, or a change in work practices following the introduction of new systems and technology. For an individual employee, the scale of the change may be as small as an unfamiliar voice on the helpline or as large as the loss of their job. Any change will make people nervous. Within limits, project directors thrive on uncertainty, or they don't become project directors. Don't assume the rest of the organisation has the same tolerance level.

Within limits, project directors thrive on uncertainty, or they don't become project directors. Don't assume the rest of the organisation has the same tolerance level.

Managing employee exits may not fall within the scope of work for your project team: the head of human resources is likely to regard it as central to their job description. Government normally tries to be supportive in these circumstances, and redundant employees will often be offered redeployment, career counselling or assistance in applying for other jobs. If employees are not being made redundant but will be transferred to the contractor, whether pursuant to legislation on transfers of business or by agreement, then you will have to ensure this is properly provided for in the contract. Organisational change management is a whole field in itself, but in general terms, the best thing you can do is provide regular, accurate information on what is happening with the project and what employees can expect. Develop and communicate a realistic schedule, then deliver it. Minimising uncertainty minimises stress.

Where the impact on employees is not a matter of losing their jobs but of having to do their jobs differently, communication is also critical. You need to think about it not just in terms of information provision but of how to engage employees in the contract delivery process without making life unnecessarily difficult for the contractor. You want them to support the project, not just be resigned to it.

In any procurement of trains, for instance, it is essential to the success of the project that the drivers like the trains. (Unless, of course, you are procuring driverless trains, but that is often not an option.) Trains need test crew. The approach chosen for the Waratah train procurement was for the test crew to be provided by the Agency rather than the contractor. The Agency called for volunteers and selected a team of the very best crew. Their knowledge of local railway operations was of real benefit to the contractor, and the in-depth understanding of the new trains that they developed during the testing phase was of real benefit to the Agency.

Just as importantly, it created a group of respected and influential train crew who were enthusiastic about the new trains. It is easy to think that, just because the shiny new whatever that the contractor is delivering for you is shiny and new and in every way better than the old, it will automatically be received by everyone as the greatest thing since sliced bread. Easy but wrong. Anyone with experience of change management knows people cling to the old with irrational tenacity and are quick to credit rumours that the new is inferior or unsafe or uncomfortable. I know of one train delivery where the drivers protested so energetically that the train had to be taken back and modified (at considerable expense) to move the master controller handle from one side of the driver's desk to the other. Your project will not be considered a success if everybody hates the product, even if it arrives on time and on budget. Involving the Agency operating business in the delivery of the project can turn potential critics into friends and supporters.

Your project will not be considered a success if everybody hates the product, even if it arrives on time and on budget.

Evaluation Training

The tenders received by the Agency will require a significant spread of expertise in order to evaluate them properly, particularly if your project involves a large asset or collection of assets that the contractor will finance, design, build, maintain and operate. You are likely to have to involve employees from across the Agency, not just the immediate project team.

One of the things you should consider is providing your evaluators with some training. The public sector is very concerned to treat tenderers fairly, partly because being unfair is what causes tenderers to sue you, but also because probity and fairness are part of the public service ethos. Unfortunately, ethos does not always translate into effective action. There are any number of public sector myths about what probity does and does not require, and you do not want these cluttering up your evaluation process.

There are any number of public sector myths about what probity does and does not require.

Your Agency's standard training package may be perpetuating some of the public sector probity myths.

Make sure the training is specific to your procurement. Your Agency's standard training package may be perpetuating some of the public sector probity myths. For instance, the standard package may tell you that 'probity' requires you to have at least three bids. It is true in general that having a number of bids makes it harder for a corrupt official to award a contract to a mate and makes it more likely that you will get genuine price competition. It is not true that a process involving fewer than three bidders is necessarily invalid or corrupt. On a really big contract, bidders need to invest millions in the tender process. They will not make this investment unless there is a reasonable chance of winning the contract. In this context, when you are shortlisting bidders to be invited to give you a price, three should be a maximum rather than a minimum, and you may well generate fiercer competition with just two bids.

Your training should explain what the evaluators will have to do and how their work fits into the process. Teach the evaluation methodology you are actually going to use, not some generic methodology that will not apply. Explain what the security restrictions are intended to achieve and why they are important, to secure commitment to their implementation.

Training will only be effective if you go about it in the right way. It should demonstrate to the project team (and everyone else) your commitment to running a proper process. You and your senior evaluators should do the same training as those with less experience, and you should not run a special session for important people only. Mix senior in with junior, so the juniors can see the commitment and the seniors can generate quality debate. If juniors think seniors don't care, they may not bother to raise issues when they see them. Don't think you are going to be able to spot all of the issues yourself. You need everybody.

Don't just attend, listen. Use feedback from the training sessions to improve the evaluation process.

BIAS

Standard procurement training will often focus on the importance of avoiding conflicts of interest. While this is indeed important – a conflict of interest is likely to generate at least a perception of bias – bias can and does exist without any conflict of interest being present at all. Your training package should acknowledge and deal with this.

The biggest single problem in contracts for services is likely to be incumbent bias: the bias may be for or against the incumbent, but it will exist. Once the possibility of unconscious bias has been recognised and acknowledged, most people are reasonably capable of suppressing the bias and judging fairly. Anonymity of bids is usually impracticable to sustain in procurement on this scale so the better thing to do is bring the bias out into the open and discuss ways of recognising and countering the problem.

The biggest single problem in contracts for services is likely to be incumbent bias: the bias may be for or against the incumbent, but it will exist.

Akin to bias is the problem of people taking irrelevant considerations into account. If your training for evaluators doesn't explain the process adequately, you risk having your engineers marking a bidder down for the quality of their widget on the irrelevant grounds that the bidder's project manager is incompetent. The incompetence of the project manager is of course not irrelevant to the evaluation as a whole, but is unlikely to be assessed under the same criterion as widget quality. If people don't understand what is being evaluated where, you run the risk of matters being 'double counted', which will not help you demonstrate that the losing bidders were treated fairly.

Personal Probity

The project director is uniquely placed to influence the outcome of the tender process. If bidders are given any reason to doubt your integrity, the entire process is at risk. If the process is overturned, your career is at risk. You probably take your integrity for granted. Bear in mind that others may not.

If you gamble, give it up for the duration. If you can't give it up, you're in the wrong job. If you drink, never get drunk. Do not break the law: even a speeding ticket shows a cavalier attitude to regulation that may count against you. Do not meet with lobbyists, do not give more of your time and attention to one bidder rather than another, avoid accepting even trivial favours. Do not let your spouse or children accept favours. Keep file notes of telephone conversations with bidders and avoid meeting bidders without someone else in attendance, even in obviously social situations.

If you are uncertain about whether something is acceptable or not, seek advice. But if you need to ask, you probably shouldn't be doing it.

Rewarding Employees

The theory is that a job well done is its own reward. This is not much of a reward unless somebody else notices.

The public sector generally doesn't do bonuses. The theory is that a job well done is its own reward. This is not much of a reward unless somebody else notices. The project team is going to deliver something seriously impressive. Your job is not only to recognise their contributions, but to make sure other people do too.

Scout around for public awards that give you an opportunity to nominate individual team members or the project itself. The Agency may have an awards programme for its own employees and you shouldn't rule out the national honours system as a means of providing recognition to outstanding individuals. Various industry associations have project awards that you should be able to nominate the project for once the contract has been signed.

Enlist your bosses in this endeavour. Chief executives and Ministers do not rise to be chief executives and Ministers without learning ways of saying thank you that make people feel appreciated, but they don't always know who to say it to. Tell them.

Advisers

Not all of the individuals you will need to set up the contract will be employed or contracted directly by the Agency. There will also be firms of advisers who will provide you with services in specialist areas. Individual advisers are responsible to their own firms rather than working directly to you.

On a day-to-day basis you may notice very little difference as you seek to meld everyone into an effective team, but you do need to remain conscious of the distinction. Employees are given directions, advisers are given instructions: the firm's professional reputation for the quality of their advice and services needs to be on the line at all times.

The next two chapters examine how to select and manage your advisers for the best results.

Chapter 10
The Lawyers

A contract is an instrument that creates legal rights and obligations. If you're building a bridge, you need engineers. If you're building a contract, you need lawyers. If you're building a contract to deliver a mega-project, you need a lot of lawyers.

And no lawyer jokes, please. When I was advising Eastern European Governments on how to adjust their legal systems to support a capitalist economy, it was fascinating to see the impact of things we take for granted. They had no mortgage laws, for instance: in a communist society people can't own property, so they can't use property as security for loans and you don't need a mortgage law. In a capitalist society, people want to buy homes and start businesses, but without security, lenders won't lend. No law of mortgages, no capitalist economy. You need bankruptcy laws (recycles unproductive assets, also good against debt slavery), corporations laws (limited liability enables bigger business), trading laws (discourages the unscrupulous from cheating the uninformed) and all sorts of other laws if you want to live the kind of life people generally want to live. Law is the foundation of society. No lawyers, no law, no joke.

That doesn't mean there aren't some pretty rubbish lawyers out there, but there's no reason for you to engage one of those.

That doesn't mean there aren't some pretty rubbish lawyers out there, but there's no reason for you to engage one of those.

In-House Counsel

Any Agency big enough to be embarking on a mega-project will employ its own lawyers. The relationship you have with the senior in-house lawyer, often given the title General Counsel, will shape the approach to legal advice for the project.

It is highly unlikely the General Counsel will want to do the legal work for your project without the assistance of external lawyers, even if they have a team of in-house lawyers of their own. They do not pretend to the extensive range of legal expertise that is required to advise on a major Government contract and they are sensitive to the potential for criticism if things go wrong. They also know lawyers on a large transaction are expected to work long hours without reference to the demands of their private lives: many General Counsel gave up working for law firms precisely to get away from this. That doesn't mean they will be happy to be bypassed entirely, nor should you be happy if that is the approach they take. You will need them.

> *If anybody knows where the bodies are buried in an Agency, it is the General Counsel.*

When trouble strikes an Agency, the General Counsel is the first port of call. They know which departments have trouble with their contractors, which employees have been investigated for what, who writes aggressive letters in disregard of courtesy and common sense, who runs for cover at the first hint of a problem, and who picks up the pieces. If anybody knows where the bodies are buried in an Agency, it is the General Counsel. Think of them as a 'dial before you dig' service. Call them before breaking new ground. They may not be able to tell you all they know, because much of what they do is confidential, but their recommendations are worth listening to.

Apart from their expertise in finding or avoiding concealed cadavers, the areas where you can expect the General Counsel to be of the greatest value to you are in:

- selecting the external lawyers
- administering the external lawyers
- advising on Agency authority
- dealing with parliamentary counsel.

The General Counsel is also likely to run the secretariat for the Board (if there is one) or whichever internal committee is at the top of your governance framework.

SELECTING THE EXTERNAL LAWYERS

In-house legal departments are in essence a law firm that has only one client. Over time, people tend to look like their pets. Lawyers tend to look like their clients. The physical resemblance may be slight, but the culture rubs off. The General Counsel's approach to procuring external legal advice will tell you a lot about the Agency's culture and its attitude to procurement in general.

With a bit of luck, they will take it for granted you will run a competitive tender process that gives the law firms with the relevant expertise a fair opportunity to be selected.

That doesn't always happen. If you are instructed to use a particular law firm (or indeed any other adviser) without following any kind of tender process, take it as a warning. It does not mean the firm will not be competent, nor that anyone is corrupt. It may mean that cosy relationships with suppliers are tolerated within the Agency. It may also suggest that in weighing the balance between process assurance and convenience, there will be a finger pushing down the scales on the side of convenience. Convenience is good, but you need assurance more: don't let yourself be nudged into omitting important activities just because they require a bit of effort.

Convenience is good, but you need assurance more.

ADMINISTERING THE EXTERNAL LAWYERS

The selected lawyers will almost certainly do work for the Agency on other matters, and the General Counsel will probably prefer to administer legal services and invoicing across the portfolio, including your project. Let them. So long as you see and check the invoices for the work being done for your project, that is all you need on the administration front.

Administration is one thing, management is another: management of the lawyers on the project is something you need to control. If it suits both of you, it can be productive to use the General Counsel to manage the lawyers on your behalf, but it must be on your behalf. Occasionally, you come across a General Counsel who wants to be the sole channel for all instructions to the external lawyers and refuses to allow them to talk to anyone else. Squash this fast. The external lawyers are key members of your team. It is not acceptable for you to be prevented from dealing with them directly.

ADVISING ON AGENCY AUTHORITY

In any project, the project director has the authority to make most of the decisions about the conduct of the project. But not all. Since it is invariably the biggest decisions that are withheld from your authority, your most important stakeholder is the person or body that makes the decisions you are not authorised to make. One of your priority tasks should be to discover who this is. It may not be obvious.

In a private sector company, authority comes from the Board of Directors. A resolution of the Board is normally all it takes to authorise even the biggest contract.

There may be a need for shareholder approvals in special circumstances, but for all practical purposes the Board is God. The public sector offers a greater variety of deities. Government agencies may have unique powers and structures since they can be created by specific legislation rather than established under the regular laws governing companies. If you come from a private sector background, the arcane intricacies of identifying sources of authority in a public sector environment may seem bizarre. Even for a contract worth billions, some private sector counterparties may not bother to confirm whether the Agency has authority to enter into the contract, no doubt feeling that reliance on ostensible authority is probably good enough and certainly less complicated. But some will check.

If you come from a private sector background, the arcane intricacies of identifying sources of authority in a public sector environment may seem bizarre.

Seek advice from the Agency's General Counsel. The senior in-house lawyer may come from any one of a number of different legal backgrounds, but will always be the world expert on the level of authority held by the Agency and how it must be wielded. What delegations does the chief executive have, what is the usual form for Ministerial delegations, who holds authority to do what? Which statutes grant and limit powers? Does the Board have authority or is it only there in an advisory capacity? If the Minister has the power to issue directions, how is it exercised?

The $3 billion contract for what is now known as the CLEM7 tollway was let in 2006 by Brisbane City Council, the largest local Government authority in Australia, with 26 wards, 27 councillors and no legal capacity to delegate the award decision. Obtaining authority was not just a matter of turning up at a Council meeting: even for Australia's largest, a $3 billion contract was never going to be a routine decision. To preserve the confidentiality of the final deliberations, which took about three days, the councillors agreed to be sequestered for the duration. This is not the kind of thing you want to be setting up without notice.

Never attempt to deal with difficulties in identifying the correct authority by making all decisions yourself without regard to whether you have the necessary delegations. This tactic works quite well on small procurements, but in the context of a mega-project is not a good idea at all.

You may be used to a culture where it is considered better to seek forgiveness than permission, but in a public sector context that is not enough. No project director, no matter how experienced or how competent, will have the authority to commit the Government to expenditure measured in billions. Forgiveness may protect your employment status, but it will not protect project decisions from legal challenge. You need permission: that is, you need to ensure project decisions are properly authorised.

Occasionally you may find it necessary to secure authorisation retrospectively. Retrospective authorisation is like forgiveness, but it requires more paperwork. Consult the General Counsel.

Retrospective authorisation is like forgiveness, but it requires more paperwork.

DEALING WITH PARLIAMENTARY COUNSEL

One of the things that distinguishes Government contracts from private sector contracts is that sometimes you need to pass laws in order to enter into the contract or meet your obligations under it. Try to avoid anything that requires an Act of Parliament. Orders or Regulations that can be signed into law by the Minister are relatively easy to organise. Something that needs to pass two houses of parliament will have to fight its way onto a packed agenda and may require humiliating concessions to some raving nutter who by electoral happenstance is gleefully holding the balance of power.

Fortunately, you will rarely find yourself in this position. New Acts of Parliament are sometimes necessary: the UK privatisations of the 1990s of the railways and utility companies were accompanied by legislation to provide regulatory frameworks for what were effectively new industries. However, something on that scale will normally be separately dealt with by the policy makers before the contracting phase commences. You may have to deal with the consequences of poor legislative drafting, but getting the drafting done won't be on your To Do list.

More commonly, it may be necessary to issue a Regulation, for example to create a new subsidiary under the Act of Parliament establishing the Agency, or to make an Order extending the list of persons having powers under another Act of Parliament to make certain administrative decisions. This *will* be your problem. It will be drafted by parliamentary counsel on your behalf, but somebody from the Agency has to give them instructions and review the drafting before the Order or Regulation is brought into force.

Your General Counsel should be both willing and able to organise this for you. They regularly receive requests from Government checking whether the Agency foresees a need for any legislative instruments, so that these can be programmed into parliamentary business as required. It is always better to go through these channels if you can. It is possible to ram through unscheduled legislative instruments, but that may require more political capital than your Minister's office is willing to expend.

The other reason for going through the General Counsel is their world-class expertise on the special laws applicable to the Agency. Parliamentary counsel are not infallible: your General Counsel will pick up things they may miss.

BOARD SECRETARIAT

The General Counsel is often responsible for running the secretariat for the Board or other important governance bodies within the agency. They will be able to advise you on the correct form for submissions and, perhaps more importantly, the idiosyncrasies of the members. If members prefer 14 point type so they don't have to put their reading glasses on, indulge their vanity. If members are intolerant of eccentric grammar, make sure papers don't contain any. Every now and then a Board, weary of deciphering badly-written pleas for its attention, will bounce papers to the next meeting just because the presentation isn't up to scratch, regardless of the substantive merits. Eliminate this risk from your schedule by putting forward good quality documents. On time. Late circulation of papers makes the secretariat look bad. Since you will need the General Counsel's goodwill, be meticulous about getting papers in on the due date, in the correct format. You are supposed to have project management skills. Don't damage your credibility by making a dog's breakfast of managing Board submissions.

Don't damage your credibility by making a dog's breakfast of managing Board submissions.

External Lawyers

Generally, it is better to select a single law firm for all external advice on the procurement. There is less risk of matters falling through gaps and more chance of issues being considered holistically rather than in isolation. You also avoid the risk that one set of lawyers will seek to amend the documents of another set of lawyers for no better reason than to prove they are paying attention, or because they prefer a different style of drafting.

Heavily negotiated documents usually become increasingly incomprehensible as negotiations progress. In the New South Wales Integrated Ticketing case, the judge was extremely critical of the wording of the call for tenders: 'It seems almost impossible that the Call was drawn by a lawyer, having regard to the obscurities and confusion of even the most important provisions.' Insider accounts suggest the problem was too many lawyers, not too few.

Sometimes you may need to use a different law firm for some aspect of the transaction, perhaps because of other things going on within the Agency. If there are industrial relations negotiations in progress, for instance, you may want to filter all industrial relations advice in connection with the project through the law firm advising on the negotiations. Make sure each law firm knows who is advising on what.

If a single law firm is going to give you all of the advice associated with setting up a contract for a mega-project, it will need to be a big one, because the range and depth of expertise required is considerable.

The range and depth of expertise required is considerable.

THE LEAD PARTNER

The most important thing you need is confidence in the lead partner on the project. This person has to be able to operate at the highest levels of your organisation. They will not normally be discussing the project with your chief executive or Minister unless you are there too, but you don't want to have to provide a translation service. You certainly don't want your own credibility threatened because they are tactless, or too lazy or too busy on other matters to be properly on top of the transaction, or just plain not up to the job.

These characteristics are also undesirable in the more junior lawyers, but juniors in any organisation tend to model themselves on the boss, so make the lead partner your primary focus. The lead partner is the most senior partner actually doing the work on the project: a 'client partner' may only be there to give you a nice warm feeling and someone to complain to if the lead partner isn't up to the job.

The qualities of the lead partner can be difficult to establish in a selection process, because confidence and trust really only develop after a period of working together. The General Counsel will probably know more lawyers than you do and may have experience of those tendering. While an incurable waffler is easily spotted, character is hard to judge from a written response and limited interview. But character is critical.

The application of the law to any particular situation is rarely unequivocal. You want a lawyer who will set out fairly the possible range of outcomes and then apply their judgment. *Their* judgment. A lawyer who only gives you the advice they think you want to hear is not a lawyer you want to engage. If they give you their own judgment, that is a significant factor you will take into account in making yours. If you know they tend to be overly conservative, or unduly sensitive to particular risks, you may adjust your judgment accordingly. But if they give you what they think will be *your* judgment, they have added no value and may well be wrong anyway.

A lawyer who only gives you the advice they think you want to hear is not a lawyer you want to engage.

One other thing on the subject of legal judgment. I'm trying to keep you from being sued, but if the worst happens, distrust any lawyer who tells you their judgment is you have a 70 per cent chance of success. Litigation lawyers do this as a matter of course. Seventy per cent is big enough to make you think the matter is worth taking to court. The implied 30 per cent chance of losing is big enough that they won't look too stupid if you do in fact lose. The figures bear no relationship to your actual chances of succeeding in the litigation.

SOLVING CLIENT PROBLEMS

Any legal firm submitting a proposal for their services will tell you they are good at solving problems. They are certainly very good at identifying them. Legal training is rigorous. When presented with a wood, your lawyer will unerringly spot the fungal blight on the third tree from the left. Fungal blight can certainly do a lot of damage. However, the bushfire raging across the gully may be of more immediate concern.

To a lawyer, finding problems comes naturally. That is rarely where they add most value: problems will find you without their assistance. You need rather more, so probe a bit deeper when they tell you they are also good at solving problems. You want lawyers who have developed a sense of what is important and what is urgent. It is your job to decide on solutions, but law firms that can help you set sensible priorities and find palatable options for taking action are invaluable.

TEAM MANAGEMENT

The efficiency with which this is done – or lack of efficiency – will be one of the biggest drivers of your legal costs.

It is important to understand how the external law firm will manage its own activities. The core team dedicated to the project may be no more than four or five lawyers, but a lot of different specialist advice will be required at various times. It may be necessary to manage the contribution of one or more tax lawyers, planning lawyers, property lawyers, intellectual property lawyers, industrial relations lawyers, litigation lawyers, regulatory lawyers, and so on. The efficiency with which this is done – or lack of efficiency – will be one of the biggest drivers of your legal costs.

This is an area where the past experience of the firm really counts. All these specialist legal areas generally operate as separate practices. If the firm regularly advises on really large projects, the specialist areas will have some understanding of large project dynamics and will be responsive to the core team. Similarly, the core team will have worked out ways of keeping specialist areas up to speed on the transaction without charging you for 50 expensive lawyers to attend a weekly update meeting. Probe this at interview. For the legal team, large projects are as much about logistics as about legal advice. When you come to sign the contract, it won't be a single document. On a privately-financed deal, the boardroom table will probably be invisible beneath the spread of folders: it is not uncommon to set aside an entire morning or afternoon to collect the necessary signatures. Bringing all of these documents to the point of signature on the same day, both in terms of negotiating them and of producing the paperwork, is a significant logistical challenge that can be extremely expensive if done inefficiently. Make sure you select lawyers who are up to the job.

COST

Lawyers are often selected primarily on the basis of their hourly rates. This is a truly dreadful idea. You may even be offered a selection process that involves plugging hourly rates into a model that assumes so many hours of work from a partner, so many hours of work from a junior, with the same number of hours assumed for each law firm tendering. Find another process. Hourly rates are not a remotely reliable guide to total legal costs on a major procurement.

The two key drivers of legal costs are the lawyers' ability to manage themselves efficiently (which should be one of your selection criteria) and the Agency's ability to give them quality instructions (which is up to you, not them). If either of those factors is out of control, your costs will go through the roof, no matter what rates are offered.

If either of those factors is out of control, your costs will go through the roof, no matter what rates are offered.

Nonetheless, you will be spending a lot of money with your chosen law firm on this project, and you should expect them to offer competitive rates, not just the standard rates they may be charging the General Counsel for other matters. On big projects, there will be lawyers full time on the job for extended periods. Law firms calculate their standard fee rates on the assumption that individuals will work a certain number of hours in the day (20 years ago it was five or six, these days more likely between six and eight), and they don't pay overtime to their solicitors. Fees for hours in excess of the planned number go straight to the bottom line, so they can afford to give you a discount.

Put a cap on the daily or weekly hours any one lawyer can charge. This is partly about saving money. The individuals have to meet targets for chargeable hours, and will be tempted to work on into the evening when it isn't necessary. They work less efficiently when tired, so you end up paying more than if they went home at a reasonable hour and started again in the morning. The other part of this is occupational health and safety. On one major New South Wales Government contract, the completion had to be postponed because a key adviser (not one of the lawyers) collapsed from exhaustion. Fatigue management is normally the legal responsibility of the employer, not the client, but a) that may not last and b) do you really want to be encouraging people to work themselves to the point of collapse?

Giving Instructions

People who complain about the quality of the advice they receive from lawyers never attribute the deficiency to the quality of their instructions. Dare to think the unthinkable. It may be your fault.

Suppose, for instance, there is a report from the building site for the enabling works that a worker has found a colony of Green and Golden Bell Frogs, the same critter that caused the Sydney Olympics project to relocate the tennis centre. You are scheduled to send in the bulldozers on Friday, but aren't sure if you should. If your instructions simply ask what the law is on endangered species, don't blame the lawyer if the answer is unhelpfully broad and doesn't arrive until Monday.

The best instructions tend to consist of both a conversation with the lawyer and an email. The conversation may give you a good enough answer on the spot and should at least help to pin down what the problem really is. Although I just told you not to blame the lawyer for poor instructions, any halfway-competent lawyer faced with the question, 'What is the law on endangered species?' ought to respond, 'Why do you ask?' Give them the opportunity to elicit what they need to know in order to give you meaningful advice. The email is to confirm what it is you want them to do, to reduce the possibility of misunderstandings and give you both a record of it. It also makes it easier for the lead project lawyer to delegate the matter to another lawyer. (Easier generally equals cheaper.) If the matter is exceedingly sensitive, you may prefer to dispense with the email until the lawyer has done some preliminary digging, but that should be rare.

Any halfway-competent lawyer faced with the question, 'What is the law on endangered species?' ought to respond, 'Why do you ask?'

All instructions to the law firm should come from you and go to the lead project partner. Make sure the teams know this. The lawyers should keep a list of the matters they are advising on, and nothing should come on or off that list without you and the lead project partner agreeing it should happen.

This is not about preventing your people from talking to the law firm directly. If there is an issue with title to land, for instance, there may be an in-house property lawyer better placed to give the detailed instructions and deal directly with the external lawyers to solve the problem. But you don't want anyone giving new instructions you don't know about or that the lead project lawyer doesn't know about:

- It's your job to be across all the issues so that they can be prioritised and dealt with appropriately in the overall context of the procurement: you can't do it if people aren't telling you about them.

- Little issues can turn into bigger issues when someone digs a bit deeper: if you are not aware of what is being investigated, you may be blindsided by your own team.

- The same issue is likely to crop up in various different contexts: to avoid cost and confusion, you want one advice on the subject from the lawyers, not several.

- You will look a complete idiot when you discover the chief executive knows about the issue and you don't.

Share the issues list with your General Counsel. Just because something is creating a problem for your procurement doesn't mean it isn't also creating a problem elsewhere in the organisation. There may be a ready-made solution already out there, or you may do better coming up with a joint approach.

Securing Good Advice

To get the very best advice ... build a relationship with the lawyers that enables them to speak frankly to you.

To get the very best advice, you not only have to give good instructions, you also need to build a relationship with the lawyers that enables them to speak frankly to you. You don't want your lawyers doing work without instructions. Equally, you expect a good lawyer to spot issues for themselves and suggest that you might like to instruct them to look into it. The extent to which they do this is as much about the relationship as it is about the competence of the lawyers. It is when things go wrong that you need the relationship most.

In the InterCity West Coast franchise case, the UK Department for Transport advised bidders of the amount of the subordinated loan facility each would have to provide if successful in the tender. The amounts were calculated using a process that was not in accordance with advice previously given to the bidders.

The external lawyers were not represented at the meeting where the decision was taken. The lead partner found out about it after the amounts had already been notified to the bidders and did raise a concern both with the project team leader and separately with the internal lawyer. The concern appears to have been expressed in relatively low key terms and no one escalated the matter within the Department for Transport. The external lawyers formed the view that the issue was closed and that it would be 'unhelpful' to provide further advice.

> *They are acutely aware that ... advisers whose advice is too inconvenient may not be welcome back.*

External lawyers are not fully independent. They make a lot of money advising Governments and wish to be seen as helpers rather than troublemakers. They are acutely aware that their advice is sometimes inconvenient and that advisers whose advice is too inconvenient may not be welcome back. If you react badly to anything that could remotely be taken as criticism, or regard suggestions for instructions as crass attempts at fee-generation, or make it clear you would rather not know about anything that would require you to do something painful, you will inhibit them from giving advice you really need.

While any lawyer will make a reasonable attempt to discourage a client from doing something stupid, they are in a much more difficult position if you already have. Build a relationship where the lawyers feel able to tell you that you have made a complete bog-up of something. Better to hear it from them than read about it in the statement of claim.

If your lawyers are concerned about giving unhelpful advice, you may wish to indicate to them that certain things are more unhelpful than others, such as:

- advice that the form of words they recommended for the authorising resolution is inadequate, so you need to go back to your Board (or worse, Cabinet) to get it right;
- any other advice that contradicts the advice they gave last week, especially if you have already passed it on to your steering committee or the Minister;
- advice halfway through the tender process that you will need to engage in a previously unscheduled public consultation before concluding the contract;
- advice that contradicts public statements made by the Minister.

This does not mean the unhelpful advice should not be given. It is better to deal with unpleasantness now than end up in court later.

But when it comes to advice, legal or otherwise, 'no surprises' is a good rule for advisers to follow.

WRITTEN ADVICE OR ORAL?

Consider whether you should be getting advices in writing or orally. This is a trade-off: certainty and evidentiary value against cost and time.

If the advice is in writing, you can call upon the lawyers' professional indemnity insurance if the advice turns out to be wrong. If the decision you are making is likely to be subject to challenge, and you want to be able to show you took independent legal advice into consideration in making the decision, you need that advice in writing. Because written advice attracts insurance claims and court cases, the advice will be meticulously researched and quite likely subject to independent check within the law firm.

On the other hand, this kind of thing uses up a lot of time. Lawyer time is expensive and your time is valuable. If all you really want is to be sure you are not mis-stating the law in a note to the steering committee on a particular issue, ask the lawyers to review the note rather than create a written advice you then have to paraphrase. Very often, all you need is a steer to help you make a decision and move on.

Just make a point of thinking whether you need the advice in writing at the time you give the instructions. Once the issue has come back and bitten you, it will be too late to change your mind.

Data Room Services

It is customary to use the lawyers to manage the 'data room' containing information about the Agency that tenderers will need to inform their bids. In days gone by, paralegals and junior lawyers used to sit in a room at the lawyers' or client's offices for hours on end, checking who came in and out and making sure things weren't removed. These days, data rooms have gone virtual, but lawyers still run them, because they are the advisers who have made the investment in secure data storage and document tracking. The software will normally also support question and answer facilities. This can be used after the issue of the call for tenders, when bidders will have questions for you, and also after the submission of bids, when you will have questions for them.

These days, data rooms have gone virtual, but lawyers still run them, because they ... have made the investment in secure data storage and document tracking.

Government e-tender websites do allow bidders to download documents but do not have equivalent facilities for indexing, download tracking and document management. The law firm sites enable you to set up separate sections for each tenderer so you can deal with bidder-specific confidential information separately if required. If it does come to a lawsuit and you need to evidence who downloaded what when, you will be much better off with a dedicated electronic data room. You can still use the Government e-tender website for advertising the tender process.

Do not be tempted to let the Agency computer people set up the electronic data room for you: this is not something to deal with on a one-off basis and you don't want to play guinea pig. You have enough to do without managing a software project. Bidders trust the security of the systems run by the law firms. And if something does go wrong, the problem will not spend long on your desk: the lawyers know they have to sort it out pronto or their whole major projects practice is under threat.

Lawyers for the Tenderers

Tenderers faced by mounting bid costs have made considerable efforts to reduce the amount they pay their lawyers. To some extent Government has assisted this process with the increasing use of standardised contract provisions. Greater reductions have probably been achieved by tenderers leaning on the law firms to cut fees, do work using more junior staff or simply do less work. A side effect of these cost-cutting efforts is that you are more likely now to encounter a disconnect within a bid in the material produced by the legal and technical teams. If the tenderer's technical team is promising software updates every six months, their legal team should not be marking up the contract so they have no obligation to provide software updates at all, but it happens. If multi-national tenderers are using in-house lawyers to the exclusion of external lawyers (increasingly common, although less so on the very largest tenders), their lawyers may even be located in a different country, which increases the risk of disconnect.

You need to make sure there isn't an equivalent disconnect within your own team when reviewing the bids. That does not mean having your external lawyers review every single page of technical documentation submitted by the tenderers: expense must bear some relation to risk. But you need to feel confident your evaluation process will pick up significant discrepancies. It is annoying to pay your lawyers to deal with errors the tenderers should have

> *It is annoying to pay your lawyers to deal with errors the tenderers should have paid their own lawyers to fix. Live with it.*

paid their own lawyers to fix. Live with it. The alternative is a contract that doesn't do what you thought it said on the box.

Post-Contract Review

Clients often fail to give lawyers much in the way of feedback, in part because giving feedback is something a lot of managers are bad at anyway, in part because they fear the lawyer will charge them for the privilege. (This doesn't explain why clients fail to say 'thank you' – please don't omit the elementary courtesies.) Once the contract has been signed, invite the external lawyers to join a post-mortem session with you and the General Counsel on a no-fees basis. Look at what went right, what could have been done better, what should not have been done at all. The lawyers are unlikely to refuse to participate. What they learn will make them more likely to win future work from you and other Government clients. What you learn will help you do better next time. Win–win.

Chapter 11
Other Advisers

Lawyers constitute the irreducible minimum when it comes to the external advisers you will need in order to set up the contract, but it is unlikely you will manage without anyone else. How many other advisers you engage is up to you – and your ability to pay them. There will never be as much money available as you would really like, but setting up this contract is not something that should be done on a shoestring budget. Cheap bad advice costs more than expensive good advice. Expensive bad advice costs even more, but the point is not how much you are paying, it's whether you are getting value for Government's money.

Cheap bad advice costs more than expensive good advice.

Although requirements will vary from project to project, it is likely you will need both financial and technical advisers.

Financial Advisers

Just as you consulted with the General Counsel in relation to legal advice for setting up the contract, you need to consult the chief financial officer in relation to financial advice and assistance. Some of the help you need will be with internal budgeting and reporting: this capability should be set up within your own team. Do make sure you have a ring-fenced budget for setting up the contract. Accounting practices can lead to perverse outcomes. If the costs of setting up the contract will be deducted from the Agency's operational budget if the contract is not signed, but from the capital budget if it is, you can come under unhelpful pressure to conclude a poor contract just to protect the operational budget.

The greater part of the financial expertise will be required in relation to the structuring of the commercial deal to be offered to the market and in evaluating and negotiating the financial aspects of the bids received. For this you will probably need external help. It is unlikely, although not impossible, that sufficient expertise will be available within the Agency. The UK Department for Transport decided to manage without external financial advisers in its failed attempt in 2012 to set up the InterCity West Coast franchise. Although the Department had previously set up many franchises, it was attempting to implement for the first time policy changes that significantly affected the risk allocation on a £5.5 billion franchise contract. Managing without financial advisers was always going to be a somewhat courageous call. They might have got away with it if the internal financial team had agreed terms of reference or deliverables for the project, but no one took responsibility for the use (or misuse) of the financial model, which was neither audited nor fit for purpose, and the tender process had to be cancelled.

FEES

Financial advisers are normally paid hourly rates, although you may negotiate a fixed fee for discrete pieces of work. As with lawyers, the rate per hour has only a tenuous relationship with the total cost to Government, so do not allow the rate to drive your selection.

Although hourly rates are usual, financial advisers are more likely than other advisers to seek a success fee, particularly where the Government is selling assets or businesses rather than setting up a project, whether the sale is done by way of a public offering of shares or as a negotiated or tendered trade sale. In such cases, financial advisers may want part of their fee calculated as a percentage of the sale price, usually payable as a bonus on completion so you feel you are getting something for the money. You are not obliged to agree to this. Consider whether the lower up-front payments and any extra level of service you are offered will be worth the bonus. It is embarrassing to Government when the reward to an adviser appears to bear no relation to the value achieved.

It is embarrassing to Government when the reward to an adviser appears to bear no relation to the value achieved.

If you adopt success fees in any form, be extremely careful how you define success. Construction contractors are not the only ones who follow the money. The last thing you need is a financial adviser with an incentive to close a poor deal. One of the criticisms made by the National Audit Office of the Royal Mail privatisation in 2013 was that the independent corporate financial adviser was only incentivised to achieve the sale, not to optimise value for the taxpayer. Since the shares rose 38 per cent on the first day of trading, and remained 72 per cent above the issue price five months later, it is unsurprising the National Audit Office found the Government could have achieved better value. One cannot, of course, blame the share price entirely on the structure of the financial adviser's role, but there was clearly scope for a better alignment of incentives to result in a better outcome.

MANAGEMENT OF FINANCIAL ADVISERS

You need within your team someone who is capable of managing the financial advisers. Anyone can learn to kick tyres on advice submissions – one of the characteristics of the best executives and project directors is an ability to ask penetrating and revealing questions on subjects they know nothing about – but ideally you want someone capable of looking under the bonnet and understanding what they see. You get the best results when a genuinely independent adviser examines and explains the advantages and disadvantages of the available options and the client is capable of making a judgment on the professional skill with which the analysis has been conducted. The ability to press advisers to do better is partly a function of understanding what they ought to be capable of.

The ability to press advisers to do better is partly a function of understanding what they ought to be capable of.

You may not have a finance person reporting to you at the relevant moment, because in the public sector it often takes a lot longer to run a recruitment process to engage a finance employee than to run a procurement process to engage a financial adviser. If you are in this position, connect with the chief financial officer to secure assistance in defining the terms of reference for the financial advisers and in selecting and managing them until you have the necessary expertise within your team.

CONFLICTS OF INTEREST

If the transaction involves financing, you need to be particularly careful to define the role of your financial advisers to avoid any problems associated with conflicts of interest. Conflicts become more and more dangerous the more money is at stake. Even where a conflict is properly managed, reputational risk persists.

The independent corporate financial adviser in the Royal Mail privatisation in 2013 was paid £1.5 million in fees. Another company in the same group was selected as one of 16 'preferred investors' and received a priority allocation of six million shares in the privatisation. Precautions were taken to manage the potential conflict of interest and neither the National Audit Office nor the Business, Innovation and Skills Committee of the House of Commons, which investigated the privatisation, reported any impropriety. Nonetheless, media reports that the six million shares were promptly sold for a profit of around £8.4 million did nothing for the reputation of anyone involved.

FINANCIAL MODELLING

> *Financial models can be dangerous without the application of common sense and a healthy dose of scepticism.*

Any project on this scale will involve financial modelling, so modelling capability should be one of your criteria in selecting a financial adviser. While you will naturally want to engage the best available, do not allow yourself to be overawed either by their expertise or by the complexity of the models they produce. Financial models can be dangerous without the application of common sense and a healthy dose of scepticism. Neither of these qualities requires you to be a hotshot spreadsheet jockey, so don't let any deficiencies in your spreadsheet skills put you off exploring the issues with the modellers.

Your first task is to decide what the purpose of the model is. It is no use seeking warranties from your advisers that a model is fit for purpose if you fail to define what the purpose is. Typical purposes would be:

- establishing a business case for the choice of project or procurement option;
- modelling costs and benefits of risk management options;
- evaluating the financial impact of tenders received;
- building a 'public sector comparator' to determine whether better value could be achieved by retaining activity within the public sector rather than outsourcing.

It is possible for a model to serve more than one purpose. It is not necessarily a good idea. In the Intercity West Coast franchise case a model was developed to assess the risk of franchisees becoming insolvent in various economic scenarios, in order to test and calibrate a contract mechanism intended to allocate to the Government most of the risk of changes in GDP. (Passenger train revenues are highly correlated to GDP, because of the high proportion of commuter journeys. In recessions, there are fewer jobs and therefore fewer commuters, no matter how attractive the service provided by franchisees.)

The same model was then extended to calculate the amount of a subordinated loan facility to be provided on behalf of the franchisee: it was not fit for this purpose. The Department for Transport didn't like the output and decided not to use it. Failure to use something not fit for purpose ought to have been a good idea, but unfortunately they had represented to the bidders that the model *would* be used, so everything came unstuck.

The size of the spreadsheet workbooks is not a guide to the usefulness of a financial model.

The size of the spreadsheet workbooks is not a guide to the usefulness of a financial model. Always review closely the underpinning assumptions. A supplier seeking a negotiated outsourcing deal once provided me with an ingenious set of spreadsheets supposedly demonstrating it could carry out hundreds of millions of dollars' worth of maintenance activity 25 per cent more cheaply than the Government agency responsible. I was interested to know where they thought savings could be made, but the spreadsheets left me none the wiser: they gave an inaccurate estimate of figures for the current activity, then applied a 75 per cent multiplier throughout. Not so much ingenious as ingenuous. Needless to say, the Government agency decided to pass up the opportunity.

Ask your modellers where input figures have come from. If they are from 'comparable' projects, think about the comparison. Cost per metre for tunnelling through sandstone will not be comparable to the costs of tunnelling through basalt or gravel. Cost per helicopter for an order of two helicopters will be higher than the cost per helicopter for an order of 200. A development in the suburbs is unlikely to generate the same revenue as a similar-sized development in the central business district. You do not have to dig these things out of the model yourself. Sit the modellers down with their list of assumptions and ask them to talk you through it.

If your large project is part of an even larger portfolio of projects, check your assumptions are not out of line. If an airport is to be served by new road and rail links, an assumption of a road market share of 80 per cent, even if not unreasonable, will embarrass the Government if the rail link contract has just been awarded on the basis of a market share of 35 per cent.

Monte Carlo simulations

More complex financial models can deal with uncertainty through the use of probability simulations. Where cost or revenue items are uncertain, you can assign different probabilities to different outcomes for each line item. Probabilities can be linked to show correlations: for instance, prices of different manufactured inputs may be likely to move in the same direction.

The computer will 'roll the dice' thousands of times (hence the name 'Monte Carlo simulation') and come up with a range of answers for the overall financial outcome. The 'P90' cost is the point where 90 per cent of the scenarios predict the project will be completed for that amount or less. It is not a promise that reality will not align with the other 10 per cent. Look at the distribution curve to get a flavour of the possible financial outcomes: see for example the probability cost curve shown in Figure 11.1. The P50 is not in the middle of the range and the P99 is a great deal more than 9 per cent higher than the P90. There are very few ways to bring a project in more cheaply and lots and lots of ways to have a cost overrun.

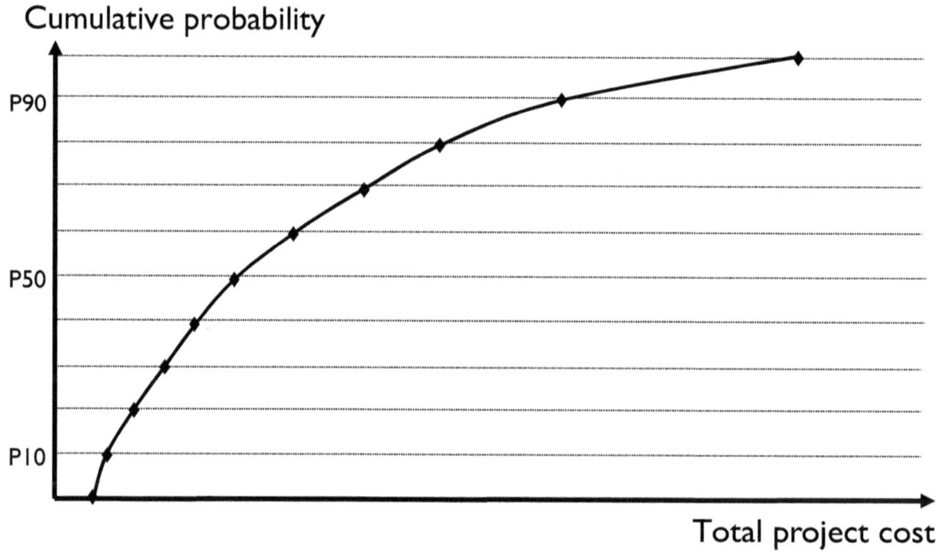

Figure 11.1 Probability cost curve

Don't be complacent if the P90 looks good. Just because the software will calculate to ten decimal places doesn't meant the estimate is accurate to ten decimal places. Or even one. Bear in mind the outputs can be no better than the inputs. The probabilities were only estimates, failure to correlate risks correctly can make a huge difference and you have yet to make the acquaintance of the 'unknown unknowns'.

Lies, damned lies and financial models

Any financial model is capable of being manipulated to give a particular outcome, which is why you need to be so careful about the assumptions. It doesn't take much. Reassessment of a few key probabilities. Choosing the P75 rather than the P90. Finding a reason to prefer the more optimistic demand forecast. Deciding certain costs are more properly allocated to someone else's budget. These are all matters of judgment and anything that requires judgment has a range of defensible choices. A tweak here and a tweak there can push the dollars all over the graph.

A tweak here and a tweak there can push the dollars all over the graph.

It is probably not entirely a coincidence that once a project has been announced by the politicians, the public sector comparator never demonstrates better value for money than the proposed outsourcing and the updating of the business case to reflect the selected tender never shows the project isn't worth doing. Models can be manipulated, and they are.

Often it doesn't matter. Window dressing is not important. Crafting attractive numbers for the media release is the same as crafting attractive words. Everyone knows the words and numbers are being chosen to give the project the best possible look, and any complexities are being glossed over. A media release is no place to try and explain the difference between real and nominal costs or what a net present value is. If the politicians are keen on a particular headline number, there is usually a way to make the number fit.

Asking your financial advisers to make the numbers look attractive is one thing. Asking them to make the numbers come up with the wrong answer is quite another. When you are using a financial model to make choices between strategies or between bidders you want those choices to be clean: no error and no bias.

Cleaning out error involves having the model independently reviewed. Even experienced modellers can make simple mistakes, entering a plus sign instead of a minus sign or referencing the wrong cell. The model in the Intercity West Coast franchise case was later found to use a different GDP baseline index from the one used in the franchise agreement for the GDP risk sharing mechanism, which rather undermined its fitness even for the original purpose it had been designed for. An independent check is ordinary good practice, not a vote of no confidence in your modellers, so there is no need to feel shy about it. Quality assurance is in everyone's interest.

Bias can be harder to eliminate than error. Run scenarios with different parameters to check the sensitivities of the variables. Push the parameters to extremes to see what happens. What variables make the most difference to the outputs? Do you understand why? Are the outputs plausible? Be honest with yourself about what results you are hoping the model will provide – and be deeply suspicious of assumptions that support those results. Demand forecasting is notoriously over-optimistic. The operators of two motorway tunnel projects in Sydney, the Cross City Tunnel which opened in 2005 and the Lane Cove Tunnel which opened in 2007, each went bust within three years of opening because traffic was less than half the original forecast. London's Millennium Dome revised its visitor projections from 12 million to 4.5 million within months of opening. If you are basing assumptions on a project similar to your own, the similarity should be between the actual projects, not between the demand achieved by the other project and the demand you are hoping to achieve for yours.

OTHER USES OF FINANCIAL ADVISERS

In any procurement, there needs to be an avenue for tenderers to express concerns about the process.

In any procurement, there needs to be an avenue for tenderers to express concerns about the process. Bidders often prefer not to complain directly to the project director, since they are in marketing mode and wish to radiate an aura of enthusiasm and cooperation. The UK does not follow the Australian practice of appointing an independent auditor of the procurement process, who will field any process issues raised by the bidders.

Financial advisers are traditionally the ones to fill this gap. If there is any problem with the process, the financial advisers to the bidders will be on the phone to the Government's financial advisers, or the investment bankers will be having slanging matches in the corridor (few investment bankers are shy and retiring). You should select financial advisers capable of holding their own in the corridor stand-offs but also capable of listening to concerns and coming to you with suggestions of how to deal with genuine problems.

Although it wasn't picked up in the Laidlaw Inquiry, I suspect this may have been an issue in the InterCity West Coast franchise case: the decision not to use external financial advisers was a problem not only because financial errors went unnoticed but also because it took away the traditional intermediary for sorting out process issues. Not understanding that people have more than their obvious function commonly ruins organisational change exercises. I call it the screwdriver error: most screwdrivers are vastly over-engineered for turning screws, but good hardware shops don't sell the cheap thin ones – customers complain because the screwdrivers break when they use them to lever the lids off paint cans.

Technical Advisers

With lawyers and financial advisers, you expect that their work will essentially be over once the procurement phase is complete. Yes, you will need to get the lawyers back if a dispute arises; yes, you may need financial advice from time to time, particularly if there are variations on a contract involving private finance. But technical advisers are much more likely to have an ongoing planned role during the delivery phase.

When you are preparing to set up the contract, technical help is primarily required with the specification: working out what you need to ask for; how to ask for it in a way that means tenderers will understand and give it to you; and whether the bid submissions match the requirements of the specification. It is absolutely critical to get this right.

Contract variations put up costs, delay delivery and diminish accountability, yet they usually result from things people could have sorted out when the specification was drafted, if only they had made the effort.

> *Contract variations ... usually result from things people could have sorted out when the specification was drafted, if only they had made the effort.*

Failure to understand the market, failure to involve the right stakeholders, failure to incorporate the winning design into the contract correctly, unwillingness to deal with an issue that was never going to go away: all of these things lead to unnecessary variations. The right technical advice during the procurement phase can make all the difference.

There is often also a requirement for technical advice during the delivery phase. It is tempting to believe all you have to do is sign the agreement, leaving the contractor to deliver on its obligations without any level of review or audit or inspection on behalf of the Agency. Tempting but foolish. A contractual right to refuse a delivery that isn't in accordance with the specification is easy enough to enforce when the delivery is a van load of office supplies. You don't get a second chance at a mega-project. Trains that are two tonnes overweight when presented for acceptance will not become two tonnes lighter when you discover they don't match the specification, and good luck with refusing delivery if the politicians want the trains in service before the next election.

If you don't want to be caught out, the contract manager will need to undertake at least some level of review or audit of work in progress during the delivery phase. Sometimes the Agency will have internal resource to undertake this, but often it won't.

This is not simply a matter of expertise. Government agencies may have restrictions on travel that make it difficult to use employees to conduct audits or inspections at foreign manufacturing plants. Assistance from technical advisers may be needed to review the contractor's project plans and schedules, assess design documentation, or inspect units or work stages presented for acceptance.

ENGAGING THE TECHNICAL ADVISERS

Given that technical assistance may be continuously required throughout the project, should you run three separate competitive tenders to engage technical advisers for specification development, evaluation support and delivery support, or should you set up a single contract covering the entire period of the contract?

Spending money on consultants is one of the things that gets Government a bad press.

There are various factors affecting your decision. Mega-projects last for years. The Agency may baulk at setting up a long term advisory agreement. Spending money on consultants is one of the things that gets Government a bad press, so agreements of this type may require specific authority from the Minister. The quantum of money you will pay out over a period of years will be tiny in comparison with the overall value of the project, but in absolute terms may involve a larger commitment than the Agency is willing or authorised to undertake. On the other hand, a firm selected for the first part of the process is extremely well placed to secure the advisory contract for subsequent phases. Awarding only a small contract for the first phase starts to look like order splitting when the firm keeps being re-engaged, which can cause the auditors to give their frown muscles a serious workout.

Because the task of the technical advisers will be significantly different in the procurement and delivery phases, a possible compromise is to split the engagement into three parts, but use only two contracts. The first two parts, specification development and evaluation support, are the most closely linked: the technical adviser responsible for assisting in specification development will have a deep understanding of the requirements that will be particularly valuable in evaluating the tenders received. Procure the first two parts through a single tender process, with the second part structured as an option (to give you an easy way to dispense with their services if the advisers don't measure up) then run a second procurement process to cover the support required in the delivery phase. Whether this approach is sensible will depend to some extent on the state of the technical adviser market. Since you need to have the delivery phase team poised and ready to run at contract award, your second procurement process would take place while the tender for the main contract is still in progress, so any firm then assisting the bidders would be conflicted out of working for you. If that is a problem, you will have to work out a different contracting approach.

The need for technical advisers in the delivery phase can be greatly reduced (although usually not eliminated) by including an independent certification process into the contract. An independent firm is appointed jointly by the Agency and the contractor and is there to certify whether or not the contractor has done various things in accordance with the contract. They would commonly provide a certificate that designs produced by the contractor will meet the contract requirements; that a proposed testing programme will demonstrate whether or not the deliverables have been properly completed; and that the deliverables have passed the testing programme and meet the requirements of the contract. Other certificates might be required whenever the contractor is to receive payment for completion of a package of works.

The system is a good one. Contractors are under enormous pressure to meet their monthly budgets. If a deliverable attracts a payment, the importance of collecting the payment may lead them to put forward a deliverable which is not really complete: a project plan that is poorly developed, a design without evidence that community consultation has been taken into account; 'completed' works that omit the site clean-up. I know of one contractor who put a stage of works forward for acceptance when there were more than a thousand items on the 'snagging list' – and got away with it because of the political pressure to declare a success ahead of the forthcoming election. The requirement for independent certification before submission goes some way to discourage this practice, and certainly takes much of the headache of dealing with it away from the Agency. You do need to have confidence in your specification: if the requirements are ambiguous or inaccurate, the involvement of an independent certifier will complicate the issue rather than make life easier for the contract manager.

Contractors are under enormous pressure to meet their monthly budgets.

RELIANCE ON REPORTS

Sometimes it will be convenient for the bidders to rely on technical reports obtained by Government, such as geotechnical surveys. If you want the bidders to be able to do this, make sure it is included within the brief when you engage the relevant adviser. Part of what you pay for with professional advice is the benefit of their professional indemnity insurance. If a third party is to be

Part of what you pay for with professional advice is the benefit of their professional indemnity insurance.

able to rely on the report, the advisers must supply the report on that basis or the insurance will not cover it.

FEE STRUCTURES

If you use any fee structure other than hourly rates or fixed fees, make sure you understand the implications.

The UK National Audit Office (NAO) report in 2000, on the Holyrood project for the construction of a new Scottish Parliament building, found that fees for project consultants had risen from £10 million to £26 million, largely because the fees were calculated on a percentage of construction costs, and construction costs had more than doubled. The increase in construction costs was not foreseen, but the NAO pointed out the risks would have been shared more fairly if a mechanism had been included to reduce the fees as a proportion of construction cost as the level of cost increased.

No action was taken to renegotiate the fees with the Holyrood consultants until 2003, which was unfortunate, as construction costs went up a further 220 per cent. By the time of the NAO's next report in 2004, the fees had risen to £50 million.

AGENCY TECHNICAL EXPERTS

Difficulties in the technical field tend to arrive from opposite directions: either you have an Agency that is completely clueless about the subject matter of the contract or an Agency that is stuffed full of opinionated technical experts. A different approach to the engagement of advisers is needed in each case.

The trouble with being clueless is that you have no way of telling whether you are being right royally ripped off. The less expertise the Agency has, the more it is obliged to delegate to the advisers and the less well equipped it is to know whether the advice it receives is any good. With zero expertise, decisions effectively become the decisions of the adviser, not of the Agency. This is usually bad news, even if the adviser is genuinely expert, because what they are expert in is the technology. Technology expertise is only one input into making good decisions. It is not necessarily the most important one.

If you find yourself in this trap, your first objective should be to recruit one or more suitable experts onto the Agency staff. If this doesn't work (and it might not, particularly if you are unable to offer the going market rate) look around for an individual consultant who is well regarded in the industry. You need someone with in-depth knowledge and experience: grey hair

You need someone with in-depth knowledge and experience: grey hair usually comes with the package, but this is not essential.

usually comes with the package, but this is not essential. A single individual will of course not be able to provide you with all the technical support you will need for a project on this scale. What they are able to do is help you understand what support you need, pin it down into terms of reference for the technical adviser and help you to select a firm that can do the job. They can later provide an independent review of the technical adviser's work. You may also want to use them as an independent member of the Evaluation Committee for the main contract.

While the use of an independent certifier will reduce your dependence on technical assistance during the delivery phase, it does not mean your contract manager can cope without technical support. There are two issues.

The first is that the independent certification process only kicks in when there is something to certify. If the contractor is falling behind schedule and isn't giving you a plausible explanation, you can't send in the independent certifier to find out what's going on.

The second is that while you may trust the independent certifier to be intelligent, expert and unbiased, if there is disagreement between you and the contractor, would you really feel comfortable that the independent certifier would decide the issue without receiving submissions from both parties?

The normal practice is for the contractor to be required to copy the Agency in when it makes a submission to the independent certifier, giving the Agency an opportunity to comment before the certificate is given or refused. You won't want to conduct the same detailed checks that will be undertaken by the independent certifier, but you do need the capability to understand what you're looking at. There may be a fine line between a minor defect that can be fixed later and a major defect that needs to be fixed before you move on: don't expect borderline cases to be decided in your favour if you don't have the expertise to comment to the independent certifier.

Having a great deal of expertise within the Agency is generally a much better idea than being clueless but it does carry its own problems. Experts are people who have opinions on their area of expertise. Unfortunately, many people have opinions on areas of expertise in which they are not expert, a phenomenon that wastes a lot of your time when it manifests itself on your steering committees. But experts have expert opinions. Inconveniently, they don't all have the same ones.

Experts have expert opinions. Inconveniently, they don't all have the same ones.

Some of the divisions arise between experts on widgets and experts on the cost of widgets. Engineers are always accused of wanting to 'gold-plate' assets. It is obvious to an accountant that it is better to buy four widgets with a design life of five years than one widget which has a design life of 20 years but is more than four times as expensive. It is less obvious to the engineer, who has to organise four installations instead of one, or more likely see a slender maintenance budget burdened with making five-year widgets last 20 years because some scrooge of an accountant won't cough up the promised capital for replacements.

The problem that often arises is not that you have to persuade the Agency engineers the accountants are right, it is that you have to persuade them their own opinion doesn't matter. Experts hate being irrelevant. But if you are going to market with a 20-year contract, and widget failure is a risk allocated to the contractor, then it is up to the contractor's experts, not the Agency's experts, to make the call on whether to buy four five-year widgets or one 20-year widget.

If you ask an independent technical adviser to tell you whether a bidder's design is in accordance with the specifications, then that is the advice they will give you. If you ask the same question of an Agency expert, they are quite likely to tell you whether the design is in accordance with their personal view on the best way to meet the specification, which is not necessarily the same thing at all. External advisers are not immune from this syndrome, but can usually be more objective. Agency experts may find it difficult to set their personal opinions to one side, particularly if the contract involves outsourcing and their jobs are the ones that will be lost. The presence of a respected external adviser to assist them can be helpful.

How often in a lifetime does an engineer have the chance to design an iconic bridge, or a fleet of submarines, or a bullet train?

In times gone by, Agency experts would usually do part of the design work and sometimes even all of it, with contractors being engaged merely to construct to the Agency's design. Many an Agency expert wishes this was still common. When I was growing up in Sydney, I learned about the engineer John Bradfield and thought how amazing it would be to be able to point to the Sydney Harbour Bridge and say, 'I did that.' Mega-projects give a lot of people that kind of buzz. How often in a lifetime does an engineer have the chance to design an iconic bridge, or a fleet of submarines, or a bullet train? These days the Agency experts generally have to sit back and watch a contractor's employees have all the fun. The temptation to join in can be hard to resist, so if you decide to run with internal experts only at any stage, reduce the risk by agreeing their remit as you would for an external adviser.

Finding Other Advisers

Depending on the nature of your project, you may need more advice and assistance than can be provided by your main legal, financial and technical advisers. There is no area of mega-project expertise lacking in consultants salivating at the prospect of selling you their assistance. There are communications consultants, computer systems consultants, industrial relations consultants. Management consultants, risk management consultants, project management consultants, change management consultants, environmental management consultants. Demand forecasters, schedulers. Whatever. If there is something you need help with, there is someone out there who can help you.

There are also a lot of people who would happily charge you for their services while being of no help whatsoever. Competitive tendering for a clear scope of work is usually the best route to value for money.

If you aren't quite sure what you need or which type of firm to engage, ask around. Your procurement department should in theory be able to help, although they don't always have someone who understands the relevant market. Often the best source of information is the advisers you already have. They will have worked on projects for a range of clients and may well be able to tell you what has been done elsewhere to solve similar problems.

Do not engage anyone to produce a report unless you know what you are going to do with it. Government archives are littered with consultant's reports that were never even read, let alone acted upon.

Government archives are littered with consultant's reports that were never even read, let alone acted upon.

It can sometimes be convenient to engage advisory services through the medium of one of your principal advisers. A report on the financial strength of the companies bidding for the contract, for instance, may be better done by a firm that specialises in providing such reports than by your principal financial adviser. Rather than appointing and managing two advisers, you could include the financial strength evaluation in the remit of your principal adviser, on the basis that they will subcontract the work to the specialist firm.

Where you need advice in a hurry, it may also be quicker to arrange for it to be subcontracted by an existing adviser, who is not constrained by public sector procurement processes. Take care with that one, though: the bureaucracy may grind slowly but it is there for a purpose. Achieving an outcome more quickly is one thing; achieving an outcome that would not have been permitted under Government rules is quite another. Don't bypass the bureaucracy if by doing so you also bypass good practice.

In some cases you may consider using advisers not only as independent experts to give you advice, but also as a resource pool, a source of people who can be seconded in to work under your direct control. Where the project resource needs fluctuate significantly, it can be difficult for the public sector to be sufficiently flexible in staffing the project, leaving you from time to time with a team that is either horrendously over-worked or sitting around doing very little. A large law firm can lend you a paralegal for a week or two here and there without their own practice missing a beat. Extended secondments for more senior staff require a bit more forethought and negotiation, but don't overlook your advisers as a potential source of temporary staff as well as of advice.

MANDATED ADVISERS

Recognise that the stupendous amounts of money involved in a mega-project make your stakeholders nervous.

Occasionally a stakeholder such as Treasury or the Prime Minister's Office will foist an adviser on you, to plant someone they trust into the project because they don't trust *you*. When you are conscious of your own trustworthiness this can be deeply irritating, particularly when the adviser has to be paid from your budget, but don't take it out on the adviser. It probably isn't their fault, and even if it is, you need them to take back favourable reports. Recognise that the stupendous amounts of money involved in a mega-project make your stakeholders nervous, particularly if there has been a recent fiasco, and this is just one way to keep them happy. It isn't all downside, either. The adviser won't have won the trust of the stakeholder by being useless: take advantage of their skills and treat it as a bonus.

More often, an adviser is foisted on you because your project has interfaces with other things going on in the Agency. If your project involves outsourcing, for instance, you will need a whole stream of work around managing the employment transition and communicating with the affected employees. Where there are other changes happening in the Agency, it is likely to give a better outcome for the Agency – and the employees – if communications to employees about all of the different changes are properly coordinated and presented in a consistent format. Where communications consultants are to be used, the Agency is unlikely to want more than one firm involved. Unless yours is the first project to need the consultant, you will be expected to use the one the Agency has already selected, and someone else is likely to be managing their contract. Do not let that stop you agreeing a remit and specific deliverables: the standard services they are providing to everybody else may not be enough for you.

Chapter 12

Governance

Governance is an over-used word that means what people want it to mean. Anything which helps to deliver a good outcome, or is itself a good outcome, runs the risk of being designated as an element of governance. 'Efficiency' has been described as a principle of governance, for instance, and so has 'diversity of thought'. Both are good things, but I don't think either of them is what governance is really all about.

My own take on it, although perhaps idiosyncratic, is very simple. At some point, the culmination of all your efforts, someone is going to take up a pen and put their signature to a contract on behalf of the Agency. That's right, the contract that commits the Agency to billions in expenditure and to public vilification if it ends up in court. The question the signatory asks, often somewhat nervously, is: 'Am I okay to do this?' Governance is what provides the answer to that question. Can the signatory put pen to paper with confidence? Have all the bases been covered? Have all those public sector backsides been covered? Governance is how you know.

You might think the person with the pen could simply ask you, rather than faffing around with time-consuming governance processes. You are the project director, you are the one running the project. What's the matter, don't they trust you?

This isn't about personal trust. This is about humongous sums of taxpayers' money. No one should authorise the expenditure of billions without seeking reasonable assurance that the expenditure is being properly incurred. When so much is at stake, it is not reasonable to rely solely on the word of one person. The trustworthy may be mistaken and the untrustworthy are bound to cause trouble. If the person with the pen relies only on your word, they have a problem and so do you. The problem for the person with the pen is that your word can never be enough to discharge their responsibilities. The problem for you is that yours is one of the backsides that need covering.

No one should authorise the expenditure of billions without seeking reasonable assurance that the expenditure is being properly incurred.

Providing Cover

The public sector has gained a certain notoriety for elevating the avoidance of accountability into an art form. Passive verb forms such as 'it was decided' are standard in public sector memoranda. Proponents of plain English complain about this, saying it makes sentences easier to understand if you use only the active voice. Their complaint misses the point. Public sector use of the passive voice is not caused by failure to comprehend the mechanics of good communication. The issue is that if you use the active voice, the equivalent phrase 'X decided' requires you to a) know and b) disclose the identity of the X who made the decision. Perish the thought. Civil servants know perfectly well that failure is an orphan and success has many fathers. They just don't know in advance which one is going to apply. Use of the passive voice enables acceptance of responsibility for a decision to be deferred until the advisability of acceptance has become apparent.

In the Intercity West Coast franchise case, not only did nobody volunteer to take responsibility for a couple of key decisions that de-railed the £5.5 billion procurement process, the subsequent Laidlaw Inquiry, despite an extensive investigation, was unable to find any evidence at all for the origin of the decisions. Similarly, the Commission of Inquiry in the Queensland Health Payroll System case was unable to discover any evidence recording the decision to adopt a prime contractor model for the procurement. The report notes, somewhat plaintively, it 'appears to have emerged'.

> *Many public sector decisions are not made by anyone. They just emerge from some primordial swamp.*

This is fairly typical. You will find that many public sector decisions are not made by anyone. They just emerge from some primordial swamp. Everyone's backside is protected because nobody can identify which backside to kick. Unfortunately, this method of rear end protection is incompatible with successful project delivery. If you can't identify decision-makers, you can't identify who is responsible for doing things. If you can't identify who is responsible for doing things, things don't get done. And if things don't get done, projects fail.

If you are to protect the rear ends most in need of protection (which must include yours, your chief executive's and your Minister's) the way to do it is to be able to demonstrate that everything that should have been done, was done. This is not merely compatible with project success, it comes surprisingly close to guaranteeing it. If everyone does everything they reasonably can to make the project a success, it is highly probable the project will *be* a success. The role of governance is to provide the assurance that everything has been done – or at least notice if it hasn't been, in time to fix the problem.

The boundaries of governance are subject to the same lack of clarity as its definitions. You adopt various processes in managing the project: developing a business case for the project that includes appropriate cost benefit analysis; undertaking systematic risk management; securing the confidentiality of the tender evaluation; and so on. These processes can be considered part of project governance, or they can be considered as the management activities that governance monitors.

I have adopted the second approach, so for the purposes of this chapter, governance has just two important elements:

1. the governance framework; and

2. independent review.

Governance Framework

Properly constituted and managed, committees are remarkably useful.

The basic governance framework for most projects involves a project director reporting to a steering committee. For a mega-project, you will need something a little more complicated, but it will still involve committees. If your definition of a committee is a body that keeps minutes and wastes hours, do not be disheartened. Properly constituted and managed, committees are remarkably useful. Even people who supposedly hate them will happily tell you there are very few problems that can't be solved by getting the right people around a table. And 'the right people around a table' is what a committee *is* – or should be. So, what committees do you need?

You need to think separately about governance for the evaluation and governance for the project (which in this context includes the underlying project of ensuring the contractor delivers whatever it is that the contract is for).

If you have a competitive tender process, you have to evaluate the bids. The process of evaluation and selection is the process most likely to put Government on the receiving end of a lawsuit if you get it wrong. To make the evaluation process bullet-proof, you need to keep the evaluation and the evaluators segregated under very strict controls.

The project itself is much broader than the evaluation: there will be issues with things like project resourcing, whether there are schedule conflicts with other projects, and how the enabling works are coming along. This requires coordination across projects, with issues being raised in different forums. Trying to segregate a project steering committee is likely to be counter-productive.

PROJECT GOVERNANCE

Standard major project governance in a Government agency will typically have three layers. The top layer is the Board, if there is one, otherwise it is the executive committee, responsible for the entire organisation. Below that will be a committee with a name like 'Major Projects Board' or 'Investment Committee', which will be responsible for all projects above some threshold. (If by any chance you are trying to establish a contract for a mega-project in an Agency that doesn't do enough big projects to justify the existence of such a committee, or is too disorganised to have one, double your resourcing budget and get more help – the organisational support you probably take for granted just won't be there.) Below that will be the steering committee for the individual project.

> *As a rule of thumb, you want people from as far up the food chain as you can get.*

You will certainly need a steering committee. Its membership will depend very much on what the underlying project is. As a rule of thumb, you want people from as far up the food chain as you can get. If your project is large but well understood – a highways agency building a major road, for instance – you may not need to go right to the top of the organisation to find your committee members. However, if the project involves structural change to the existing organisation, with significant services being outsourced for the first time or a core IT system being replaced, then ideally you want both the chief executive and a non-executive from the Board on your steering committee. If you can attract enough of the people who constitute the Investment Committee, you can then secure agreement to bypass that committee entirely. This is helpful, quite apart from the saving in paperwork, because you will need time and focus from these people that you may not get if you are sharing an agenda with several other projects.

Bypassing any standing committees between your steering committee and the Board may be helpful. Bypassing the Board is not. The body charged with running the Agency needs to be in the governance loop. In the InterCity West Coast franchise case, which was notable for its many failures of governance, the selection decision that was later overturned did not go to the Board at all. Up to that point the franchise was referenced at Board meetings only once and the risk registers presented to the Board for review contained no specific risk in relation to the InterCity West Coast tender process. The full Board was not even aware of what the governance framework was: a subcommittee of the Board, established to supervise the scoping stages on the franchise process, subsequently revised its remit to cover the issue of invitations to tender and the award of franchises, but there was no evidence the Board ever endorsed this change. This was an advisory Board, not a true Board of Directors, but the executive committee was also bypassed. In the 26 meetings of the executive committee held during the relevant period there was reference in the minutes to rail refranchising on only three occasions and not a single explicit reference to the InterCity West Coast tender process. The people at the top were out of the governance loop and failed to see the fiasco coming.

The people at the top were out of the governance loop and failed to see the fiasco coming.

A single steering committee, ideally reporting directly to the Board, is sufficient for internal purposes, but you will need a second committee. The governance issue here is not project management but stakeholder management. Mega-projects go beyond any single Agency. You need a group that has people on it from outside the Agency, so you can keep the big end of town updated in a relatively controlled environment. The external committee is not there to override the Board's responsibility for project decisions but to give guidance, manage stakeholders and facilitate inter-Agency cooperation where required.

Membership of this committee will depend on the project, but you will need one or two senior people from your Agency, including the chief executive or, if different, the line manager to whom you report. (Your project is so big your reporting line should go to the chief executive or no more than one level below. If you have to report to someone any further down the food chain than that, pay particular attention to getting the governance framework right, because it will provide the access to senior people you will need to deliver a successful project.)

Treasury should certainly be represented. If your Agency is a separate organisation within a larger Government grouping such as transport or health you will need someone from the central organisation. Depending on the political profile of the project, you may also need staffers from the Minister's office, perhaps also the offices of the Treasurer and Prime Minister. While membership of such a committee is an excellent educational experience for a young staffer, the committee is of more value to you if the people on it know which way is up. Try to get the more senior staffers, who have mastered the art of putting items onto the Cabinet agenda. (This is a real issue when you need Cabinet approvals. Your project may seem humongously important to you, but a Cabinet with a trillion dollar budget and a possible need to declare war on the East Quango Republic may well have other priorities. If you are very unlucky, the Cabinet secretary will be engaged in a feud with the Minister's office and you will have to beg Treasury or someone else to put it on the agenda instead.)

The committee is of more value to you if the people on it know which way is up.

Generally, you as project director will be working within the Agency that benefits from the project. This is not always the case. In shared services initiatives, where the Agency's internal systems are being superseded by a whole-of-Government shared system, management of the project often sits elsewhere in Government. In such cases the external committee needs to have strong representation from the operating arm of the Agency, so that the systems implications for the operating business are properly managed.

Governance in these circumstances was identified as a major issue in the Queensland Health Payroll System case. The project was managed for Government not by Queensland Health but by CorpTech, a technology group that set up the contract while within Queensland Treasury and was then transferred to the Department of Public Works, where it continued to manage the project. The Auditor-General described the governance arrangements as 'complicated' and 'ineffective' and noted that (despite or perhaps because of the existence of a number of different governance bodies) it was 'not clear … [who] had responsibility for the overall governance and successful completion of the whole project.' The project was a spectacular failure.

External committee membership will not be your decision. Use what influence you can to secure representation from all the key stakeholders, and try to exclude anyone who does not add value, either in their personal contribution to discussions or in their ability to influence the stakeholders they represent. The more people on the committee, the greater the risk of leaks to the media or to people who do not wish the project well.

The more people on the committee, the greater the risk of leaks to the media or to people who do not wish the project well.

A typical framework for project governance is shown in Figure 12.1. For governance of the evaluation, you need the same two committees, but you need to configure the decision-making differently to take into account the role of the Evaluation Committee.

EVALUATION GOVERNANCE

Project governance is about keeping a project under control (or at least noticing when it isn't). Evaluation governance is about rendering the tender process bullet-proof, which involves keeping a clear distinction between evaluation and decision-making. A separate Evaluation Committee, normally chaired by you, produces an evaluation report which must then go to the decision-makers.

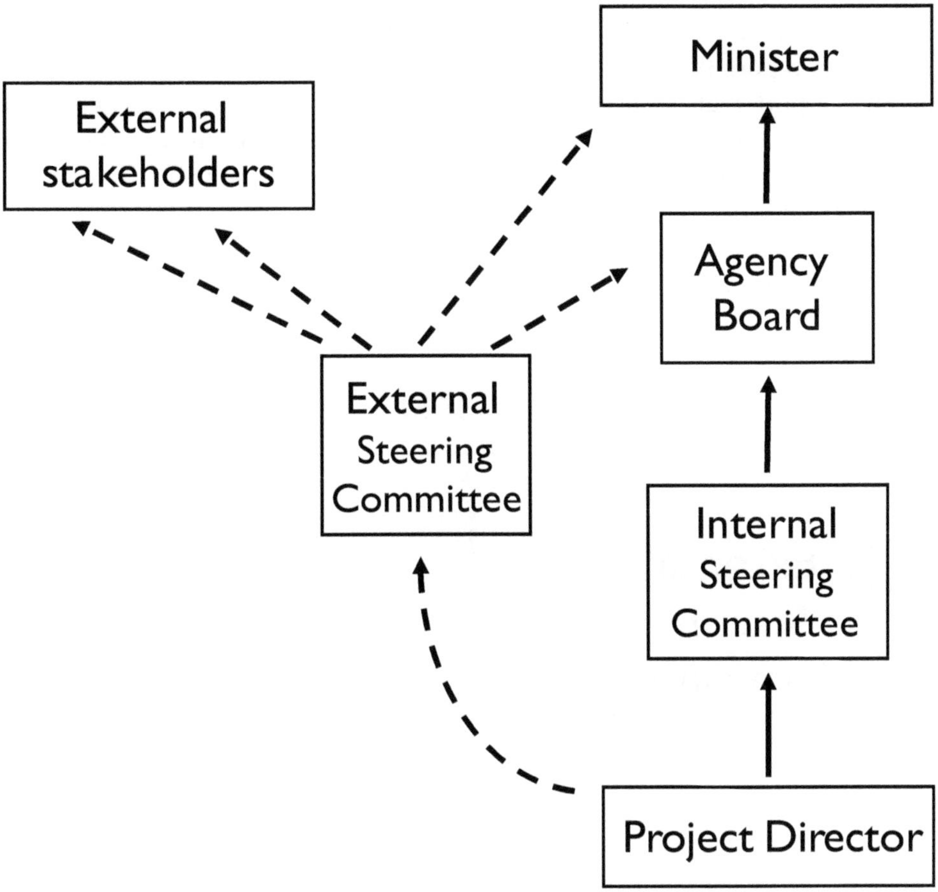

Figure 12.1 Project governance framework

For a small contract, the Evaluation Committee and the decision-makers may be one and the same. This works because the decision-makers have personally reviewed the tenders, so the evaluation report and the record of the decision are essentially one and the same thing. Your problem is that the selection decision will be made either by Cabinet itself or by someone delegated to do so by Cabinet, probably the Minister or Treasurer or both jointly. Certainly whoever is making the decision will not have reviewed the tenders personally. If their decision is based on something other than what is in the evaluation report, it may be at risk of challenge because of being made using a discretion the decision-maker didn't have, or on the basis of matters that were not relevant.

If the decision-maker is not happy to make a decision on the basis of the evaluation report, the correct course is to send the evaluators back to produce another report that properly deals with whatever the decision-maker was concerned about. To limit the risk of the decision-maker instead going off on a frolic of their own in disregard of the report, the governance framework should be designed to give sufficient confidence that no one will feel any need to second-guess the report's recommendations. The basic structure I prefer is shown in Figure 12.2.

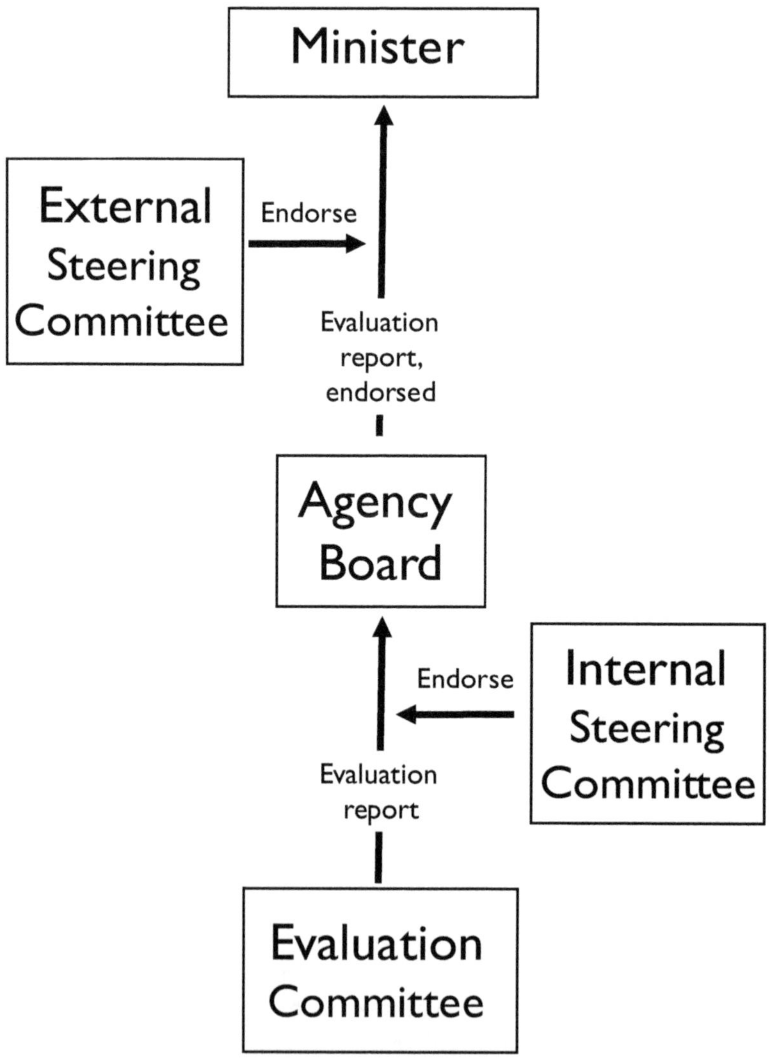

Figure 12.2 Evaluation governance framework

The evaluation report goes direct from the Evaluation Committee to the internal approvals body, the Board if there is one. It goes with the endorsement of the internal steering committee, which will give the Board comfort that process has been followed on the evaluation and that the organisation is ready to enter into the contract once a decision has been made. (Further comfort will also be obtained from independent review reports, discussed below.) The Board then adds a note endorsing the report to the Minister, and the external steering committee endorses the Board note and report. The Minister gets comfort that the Agency is satisfied with the process and ready to go, and also gets comfort that all the Government stakeholders are happy bunnies.

The framework may have more layers in it if the Minister does not have delegated authority from Cabinet to make the decision, or the Board wants endorsement from the regular Investment Committee, but the principle is the same. The evaluation report should be unchanged in form all the way from the Evaluation Committee to the ultimate decision-maker.

The evaluation report should be unchanged in form all the way from the Evaluation Committee to the ultimate decision-maker.

TERMS OF REFERENCE

There is no universal perfect governance framework. Whatever structure is selected, the most important thing about your governance framework is that you should know what it is. This sounds obvious, but it was yet another failing in the InterCity West Coast franchise case. The internal auditors produced a 'Rail Governance Map' about a week after the tenderers had submitted their bids – that is, when the tender process was in full swing – yet the subsequent report from the National Audit Office found the actual governance framework to have been quite different.

The actions of a 'Contract Award Committee' ultimately caused the tender process to be cancelled, since it determined the amounts of the subordinated loan facility in a manner not in accordance with the guidance provided to bidders. But its terms of reference said its role was 'providing assurance on the procurement process'. Determining the subordinated loan facility amounts was hardly an assurance role. It seems the committee members based their belief in their authority on the process charts issued with the guidance to bidders. But none of the inquiries managed to establish who took or approved the decision to issue the guidance in the first place.

Any committee set up or used in relation to your project should have written terms of reference that make its role clear, and also define critical elements such as membership, quorum and meeting frequency. The Contract

Award Committee for the InterCity West Coast franchise failed to meet for five months during the tender process. During those months the project was without a designated Senior Responsible Officer for an extended period (this unfortunate omission was eventually picked up by an external review) and in that time 'emerged' the critical, unattributed, decision around using a financial model that was not fit for purpose. A committee that is supposed to provide assurance but fails to meet and is mistaken in its remit is unlikely to produce much in the way of assurance, and so indeed it proved in this instance. Written terms of reference approved by the Board and formally adopted by each committee go a long way to avoiding such confusion.

A committee that is supposed to provide assurance but fails to meet and is mistaken in its remit is unlikely to produce much in the way of assurance.

CARE AND FEEDING OF COMMITTEES

Many managers are impatient with governance committees, largely because such committees are often very badly administered. The manager prepares a paper in the prescribed form, has the paper rejected because the prescribed form has changed without notice, resubmits the paper a month later with the required 15 signatures, discovers the committee failed to meet, et cetera, et cetera, et cetera. This kind of thing gets governance a bad name. A competent chair for each committee is a valuable asset, but that appointment will not be in your gift, so you could be unlucky.

One of the advantages of the framework I suggest is that the internal and external steering committees are specifically constituted for the purposes of the project, which means you as project director will be responsible for administering the secretariat function. Many a committee chair of dubious ability has been raised to adequacy by a competent committee secretary. Make it your business to see the agenda has the right things on it in a convenient order.

The committees will be under the impression they are there to see you do your job properly. This is true, but from your point of view it is more important that they do *their* job properly. The people selected as committee members will, collectively, have the ability to provide you with fantastic advice and support, which is one of the functions of a steering committee. You need them to turn up regularly, participate actively in discussions and be willing to exert themselves on your behalf with the stakeholders they represent. Make it easy for them to be supporters by providing timely and interesting papers and respect their time by structuring the agenda so meetings do not overrun.

One of the privileges of being on a steering committee is hearing the bad news first. The people on your external steering committee provide briefings to the stakeholders they represent. No one likes bad news, but you will receive a lot more support from committee members if they are carrying the bad news from you to their stakeholders, rather than hearing the bad news from their stakeholders and having to ask you what the heck is going on. 'No surprises' is the first rule of committee management.

One of the privileges of being on a steering committee is hearing the bad news first.

Where physical works are being undertaken as part of the project, include photographs in reports as evidence of progress and as a way to make the reports more interesting. One project director, knowing a concern of the committee was whether public consultation was being properly carried out, produced a photograph of a happy toddler sent to him by the child's grandmother, whose objection to a proposed communications tower had been overcome by a small change in its location. The photograph was far more convincing than a mere statement that the objection had been dealt with. Boring meetings produce uncommitted stakeholders. Avoid dull. If you really can't find anything interesting to put up for discussion, at least provide party pies so committee members do not feel their time has been entirely wasted.

Boring meetings produce uncommitted stakeholders. Avoid dull.

From time to time it will be appropriate to invite your lead advisers to attend meetings of the governance committees, to give their view of progress. Even when they don't attend, be open with them about what project matters are being discussed with the chief executive and the various governance committees, and listen to their suggestions. Their client is the Agency, not you personally, and while they should have respect for your judgment on what needs to be presented, they have to consider the interests of the client. You don't want them feeling they have to raise matters privately with the chief executive because they think you are concealing significant issues from the governance committees.

Independent Review

Box-ticking is a public sector sport.

Box-ticking is a public sector sport. The intent behind it is entirely good: a checklist is an enormously powerful tool that has improved safety and efficiency in areas as diverse as surgery and aviation. But the value of the activity described in the list (such as checking that no swabs have been left inside the patient or that the oil pressure gauge is showing a safe reading) comes from doing the activity, not from putting the tick in the box. Public sector organisations have been known to lose sight of this simple truth. So have private sector ones, but they aren't your problem. Your steering committees should take the view that a tick in a box is extremely good evidence that the box has been ticked, but fairly poor evidence that the statement next to the box on the checklist is meaningful. This is not a personal insult but a sign that you have experienced and intelligent people on your steering committees.

While your steering committees will want to hear from you that you are doing all of the things associated with good project management and following a proper procurement process, they will want other assurance that what you are telling them is correct. If the committees are insufficiently experienced to ask for such assurance, give it to them anyway. That assurance protects the project against failure and protects you against recrimination.

The essence of effective assurance is independence. It is a rare author who can proofread their own copy effectively. It is also difficult to see the gaps in your own logic. In the InterCity West Coast franchise case, the project team knew that if they released the financial model they were using to the bidders, their process would be challenged. They therefore chose not to release the model. This successfully avoided the immediate trigger for a challenge, but failed to cure the process. When the losing bidder challenged the process anyway, the deficiencies in the model were revealed and the franchise competition had to be cancelled.

Independent review can be provided in three ways:

1. through the governance framework itself;
2. by using external advisers; and
3. by commissioning special audits and reviews.

If you are not using all three, you are probably in trouble.

BUILT-IN INDEPENDENCE

The different committees in the governance framework should generally have different people on them, with only a small overlap. Some overlap is helpful in ensuring consistency of understanding across the framework. Too much overlap is bad news. Apart from the purely selfish reason, namely that if you have two committees with the same membership you might as well abolish one and save yourself the paperwork, if there is too much overlap you do not get a properly independent view.

> *If you have two committees with the same membership you might as well abolish one and save yourself the paperwork.*

Where there are several internal committees, you run the risk that there will not be much independence anyway. Patterns of behaviour set in other contexts, perhaps through management reporting lines or sheer force of personality, can lead to a small number of individuals dominating the committees, with no adequate challenge. Lazy committees may let the project director push decisions through without consideration. Tempting as it may be to regard this as a plus, it isn't. Your governance committees should be populated by experienced executives with a variety of backgrounds, each with a cupboard full of T-shirts earned the hard way. You want the benefit of their experience.

If a lazy committee is likely to be a problem, or if the committee has a shortage of relevant expertise, consider persuading them to accept an independent member from outside the organisation (not from one of the external advisers to the project, but independent of them as well), with a specific brief to look for and challenge potential areas of vulnerability. You will have to pay them, but it is usually money well spent. For standing committees that come with independent members built in – the non-executives on a Board, for instance – consider having the chair designate one of the independents to take a particular interest in the project.

EXTERNAL ADVISERS

The extent to which you need to rely on external advisers will vary with the in-house expertise of the individual Agency, but it is a brave mega-project director who embarks on establishing a contract without external legal, financial and technical advisers. They will normally do these big transactions far more frequently than any single Agency does, which gives them a depth of expertise it is hard for Government employees to match. As important as their expertise, however, is their independence. They are obliged to maintain professional standards and pay large premiums to maintain their professional indemnity insurances – premiums that get even larger if they fail to meet the standards. They have their own processes for making sure key advices are independently checked by someone in the firm who is not too close to the project: an audit of a financial model, for instance, will not be carried out by the person who built the model.

You do need to make sure their professional indemnity insurance is on the line. If you want to rely on advice, you need to get it in writing. But if you ask them to provide written confirmation that a process has been followed or that a financial model correctly produces the required outputs, that is what you will get. Admittedly the confirmation will come with a load of caveats (they too have backsides that need protecting), but that is actually the point. Better a caveat you have to make a judgment about than a meaningless tick in a box from someone who hasn't bothered to check.

Better a caveat you have to make a judgment about than a meaningless tick in a box from someone who hasn't bothered to check.

Advisers are expensive, but not compared with the cost of defending a challenge to the procurement process. The National Audit Office report on InterCity West Coast franchise case estimated the UK Department for Transport spending at just £1.9 million working on the cancelled competition, but £7 million on the judicial review and the various inquiries into the debacle. The decision not to engage external financial advisers for the competition does not appear to have been made in order to save money, which is just as well, because it clearly didn't. External advisers are not immune to error, so one cannot say for certain the outcome would have been different had financial advisers been appointed, but it is hard to think they would not have added value.

One caveat: external advisers are not fully independent. They make a lot of money advising Governments. Repeat business comes from giving good advice and from not embarrassing the person giving the instructions. It is not always easy to achieve both in circumstances where the person giving the instructions has done something stupid. Encourage your advisers to err on the side of giving good advice.

SPECIALLY COMMISSIONED REVIEWS AND AUDITS

The audit most useful to you in the context of not getting sued is an audit of process: independent confirmation that the procurement process has been carried out in accordance with the terms of tender. For some reason the UK has not taken to the idea at all, which is why the process problems in the InterCity West Coast franchise case went undetected until it was too late to do anything except cancel the competition. Other jurisdictions have been more open to the idea: in Canada the people who do it are called 'fairness monitors'.

In Australia, the process audit role has been carried out by 'probity auditors'. As the name suggests, the role evolved as an anti-corruption measure, but I am not convinced probity auditors have done much to detect corruption. They are hired consultants with no special investigative powers. If someone on the evaluation team has a conflict of interest as a result of receiving a brown envelope full of banknotes, they are unlikely to declare it and the probity auditor will never know. However, despite the scandals emerging from anti-corruption inquiries, Government agencies are far more likely to treat bidders unfairly out of incompetence or inadvertence rather than corrupt intent. A probity auditor may be next to useless at discovering corrupt conduct of an individual, but is (or should be) perfectly capable of identifying whether a procurement process is fair and has been followed. And it is failure to follow a fair process, not corruption, which is at the heart of an action for judicial review. A certificate that a fair process has been followed is a valuable piece of independent assurance.

Government agencies are far more likely to treat bidders unfairly out of incompetence or inadvertence rather than corrupt intent.

One issue with the use of probity auditors in Australia has been that they customarily act both as process auditors and probity advisers. When it comes to giving advice, probity auditors are not automatically blessed with divine guidance, or even competence, particularly if they have no experience of very large projects. Choose carefully. Communications with bidders do need to be carefully handled, for instance, but while a complete ban on communications might help prevent corrupt conspiracies, it would also compromise the ability of the process to deliver a good commercial outcome or a successful project. A major change to the terms of tender while the process is in full swing is highly undesirable, but cancelling the competition and starting again is not necessarily the right answer. Any probity 'requirement' that delivers a stupid outcome is not a requirement – there will always be a way to deliver a non-stupid outcome.

Any probity 'requirement' that delivers a stupid outcome is not a requirement – there will always be a way to deliver a non-stupid outcome.

If you are saddled with an over-zealous probity adviser, seek a second opinion from your lawyers. If the advice you want relates to a major change in the process being audited, seek the first opinion from the lawyers. Probity auditors are not legal advisers and the probity advice they give may be wrong in law, but if you have let them give it, they will then have grave difficulty in giving an audit sign off against their own advice.

Gateway reviews

It is now customary for Treasury to require all large Government projects to be subject to Gateway reviews. The Gateway concept is that at each stage of the project it should be subject to external review at the point where a decision is about to be made on whether to proceed to the next stage. The project will be given a rating of Green (okay to go), Amber (some problems, fixable as you go, proceed with care) or Red (major problems, get them fixed before moving to the next stage). Different jurisdictions use slightly different versions.

The process is managed in each jurisdiction by a special Gateway unit, which organises the reviews when called upon by the Agency and selects the reviewers, usually a team of three. There will be a planning day for the reviewers, where they will be given some basic information about the project and decide whom they would like to interview – which may include people outside the Agency – and what documents they need to see. The reviewers then return, generally about two or three weeks later, for an intensive few days of interview and discussion culminating in a written report. A draft is presented to and discussed with the appropriate senior person at the Agency (normally the person to whom the project director reports), who will have been given daily updates on the review. The final report is then delivered, often the following day, so the review may be completed within a single week.

In the Australian versions of the Gateway process there are six stages, given different names in different jurisdictions: strategic assessment, business case, pre-tender readiness, tender evaluation, pre-commissioning readiness and benefits evaluation. Projects will not necessarily undergo a review at every stage, although this is encouraged. By the time a decision has been made that a contract should be set up, the strategic assessment and business case reviews should be complete. The two reviews concerned with the contract establishment process are the pre-tender review, conducted before the invitation to tender is issued, and the tender evaluation review, conducted before the contract is entered into.

It is surprising how deep into a project it is possible to get in just a few days.

I have been both reviewer and reviewed, and my experience of the process has been uniformly good, although being a reviewer is undoubtedly more fun and less stressful. It is surprising how deep into a project it is possible to get in just a few days. The team of reviewers generally brings a wide range of experience to bear and the insights generated are always fascinating. The reviewers see their role as helping to make the project a success. They are keenly conscious of the difficulties faced by a project director, often from direct personal experience, and their recommendations are generally designed to ensure the necessary support is provided. That said, there are (rare) occasions when the reviewers conclude the project director is not up to the job and have to make recommendations accordingly. This is unpleasant, not least for the project director, but it is better for Government to find out before more damage is done.

Reviewers are paid by the Gateway unit, not the Agency. This helps assure the independence of the reviewers and prevents the Agency avoiding the review on the grounds of poverty. Agencies sometimes resist Gateway reviews because of the time involved. A week is a long time in the hectic run-up to the issue of the invitation to tender, and there is also the preparation required in collecting the requested documentation. Put up with it. The reviews normally add considerable value and many a project director has seized the opportunity to secure support for additional resources.

A week is a long time in the hectic run-up to the issue of the invitation to tender.

Senior people in the Agency find reassurance in having external parties review the project. Sometimes they find too much. Gateway reviews are useful, but they do have limitations. The process is a peer review that provides a snapshot of the project, not an audit. If key people are not available to be interviewed at the relevant time, they are not interviewed at all. While reviewers are familiar with risks common to these projects and will check the risk register to see that expected risks are being dealt with, they may not be in a position to identify project-specific risks that have not made it onto the register or are not otherwise drawn to their attention.

If the Agency's internal governance framework is not up to scratch, a Gateway review is not an adequate substitute. Another of the many issues in the InterCity West Coast fiasco was that the Gateway reviews were directed at the rail franchising programme as a whole, not specifically at the InterCity West Coast franchise, which was considered a pilot for the larger programme. The equivalent of the pre-tender review was conducted after the invitation to tender on InterCity West Coast had already been issued. Yet this very high level review was treated as if it gave the level of insight that would be expected from a project-specific review.

It is no use commissioning a Gateway review, or indeed any other kind of review, if you then ignore the recommendations. The point of a Gateway review is not to tick a box confirming that you've done a Gateway review. A team of high calibre people has just given you the benefit of their considerable experience: do something about the issues they highlight.

Other reviews and audits

The project team is going to be busy, and it is better not to bother them with too many other audits and reviews unless there is a specific reason for it. But where there is a specific reason, don't hesitate.

If you use any kind of financial model, get it audited. Even minor typographical errors can make a huge difference to the output. And you will look really, really silly if you don't know whether the figures have been adjusted for inflation.

If you are relying on demand forecasts, you could also consider an audit. Alternatively, you could consider shooting yourself.

If you are relying on demand forecasts, you could also consider an audit. Alternatively, you could consider shooting yourself. I don't think I have ever come across a transport demand forecast that displayed any predictive value. The history is long and ignoble. Nine years after the opening of the Corinth Canal in 1893, demand from shipping was barely one-eighth of what had been forecast. There is a persistent urban myth concerning a road project where the supposedly conservative demand forecast, on later examination after actual demand had proved to be some unutterably pathetic fraction of the prediction, was discovered to represent the road being used at peak capacity for more than 18 hours a day, including at weekends. At least I hope it's a myth.

If you are doing something new and different, arrange for an independent review by way of a sense check. The tradesman's principle of 'measure twice, cut once' has been largely abandoned by an internet generation weaned on beta testing. Code is cheap. If you're developing an app, by all means get it out there and let the beta testers discover the bugs by watching how it fails. Innovation is a fine thing. But when the financial consequences are counted in billions, measure twice before you commit. And don't count the second set of measurements unless it is taken by someone independent.

PART IV

The Procurement Process

Chapter 13
Establishing a Fair Process

All's fair in love and war – but not in procurement. Unfairness can see your contract struck down before the Agency's corporate seal has been returned to its box in the General Counsel's cupboard.

The procurement process in its widest sense encompasses all activity from the first inkling that some new infrastructure might be a good idea right through to the unveiling of the new asset in all its glory. But when we speak of a fair procurement process, we are talking about the process of selecting a preferred bidder and awarding the contract. The people you need to be fair to are the bidders out there in the market.

Standard Process

Governments have made big efforts in recent years to set up standardised procurement processes, driven by the appalling amounts of money being wasted by Government agencies. A lot of thought has gone into these processes: surely you can adopt the standard and all will be well?

Wrong. The mantra for a mega-project is that the standard form of anything will never be fit for purpose.

> *The mantra for a mega-project is that the standard form of anything will never be fit for purpose.*

Standard processes are just that. Standard. Over thousands of contracts, the risk of the standard approach not giving the best outcome in some particular case is offset by the value generated by having a consistent approach. All good, except that no Government agency does thousands of mega-projects. You need a procurement process tailored to your particular project, because the amount of value you can destroy if you get it wrong is not capable of being offset by mere consistency.

For instance, standard terms and conditions of tender typically provide for mandatory disqualification for relatively trivial non-conformances. If you have 20 competent bidders for a small contract, it is perfectly sensible to disqualify a few for sending you two copies of their bid instead of three: why should you go to the trouble of making or requesting an extra copy for someone who can't be bothered to read the instructions? But if the bidder has just spent millions on the bid and is one of only two in the competition, disqualification will leave you at the mercy of the remaining bidder, which won't do anything for your chances of securing value for money. It may even leave you open to judicial review on the basis that the disqualification is in the circumstances unfair.

A cookie cutter process is fine if you are buying biscuits. You aren't.

A cookie cutter process is fine if you are buying biscuits. You aren't. Put the standard form procurement guidelines back on the shelf and think about what you are trying to achieve.

What Makes a Process Fair?

There is no one-size-fits-all legal definition of fairness. You always have to consider what is fair in the particular circumstances. So think about your particular circumstances.

Although anything illegal will always be considered unfair, do not start by asking what you have to do to comply with the law. First ask what will deliver the best outcome for your procurement. Then ask if it is fair to the market. Only then do you need to ask your lawyers to check whether there is anything you should do differently to make it legal. If your process delivers good outcomes and is fair to the market, the law is unlikely to stand in your way, although you might have to publish a notice or adjust a time period or two.

The potential bidders out there are looking for two things:

1. a fair opportunity to participate in the procurement process; and

2. a fair opportunity for participants to be selected.

Although these sound similar, they are not quite the same thing, and different considerations apply.

Fair Opportunity to Participate

For bidders, a fair opportunity to participate means both knowledge and entitlement – they find out about the procurement process in time to put a bid together by the deadline, and they are not unfairly excluded from the bidding process.

People finding out about the procurement process for a mega-project is not normally an issue. These days, anyone interested in Government contracts can register with the appropriate e-commerce website or subscribe to the relevant journal and receive automatic notifications of contracts in their area of interest. Provided, of course, you have put the contract notice onto the website or into the journal. Don't forget. This step is generally required by law.

Whether bidders are keen to participate depends on how attractive the contracting opportunity is. Chapter 14 looks at how to engage with the market to determine what will bring in the bidders you want. The fairness issue around participation is not how to lure the bidders you do want but how to exclude the ones you don't.

You don't want bidders who are incapable of delivering the project. They are a dangerous waste of effort. A waste of effort, because you will have to spend valuable time establishing and documenting their incompetence, and dangerous, because their very incompetence may lead them to offer what seems like a fabulously low price, which may seduce the Agency into awarding them a contract that will inevitably end in disaster. You also don't want so many bidders that it takes forever to evaluate proposals.

EXCLUDING UNWANTED BIDDERS

Government agencies used to have almost total control over who participated in a procurement process. If they wanted to invite a bid from only one supplier, they could. If they wanted to restrict bids to the list of current suppliers, they could. If they wanted to exclude foreign bidders, they could. And they did all of these things; sometimes fairly, sometimes unfairly and sometimes downright corruptly. Abuses and uncompetitive practices have cost Governments appalling amounts of money over the years, and these days the procurement process is hedged about with laws and guidelines designed to curb the abuses and foster competition.

Abuses and uncompetitive practices have cost Governments appalling amounts of money over the years.

There remain various ways of excluding bidders. Each may be fair or unfair, legal or illegal, depending on the circumstances and how you go about it.

Participation by invitation

The first way is the invitation-only route, where you request proposals from a limited number of suppliers of your choosing and refuse to accept proposals from anyone else. You need to have some justification for the selection of your invitation list: what is considered legitimate will vary in different jurisdictions. Even a sole tender, that is, inviting only one proposal, can be considered fair, usually when the supplier in question has a monopoly on necessary intellectual property rights. However, a sole tender is rarely desirable. The existence of competition makes it far easier to secure good terms from a contractor.

The danger with invitation-only tenders is that you will exclude good bidders merely out of ignorance or laziness.

The danger with invitation-only tenders is that you will exclude good bidders merely out of ignorance or laziness, which is no way to achieve value for Government's money. In the Air Traffic Control System case, the Australian Civil Aviation Authority invited tenders from six suppliers. When a seventh sought to participate, the Authority turned them down on the basis that to include them would add a week to the evaluation schedule. The decision was severely criticised by a later review, particularly as it was already known to the market that two of the original six bidders invited had decided not to participate, but the Authority was considered to be within its rights. Ironically, problems with the procurement process in that case meant the contract was not awarded until almost two years after the target date, which made turning down a good bidder for the sake of a saving a week look particularly silly.

Restricted eligibility

A second way of excluding bidders you don't want is to advertise the tender freely, but limit the eligibility to bid. Sometimes this will be required by law, as when trade sanctions in place against other countries prohibit dealings with certain foreign-owned businesses. Some limitations on eligibility will not be permitted: take legal advice on this.

Be careful any eligibility restrictions do not exclude more bidders than you intend. Some standard procurement terms require a bidder to be an incorporated company. This probably originated to ensure people engaged for small consulting jobs weren't treated as employees for employment law purposes. In a mega-project, bidders often take the form of a consortium. They will set up a special purpose vehicle (usually a limited company, possibly a trust) to be your counterparty to the main contract if the bid is successful, but you may also have separate agreements with the consortium members, covering guarantees and other matters. The members normally come together specifically for the purpose of tendering. At the bid submission stage the agreement between them may be no more than a heads of terms and the special purpose vehicle may not exist. Make provision in the terms and conditions of the tender to allow tenderers to be a consortium. Also allow them to change the composition of their consortium during the course of the tender process – but only with your consent. That way, you won't lose a good bidder just because they couldn't finalise terms with a minor member of the consortium, but you are protected against your counterparty turning into something substantively different from the one you thought you were dealing with.

Participation fee

A way to exclude time-wasting bidders, possibly useful if the market includes pushy vendors who have no hope of securing the contract but see the submission of a bid as a way to put their sales material in front of the Agency, is to require a deposit or bond from all bidders, perhaps refundable if the bid meets certain criteria. However, such vendors are rarely encountered at the mega-project level and the administration of managing deposits is likely to be more trouble than it is worth.

Submission arrangements

If you are going to exclude bidders, make sure it is deliberate.

If you are going to exclude bidders, make sure it is deliberate. When you have only two or three bidders in the contest – and it is possible there are only two or three parties in the entire world capable of delivering your mega-project – you can't afford to lose any through carelessness. Yours *or* theirs. Make sure the submission requirements specify the date, the time and the time zone of the deadline. Have your bidder liaison manager check personally with the relevant people on the bid teams that they know where and when and how to deliver their submissions. And if you use a web-based submission process, be very sure you know what to do if the servers are down at the wrong moment.

The technology around submissions is frankly a pain. Happy the days when tenders simply had to be placed in a locked tender box before the expiry of the submission period. Today's bidders will inevitably want to send you computer simulations of the finished project, or one-twentieth scale models, or electronic files that can only be opened with software you don't have. Work out what you are and are not going to allow, make it clear in the conditions of tender and build in some discretion to accommodate minor non-conformances so you don't exclude bidders unnecessarily.

Level playing field

Bidders will exclude themselves if they see no chance of winning the contract. Bidding for this scale of contract doesn't come cheap. Your choice of contract structure may have a significant impact on which companies participate in a procurement. For instance, when you let a single contract for the delivery of all aspects of a mega-project, you effectively prevent small and medium sized companies from tendering, except possibly as part of a consortium. If you want to ensure smaller companies have a piece of the action, you must either let a number of smaller contracts instead of one large one, leaving Government with the integration risk, or else include requirements in your large contract around smaller companies being offered opportunities to tender for subcontracts.

It is important to understand how the contracting structure you have adopted will impact the market, or you may find yourself excluding bidders unintentionally. In the Waratah train procurement, the New South Wales Government decided to include in the contract the construction of a new maintenance facility. The market for train manufacturers was international. The market for facility construction was local. There were more potential train suppliers than facility builders. If every bidder had been required to have construction capability on board from the start, the shortlisting decision would effectively have been made not by the Agency but by the facility builders, who could choose which train supplier to partner with. Instead, the Agency made it possible for a bidder to be shortlisted without having construction capability, knowing that any train supplier who made it to the shortlist would be able to attract a competent facility builder for the next phase.

A level playing field is good, but do not mix your sporting metaphors. In handicap races, better horses are made to carry weights so the poorer ones have an equal chance of winning. A handicapper triumphs when every horse in the race is line abreast at the finish, because it makes the race more exciting. You are not there to entertain the punters. The idea of a level playing field is not to handicap the better bidders but to *avoid* handicapping them. True, it generates competitive tension if you have a number of bidders with fairly equal chances of winning, but you do want the best bid to end up in front. Don't saddle anyone with an unfair handicap.

> *The idea of a level playing field is not to handicap the better bidders but to* avoid *handicapping them.*

Fair Opportunity to Be Selected

You can think of your procurement process as being designed to identify the best bidder to whom you will wish to award the contract. It is equally correct to think of it as designed to eliminate all the bidders to whom you will not wish to award the contract. Any bidder will be upset at being eliminated, but elimination is the whole point of the exercise. The fact that a bidder has been declared surplus to requirements is entirely without forensic interest. It is unfairness that will found a cause of action.

You have a lot of leeway in how you structure your process. If you have ten bidders, you can call for statements of capability, eliminate the nine least capable bidders in one hit, then spend the next year trying to negotiate terms with your preferred bidder. It isn't a recommended approach, but that is because negotiation in the absence of competition is unlikely to deliver the best value for money, not because it is inherently unfair. Alternatively, you could eliminate those nine bidders one at a time, calling for the remaining bidders to submit revised pricing with every round. Again, not unfair but not recommended. The process would take an expensively long time and a queue of impatient bidders would form at your door to demand you stop faffing around and move to a shorter shortlist in rather fewer steps.

The structure of your procurement process has a big impact on its effectiveness in securing best value for money.

Although the structure of your procurement process has a big impact on its effectiveness in securing best value for money, the issue with unfairness is not how many rounds there are, or how many bidders are eliminated at each, but the basis on which they are eliminated. A bidder will consider your process unfair if:

- there are undisclosed evaluation criteria;
- they don't have an equal opportunity to make submissions;
- another bidder cheats;
- the evaluation is biased;
- the reasons for the selection decision are improper.

EVALUATION CRITERIA

You select your contractor on the basis of evaluation criteria. Whether or not the criteria are useful in delivering the best project outcome, the issue in terms of fairness is simply that all evaluation criteria need to be disclosed before bids are submitted. This is a no-brainer. Quite apart from any consideration of fairness, how will bidders know what to offer you if they don't know what you will base your decision on?

Portcullis House, a terrorist-proof building built for the House of Commons at Westminster in the late 1990s, included what was described as 'probably the most expensive fenestration system ever'. The tender documents for the fenestration contract failed to set out specific evaluation criteria. The losing bidder had offered the lowest price and successfully sued the Corporate Officer of the House of Commons for failing to award them the contract. The House of Commons was unable to persuade the court the bidders could have worked out the other evaluation criteria from the information requested. Given the court also found the project team never did agree what the criteria were, this is hardly surprising. Always make the evaluation criteria absolutely clear.

Law and practice around disclosure of the weightings attached to the criteria varies. In many jurisdictions weightings, or at least the order of importance, are disclosed simultaneously with the criteria. In Australia, some jurisdictions disclose weightings only in the post-tender de-brief, perhaps because the Agency is not ready to make a decision on weightings when the Request for Tenders is issued, perhaps for fear bidders will seek to 'game' the criteria. You should certainly be aware of the risks of gaming and design your criteria and weightings accordingly, but you are usually better off letting bidders know what you think is important while they still have the opportunity to offer it to you.

EQUAL OPPORTUNITY

Your choices will not impact all bidders equally.

All bidders should receive the same information and have the same time available to prepare their bids. Your choices will not impact all bidders equally. An incumbent bidding for a services contract will be able to produce a bid much more quickly than others, so a short bid preparation period could favour them unfairly.

Do not allow one bidder to change a material aspect of their bid without allowing the other bidders a similar opportunity. The Holyrood Inquiry criticised the process for appointment of the contract manager. It was first decided to eliminate the two highest-priced bidders and interview the remaining two. There was a subsequent decision to interview one of the eliminated bidders after all, which the Inquiry considered unfair – not because the one was interviewed, but because the other eliminated bidder, whose price was lower, was not.

Be careful also with the amount of time bidders are allowed to present or explain their bids. Bidders, with some reason, see direct contact with evaluators as extremely valuable in putting their case. They will be quick to allege unfairness if they think another bidder is being offered more face time.

Fairness is required. Paranoia isn't. When the Department of Transport evaluators in the New South Wales Integrated Ticketing case wanted a presentation from one tenderer, they not only offered the other a similar opportunity but said they would not hear either unless both consented. Giving one tenderer a veto over the Government receiving information from another was clearly inappropriate: like the judge, I suspect the Department suffered 'excessive sensitivity to an altogether artificial notion of evenhandedness'. Fortunately for Government, even though this excessive sensitivity clearly *could* have been unfair, no *actual* unfairness resulted, so the tender process was not compromised.

CHEATING BIDDERS

A gift to a Government official may be an accepted courtesy or a criminal bribe.

Mega-projects often attract international bidders. Different countries have different standards for what constitutes corruption. A gift to a Government official may be an accepted courtesy or a criminal bribe. If your evaluators visit a manufacturing facility, they may be offered a sandwich lunch on site, or they may be offered a champagne banquet at the casino with optional extras. Avoid embarrassment and accusations of unfair influence by spelling out your Agency's policy in such matters.

While few bidders set out with intent to cheat, there are significant risks around misuse of confidential information, particularly in relation to pricing. If a bidder receives information they are not supposed to have, they should not make use of it but should destroy or return it. If the leak was inadvertent and is continuing, such as documents accidentally posted to an open drive, they should advise the source to plug the leak. If the leak was deliberate (venal Government employees have been known to offer information to bidders in return for cash) it should be reported to the appropriate authority.

Should, should, should. The world is not like that. People cannot resist confidential information. Even experienced solicitors, who ought to know better than to do something that could get them struck off, have been known to read and make use of material sent to them inadvertently. The Queensland Health Payroll System Inquiry report quotes an engaging email from a bidder's employee who heard Government had mistakenly placed confidential evaluation material on an accessible drive. Far from reporting this as a matter of concern, the email records his efforts to find the material and concludes with a regretful: '… looks like we were just a little bit too late.'

You could be lucky. Many tenderers seeking Government contracts have codes of conduct prohibiting misuse of confidential information and train their employees in ethical behaviour. In the Queensland Health Payroll System case, a tenderer was offered confidential Government costing information by one of its contractors. The information had been obtained without authorisation. The tenderer very properly drew the matter to Government's attention and terminated the engagement of the contractor. It is unwise to rely on luck. The Commission of Inquiry into the same tender process found the bid team for the successful tenderer had no such scruples and not only accepted unsolicited confidential information but went looking for more.

It is unlikely anyone will break into the evaluation room, although not so unlikely that you shouldn't consider installing CCTV: with a mega-project, enormous amounts of money are involved, and some people find ethics hard to sustain when so much is at stake. But human curiosity is almost irrepressible. People who would never lie or steal or even jaywalk will be unable to resist looking at confidential material that drops into their inbox. Electronic leaks are not the only problem. Nobody turns their ears off in lifts or corridors or cafés, so don't discuss the evaluation except in secure locations. Using code names for bidders helps limit the risk of people understanding what they hear, but is only a partial protection at best.

People who would never lie or steal or even jaywalk will be unable to resist looking at confidential material that drops into their inbox.

You may need to send copies of tender submissions outside your direct control in order to carry out the evaluation: your lawyers will normally review the contract mark-ups at their own offices, for instance. Do not send anything to anyone unless they have committed to a process to secure the confidentiality of the material and are willing to submit to a process audit.

If you don't want bidders to cheat by making use of confidential information they shouldn't have, the only sure answer is not to give it to them and not to leave it lying around. Technology has made this more complicated. Unless you make an issue of it, your 'secure' drive will be accessible not only by project team members who have signed an appropriate confidentiality agreement, but also by every employee and contractor in the entire computer division, including some who left years ago. Make an issue of it. Be picky.

Every smartphone can take legible pictures of documents and practically everyone has a smartphone, including the contractors who clean the building and have a key to the evaluation room unless you change the locks. It is so, so easy to send an email to the wrong address. No information security process is 100 per cent secure, but there are billions at stake. Set up the tightest security you can manage and don't let your team slack off.

BIAS IN THE EVALUATION

You will need to put in place arrangements to deal with conflicts of interest. Mega-projects can be a surprisingly small world: it is virtually impossible to get through a tender process without some conflict of interest arising. These are normally not a problem so long as you don't ignore them. You just need to have a process in place to ensure the conflict is identified, declared and neutralised. Take advice as necessary in particular cases.

Mega-projects can be a surprisingly small world: it is virtually impossible to get through a tender process without some conflict of interest arising.

Again, paranoia is not required. In the administration of public justice even the appearance or apprehension of bias is enough to disqualify someone from deciding a case. In the administration of public contracts it is only actual bias you have to worry about. Even then it is bias of the decision-makers giving rise to unfairness that is the issue. An expert who is perfectly sound on the relative merits of widgets may harbour highly prejudicial views on the personal competence or hygiene of a widget-maker's managers. That does not prevent the decision-maker seeking the advice of the expert in relation to the relative merits of widgets.

In the InterCity West Coast franchise case the UK Department for Transport was so concerned about a possible accusation of bias that they adopted an interpretation of bidder anonymity which the Laidlaw Inquiry described as 'unique'. I might have used a less charitable description. It excluded senior people from the tender process, people who could perhaps have prevented its failure, simply because they had seen a complaint made by a bidder. Total overkill.

Conflicts of interest are not the only form of bias. Your evaluation methodology should be structured to minimise other undesirable manifestations, such as making judgments before you have enough evidence. Quite apart from the risk of challenge, bias and prejudice rarely lead to optimal outcomes.

IMPROPER REASONS

One of the most well-established grounds for overturning a decision on judicial review is to show the reasons for the decision were improper: either the decision-maker failed to take into account something relevant, or took into account something that was not relevant. (The latter is similar to the undisclosed criteria issue that resulted in a successful challenge to the award of the contract in the Portcullis House case.)

> *Government agencies used to protect themselves against an action alleging they made a decision for the wrong reasons by never giving reasons at all.*

Government agencies used to protect themselves against an action alleging they made a decision for the wrong reasons by never giving reasons at all. This had varying degrees of success. It is difficult to establish what you took into account if you keep no records, and if you do keep records, they are almost certainly going to have to be produced in court even if they were not disclosed to bidders. In any event, transparency is now the order of the day. Your process must involve a de-brief of the losing bidders, including disclosure of the reasons for the decision.

Is it Fair to Pay Bid Costs?

Generally, Government pays bid costs only when things have gone horribly wrong. The UK Department for Transport paid out more than £40 million in compensation to bidders when it cancelled the InterCity West Coast franchise competition in 2012. If you follow a fair procurement process, you won't have to pay bid costs by way of damages. Should you be offering to pay bid costs anyway? The costs of bidding for mega-projects are after all very high. Bidders invest millions, and all but one will lose every penny. Is this fair?

Where Government is claiming intellectual property rights in work done by bidders, Government should certainly offer value for those rights. Government is acquiring something, rather than simply making a choice of supplier, so payment is fair. In other circumstances? Probably not. It may be necessary if, say, the Government or Agency has a track record of calling for bids but failing to award a contract, but in ordinary circumstances paying or contributing to bid costs is not required. Yes, on a mega-project the bid costs are measured in millions, but that merely reflects the scale of the contract. In a world where the potential profits (and losses) may be in the hundreds of millions, the scale of costs the bidders incur is not of itself unfair.

What is unfair is making those costs higher than necessary. Changing the timetable or requirements without notice, so bidders incur wasted preparation costs. Requiring unnecessary information, so bidders pay to provide stuff you don't look at. Taking forever to make decisions and respond to queries, so expensive bid teams are kept hanging around. Putting forward indefensible contract conditions or risk allocation, so bidders incur legal costs objecting to something that should never have been proposed in the first place.

This kind of unfairness will probably not found an action for judicial review except in the most extreme circumstances, but it increases your chance of ending up in court all the same. If these elements of your procurement process are sloppy and fail to consider bidders' convenience, bidders will be disposed to believe the potentially actionable elements of your process are sloppy and fail to consider bidders' rights. What is more, they are likely to be correct. Sloppiness is contagious. You are not running this procurement process for the convenience of the bidders, but if you fail to consider bidders' convenience you are probably not giving adequate consideration to their rights. Don't push up bid costs unnecessarily.

If you fail to consider bidders' convenience you are probably not giving adequate consideration to their rights.

Documenting the Process

Your process needs to be set down in writing. Failure to follow a fair process will leave the award of contract open to challenge. A written process can be given an independent check for fairness before you commit to it, which is valuable assurance. A written process can be disseminated more easily: your team needs to know what the process is, so they can follow it or draw the problem to your attention if they can't. A written process also makes it more likely the team are all following the same one. And if a challenge is made or threatened, you will find it extremely hard to produce evidence you followed a fair process if you have no evidence of what the process was in the first place.

Although your process needs to be documented, it is not a single document. The basis of your 'process contract', the legally binding terms that apply to the procurement, is the conditions of tender that you will issue to the market. Your Agency will have a standard form but, as always, the standard form will not be fit for your purpose.

Delete the reference to compliance with the code. There's bound to be one. Every standard form Agency conditions of tender I have ever seen includes a provision saying the procurement will be conducted in accordance with a code of conduct or set of procurement guidelines, often one issued by some other

Government agency. Delete it. You do not tailor the conditions of tender to your specific requirements in order to shoot yourself in the foot by importing inappropriate terms from a document you haven't read. If your process is in accordance with the code, you don't need to mention it, and if it isn't, you are in trouble if you say it is. If the code really is consistent with your process you may decide to retain the reference to keep a stakeholder happy, but don't do it lightly. And if your Agency is bound by inappropriate guidance as a matter of law or practice, get legal advice on how to exclude its effect.

Government lawyers make something of an art form of the conditions of tender.

Check everything, but particularly the extent of the discretion you have to change the process as you go along, because you will need it: nothing ever goes entirely to plan. Government lawyers make something of an art form of the conditions of tender, so Government and participating bidders become legally and irrevocably bound to … well, it varies, but basically Government can do anything it feels like, and bidders have to do what they are told.

Perhaps surprisingly, this is normally acceptable except in conditions of perceived sovereign risk, but extreme examples may prompt a bidder to include a purported amendment of the terms with their bid submission. This can be very messy indeed, because it casts into doubt whether you may consider the bid at all – is the competition fair if bidders are signing up to different terms and conditions? The conditions of tender are expected to favour Government, but avoid taking it to the point of provoking bidder revolt.

The reason bidders will usually be relatively unconcerned by conditions favouring Government is their confidence that, whatever the words actually say, you are going to be obliged to act reasonably and in good faith. And they're right. You are.

Apart from the Government-can-do-anything provisions, the key process documents are:

- the submission requirements, which form part of the conditions of tender and must be fully disclosed to bidders;
- your evaluation methodology, of which at least the evaluation criteria must be disclosed;
- your procedures for preserving confidentiality and dealing with conflicts of interest, which must be disclosed to bidders to the extent they are involved (for example, you will have a procedure for bidders to submit confidential requests for clarification).

There is no standard format. Break your process and procedures into a number of separate documents so you don't have to give everybody the entire thing. The clerk who checks the tenders were delivered in accordance with the submission requirements does not need to be privy to the evaluation methodology.

Your documents are not the last word on what the process is. Terms can be changed: by formal amendment, by exchange of correspondence, by conduct. As the police put it, anything you say may be taken down and used in evidence against you. That goes double for anything you put in writing. Never forget emails count as writing. So do text messages – they are less likely to come back and bite you than is an email, but only because people normally delete text messages irretrievably, not because they are any less efficacious in law. In the InterCity West Coast franchise case, the UK Department for Transport issued guidance to bidders on how the amounts of a subordinated loan facility would be calculated, inadvertently removing their discretion to determine the amounts in another way. It came back to bite them. In any interaction with the bidders, always be alert to the possibility that what you say or write or do could change the terms under which the process is being conducted.

Terms can be changed: by formal amendment, by exchange of correspondence, by conduct.

A Fair Process – But Can You Demonstrate It?

Having a fair process, and following it, are two-thirds of avoiding legal action on the procurement process. The other third is being able to evidence that you followed it.

Collect the evidence as you go along. When a challenger claims bias because the evaluation team had a conflict of interest, you can spend hours and days trawling back through every email and minute of meeting over the last however-many months, trying and probably failing to corroborate your very patchy memory of what (if any) conflicts were declared and what (if anything) you did about it. Or you can go to your conflicts register and see immediately what the conflicts were and what action was taken, together with the legal or audit opinion advising the action was sufficient. If you want to be able to choose the second option (and believe me, you want to choose the second option) set up your conflicts register at the start of the process and keep it up to date throughout.

In every meeting you have with a bidder, ask them whether they have any issues with the process. When they say 'no', minute their answer. It comes in handy as evidence later, when you need to convince losing bidders that what they are suffering from is not unfairness capable of founding a legal challenge, but merely the inevitable anguish of having spent months and millions failing to win the biggest contract in town. And if they say 'yes', do something about it.

Change Can Be Fair

> *A process established as fair and reasonable may not remain appropriate if circumstances change. Fairness does not require you to charge blindly on.*

You cannot foresee everything. A process established as fair and reasonable may not remain appropriate if circumstances change. Fairness does not require you to charge blindly on.

On one contract I set up, bids came back in a price range that was $50 million more than we expected. It would have been a nonsense to continue to follow the agreed procurement process, since Cabinet was never going to stump up the extra $50 million. More to the point, we had no idea why it was so expensive. After a bit of thought and some independent advice (and consultation with Treasury, always the key stakeholder on money matters), we went back to the two bidders with a proposal: we would break off the process while we consulted with them to identify what was causing the extra cost. We would then issue a revised specification and allow them to adjust their bids accordingly. The bidders had no problem with that approach. The consultation rapidly made it clear the specification required functionality we had thought was standard but would actually have required some very tricky software development. It was a simple matter to adjust the specification and request updated bids.

The conditions of tender issued in that case were, as usual, expressed to allow Government to do practically anything whether the bidders liked it or not. This would not have saved the situation if we had taken a course of action that was unfair. It was important in protecting against legal action that we told the bidders of the planned change and confirmed there were no objections. But the mere fact that the original process was changed did not make the process unfair.

Fairness is Not Enough

You want to procure a successful project. When you follow a fair process, and have evidence of your virtue in this regard, you are most unlikely to end up in court defending the award of contract. That will be small comfort if you have awarded an undeliverable contract to a high priced incompetent: it will merely delay your appearance before the judiciary.

That will be small comfort if you have awarded an undeliverable contract to a high priced incompetent.

If the project is to be successfully delivered, rather than just successfully commenced, you need a process that does more than eliminate bidders fairly. You need a process that will conclude with a binding contract, with a contractor who is capable of meeting their obligations, to deliver the project in a way that meets Government's objectives, on terms that represent value for money to Government.

Fairness is not enough. You have some more work to do.

Chapter 14
Putting Out the Call

> *The number one cause of a poor quality bid is a poor quality request.*

Government agencies often complain about the quality of tenders they receive. The quality can, indeed, be poor. But the number one cause of a poor quality bid is a poor quality request. To invert the computer programmer's mantra, garbage out means garbage in. Tenderers find it much easier to *give* you what you want if you *tell* them what you want. It also helps if what you want is capable of being provided.

Putting a clear and useful call to the market is done in three stages:

1. *Pre-tender engagement*: interaction with the market before the competition starts, often called market sounding.

2. *Shortlisting or pre-qualification*: inviting parties to compete for an invitation to tender.

3. *Selection*: inviting shortlisted parties to compete for the award of the contract.

Pre-Tender Engagement

To structure your procurement process for success, you need to understand the market. How many players are there? How differentiated are they, and on what basis? Are relevant commodity prices up or down? How tight is the labour market? Are company order books full? How easy will it be for companies to obtain financing? Are there rival technologies, or only rival companies? How familiar is the market with the particular technical challenges of your mega-project? What contract forms are standard in the industry? What drives corporate profits? How fast is the market changing?

The first thing you are looking for is potential bidders. This is not as straightforward as it might appear. Because of the scale and complexity of the contract deliverables, tenderers are usually consortia rather than individual suppliers. The procurement may bring together companies that operate in what are normally separate markets, such as the construction market and the finance market. You can allow consortia to form as they will, or you can select the best construction contractor and then join with that contractor to conduct a separate competition for the financing. Find out what is likely to deliver the best outcome for you.

If the Government has recently cancelled a major tender for political reasons, potential bidders may consider sovereign risk an issue.

The second thing you need to understand is how attractive your preferred contracting structure and risk allocation will be to the market. If the financial markets have just gone into free fall, this is probably not the time to ask for private finance. If the last three toll road contractors went bust through inaccurate demand forecasts, the market may not be keen on taking demand risk. If the Government has recently cancelled a major tender for political reasons, potential bidders may consider sovereign risk an issue.

Your chosen structure has to work for Government as well as the market. As discussed in Chapter 3, the Holyrood Inquiry into the construction of a new Scottish Parliament building found most of the problems with that project stemmed from the decision to adopt a 'construction management' approach, that is to appoint a construction manager and with their assistance award individual contracts for some 60 construction work packages. The Government was unable to manage the risks of that approach, and the project suffered very significant delays and cost overruns as a result.

If you cannot identify a reasonable number of potentially capable bidders who appear to find your contracting structure and risk allocation an attractive proposition, figure out what the problem is and do something about it. That's what pre-tender engagement with the market is for. The time to change your approach is *before* anyone has invested serious money in something that isn't going to work.

SOURCING MARKET INFORMATION

How do you find this kind of information? If your Agency has a genuine strategic procurement unit, they may be able to give you an accurate briefing on the state of the market. Bear in mind a title with the word 'strategic' in it may indicate aspirations higher than the actual competence level. If the unit is not in regular communication with major suppliers and other Government purchasers, or even if it is, think about cross-checking with your financial advisers, who will often be a good source of information. Even this may not be enough.

> *Your casual remarks may be collected like jewels, your passing thoughts treated as imperishable wisdom.*

The people with the best information about a market are the people in it. Suppliers know only too well what competition they face. In ordinary circumstances, picking up the phone and asking is a wonderful way to obtain information, but if Government has announced its intention to proceed with a mega-project, your circumstances are not ordinary. In the eyes of the market, you have just become someone with a huge contract in your gift. Your casual remarks may be collected like jewels, your passing thoughts treated as imperishable wisdom. Do not let this go to your head. Avoid giving more time to one supplier rather than another, lest you fuel allegations of bias, and be careful what you say. A casual remark about a minor difficulty with a product or service or company official may send a supplier into a paranoid frenzy. A mere conversational gambit about the state of the robotics industry may be repeated and seized upon by unions as demonstrating an intent to sack every machine operator in Government employ. The proximity of a billion dollar contract fuels a lot of rumours.

In these circumstances it can be helpful to choose more formal interactions with suppliers for your information-gathering. A managed consultation process can also get the lobbyists off the Minister's back, which may win you some brownie points. Rather than rely on informal chats with particular suppliers, issue a written request to all. Rather than limit the invitation list, issue the request through the relevant Government e-commerce website, which will be monitored by suppliers. It is perfectly proper to follow that up with an email to the players you particularly hope to hear from, to draw their attention to the site.

Don't just send out a list of questions or a blank sheet of paper and hope for the best. It is usually a good idea to invite suppliers to a presentation where you explain what you want and why you want it. And why they should give it to you. Suppliers may have the best information, but that doesn't mean they are keen to share it. Responding to a request for market information costs money and may be seen as giving away confidential information or competitive advantage for free. Why should they do more than send you their current swag of publicity material? Tell them. If you don't know, your request is not worth issuing.

TWO-WAY COMMUNICATION

You want information, but you are also giving information. The questions you ask and the reasons you give for asking them will tell the suppliers a lot about your general approach to the procurement. This is an early opportunity to

The more desirable the contracting opportunity, the better terms the bidders will offer.

'sell' the contract to potential bidders. Yes, I know you think you're the one doing the buying, but contracts go both ways. The more desirable the contracting opportunity, the better terms the bidders will offer.

Give warning to the market if you intend to do anything unusual in the tender process, or to adopt a contract structure they are not expecting. For instance, if the Agency is adopting a new policy that it will only enter major technology contracts with the original technology provider, rather than being willing to procure the technology through an intermediary, let the market know before the technology providers tie themselves to companies that will not be eligible to bid. It also gives any technology provider who prefers dealing through intermediaries the opportunity to ask you to change your mind.

ARE YOU LISTENING?

The point of a market sounding is to find out what the market is willing to tell you. If you don't take advantage of that input, the exercise will be wasted. You certainly don't have to take instructions from suppliers, but if you go out to 'consultation' with something you are not prepared even to consider amending, you will just antagonise people. Listen to what the market tells you. Make it clear you have heard what people have to say, even if you don't take up their suggestions.

WITHOUT PREJUDICE

The thing that differentiates an information-gathering or consultation exercise from the next stage of the process is that you are not going to use the information you receive to eliminate any bidder from the competition. Make this clear: if the bidders don't like what you are putting forward, you will end up with a better contract if they say so rather than tell you what they think you want to hear.

Since pre-tender market engagement is without prejudice to subsequent stages of the procurement process, it can be used to keep impatient politicians happy. I used this tactic on the Waratah train procurement to give something for the Premier to announce, at a time when it was politically important to be seen to be making progress with the project, but we were not ready to proceed to shortlisting. Government had already decided to impose a local content requirement, so we called for registrations of interest from anyone capable of doing any part of the contract, such as manufacturing train seats or air-conditioning units, and promised that any local business which registered would have its details supplied to the tenderers. Everyone was invited to attend a presentation at Government offices with tea and biscuits and a harbour view, and more than a hundred people showed up. Local businesses had a networking opportunity. The Premier had his photo opportunity. The project team had an extra-time-to-prepare-for-shortlisting opportunity. Happiness all round.

Shortlisting or Pre-Qualification

Valuable as pre-tender market engagement undoubtedly is, it will not deliver you a contract. You need to move on from the preliminary skirmishing. The next step is to issue an invitation to the market to apply for the right to tender for the project. This is commonly called a request for expressions of interest, or a pre-qualification questionnaire. What distinguishes it from earlier interactions with suppliers is that you will use it to eliminate bidders. If a supplier fails to submit a response, or if their response does not stack up sufficiently against your evaluation criteria, they are out of the competition.

Moving from consultation to assessment crosses a critical threshold.

Moving from consultation to assessment crosses a critical threshold:

- It triggers obligations relating to confidentiality and interaction with bidders that will be restrictive, so you don't want to kick off this formal part of the competition until you are ready to do so.

- If you end up cancelling the competition (whether because you've been sued or Government just changed its mind), this is the point in time from which bidders will be seeking to claim their costs.

- The invitation you issue sets the stage for all subsequent assessment of and negotiations with the tenderers: if you put yourself into a position of disadvantage, you may never be able to recover.

If bidders are eliminated from the competition at the shortlisting stage, they down tools and go and find another contract to bid on. For you, this is the only contract you have. Beware of stakeholders who say things like, 'It's only the shortlisting phase.' If your shortlist has the wrong people on it, your project will not be successful.

WHY DO YOU NEED A SHORTLIST?

On small value procurements, you may not bother with shortlisting. You put an open invitation to tender on the e-commerce website, evaluate the responses and select the party you want to contract with in a single step. That doesn't work with mega-projects.

Tenderers need to invest millions. They will not do that unless they see a good chance of winning the contract.

To develop a bid sufficiently to offer a price that is both competitive and gives a profit rather than a trip to the bankruptcy court, tenderers need to invest millions. They will not do that unless they see a good chance of winning the contract. If you set up an open tender without a shortlisting stage, tenderers have no certainty of who and how many are going to bid. Some will be put off altogether and some will submit a minimum-investment bid with lots of marketing material and very little substance. And if by some extraordinary chance they did all submit high quality bids, you would be saddled with a monumental evaluation task to deal fairly with them all. You need a shortlist. The only circumstance in which you might go straight to an invitation to tender for the contract itself would be if there are no more than three potentially capable bidders in the market: even on mega-projects, this is relatively unusual.

BASIS FOR SHORTLISTING

The shortlisting process allows you to select a small number of bidders, each with the following characteristics:

- *Government is prepared to do business with them*: if your Government is currently imposing sanctions or has other legitimate reasons for refusing to contract with particular bidders or classes of bidders, make sure your conditions of tender allow you to exclude them, otherwise you may end up in court when you shortlist someone with a poorer bid.

- *They are capable of delivering the project*: if you enter into a contract with someone incapable of delivering it, the project is doomed. Eliminate the incompetent at the shortlisting stage, so they have no opportunity to produce a superb pricing offer that blinds you to the inevitability of failure.

- *They are more capable than the ones you didn't select*: the more capable they are, the more likely your project is to be successful, and if they are demonstrably more capable than the ones you eliminate, the losers will have trouble finding grounds to sue you.

Since bidders will only make a limited investment, make sure everything you ask them to produce is directed towards enabling you to make this selection. Every mega-project is different, so be specific. Generic capability is not enough. If the contract involves maintenance of trains or ships or aeroplanes, do you need a contractor with the engineering and project management skills to design and build a new maintenance facility, or one with the industrial relations and people management skills to be able to share an old one?

When you start the shortlisting process, you will probably still be working on the detail of the invitation to tender, but if you haven't done enough to know what capabilities will be required, you haven't done enough to start shortlisting.

If you haven't done enough to know what capabilities will be required, you haven't done enough to start shortlisting.

BIDDER EDUCATION

Have an eye to the next stage of the project. Although bidders will be reluctant to invest too much at the shortlisting stage, those who are confident they will make the cut will be planning ahead. The more preparation they undertake, the better quality the bids you will eventually receive. Make it easy for them by letting them know what to expect.

Limit the material you request from bidders to what is necessary to enable you to make the shortlisting decision, but the material you hand out doesn't need the same restraint. You will be setting up a data room, these days normally an electronic data room run by the external lawyers, to include all the information tenderers will need to price their bids. Although much of this information will not be needed for the shortlisting stage, there is normally no downside in making it available early. The area to watch is service contract information which may be confidential to an incumbent: in these circumstances you will need to make special arrangements to be able to release the information and may be better off waiting until you have a shortlist.

Include a document explaining the contract structure you intend to adopt. Take the opportunity to sell the deal and start getting the bidders comfortable with the risks you will be asking them to take. Risks they don't understand will be mispriced, which does you no favours even if the price is too low rather than too high. You will need to put appropriate caveats into your conditions of tender – bidders should be permitted to rely only on the terms of the contract you issue in due course, not your explanatory document – but that is easy enough and the value of having the bidders understand your intentions is considerable.

Selection

The final stage is when you call for an offer that will enable you to award the contract. There will sometimes be a second or even third round within this stage, if the tenderers on the shortlist are allowed to make further refinements to their bids, but the essence of this stage is that it will conclude with you awarding the contract to one of the bidders.

The essence of this stage is that it will conclude with you awarding the contract to one of the bidders.

The Request for Tenders normally comprises a number of different documents. These can be grouped in three categories:

1. the conditions of tender;

2. documents that will form part of the agreement with the successful tenderer, including the technical specification and the draft commercial terms;

3. returnable schedules that, completed by the tenderers, will form part of the bid submissions.

You will also need to update the data room to add any necessary background material that has not already been made available.

CONDITIONS OF TENDER

As in the shortlisting phase, you will issue a document with the Request for Tenders setting out the ground rules for the process. A lot of it will be in more or less identical terms to the one you used for the shortlisting, but some things you need to think about are specific to this stage of the process.

EVALUATION CRITERIA

A new set of evaluation criteria is required. Shortlisting was all about capabilities. Now you will choose between the bidders on the basis of a rather different set of criteria, including the cost to Government.

One area you may need to consider is the approach you will take in circumstances where the company running the successful bid will not be the party that enters into the contract. On a privately-financed deal, the party entering the contract will be a Special Purpose Vehicle (SPV), a company or trust set up with no other business than the contract. The SPV would simultaneously enter into subcontracts, often called the core contracts, with the entities that will actually carry out the SPV's obligations under the contract with the Agency.

Since the SPV does not exist before the commencement of the tender process, it is open to Government to dictate or influence the SPV's composition and governance through the use of specific evaluation criteria.

Why might you want to do that? Ask London Underground. A consortium called Metronet won the contracts for two of the three controversial Public Private Partnerships for the modernisation of London Underground's infrastructure and in 2003 set up two SPVs, one for each contract. By 2007 their costs were, between them, some £2 billion over budget. While some could be claimed against the contracts as not having been anticipated in the bids, the independent PPP Arbiter would only award costs that would have been incurred by a contractor performing in an efficient and economic manner. An interim review by the PPP Arbiter indicated the amount recoverable could be less than £500 million. The balance, a billion and a half pounds, represents a staggering amount of inefficiency and miscalculation.

The balance, a billion and a half pounds, represents a staggering amount of inefficiency and miscalculation.

A major problem was a 'tied supply chain': all five members of the consortium had contracts to perform work for the SPV. This was not of itself the issue. They had, after all, formed the consortium precisely because they wanted to win the work. But having won it, they awarded themselves subcontracts that were not on fully arms' length terms. One contract, with the rolling stock manufacturer, was found by the PPP Arbiter to be operating efficiently and economically after a somewhat rocky start, but the other contracts were subcontracted through another SPV, Trans4m, owned by the remaining four shareholders. The contract with Trans4m gave Metronet very little in the way of enforcement levers – invoices had to be paid when presented, with no withholding rights for performance failures – and there was little opportunity to contract work elsewhere on more reasonable terms. The chairman of Metronet was reportedly threatened with litigation when he sought to reduce the amount of work going to the shareholders.

You could simply perceive this as Metronet's risk, but when a risk is too big for a contractor to manage, it comes bouncing back to Government. Metronet went bust and the UK Government had to pick up the pieces. In addition to the direct costs, estimated by the National Audit Office as being up to £410 million, 95 per cent of the Metronet debt finance had to be paid off by the Government immediately. That money would have been paid gradually over the lifetime of the contracts in any event, but an un-programmed payment of £1.7 billion makes a dent in anyone's budget. Treasury was not amused.

Very often the bidder in a Public Private Partnership will effectively be driven by the party seeking to win the main construction contract.

Very often the bidder in a Public Private Partnership will effectively be driven by the party seeking to win the main construction contract. The Metronet debacle alerted Governments to the issue of SPV governance and since then most bidders will point smugly to a proposed SPV structure that doesn't give the contractors a majority stake. That will not give you much comfort if the SPV shareholders' agreement is weighted heavily in favour of the bid sponsors. On at least two Australian privately-financed projects, the SPV Board members nominated by the equity investors representing the construction contractor were, under specific governance provisions, entitled to be present at and participate in SPV Board meetings, and perhaps even vote, even when the subject under discussion was the enforcement of the construction contract against the very contractor they were representing. Both projects suffered from significant delays in construction and associated cost overruns.

Who are the SPV personnel? If they are all on secondment from a core contractor, can you really expect them to enforce the core contract effectively? And who looks after the majority interest? The final equity investors may be brought into the project by the financial bid sponsors either late in the tender process or only after the bid has been won, which limits their ability to influence the governance arrangements. Probably the most reliable indicator of a bidder that genuinely takes governance seriously is the early appointment of a strong independent chair for the SPV Board of Directors, and this is something you should look for.

It is not advisable to mandate any particular structure for the bidders, since every consortium is subject to different pressures and it may also not be in Government's interest to limit the use of other structures that may be more efficient for financing purposes. But you need to know your bidders are putting forward, as the proposed party to your contract, an SPV that has both the will and the capacity to manage its core contractors effectively. Make it clear the governance of the SPV and the relationships it has with its core contractors are matters you will take into account in the evaluation.

Return date

You need to specify a date for the return of bids. Give bidders a reasonable amount of time – measured in weeks or months, not days – to absorb the information in the data room and produce their bids. Take account of holiday periods. A bidder will achieve more between 24 October and 2 November than they will between 24 December and 2 January. Let's face it, requiring bids to be submitted on 2 January is just plain nasty. Don't do it.

Where bidders will have to approach subcontractors for pricing on elements of the bids, you need to allow enough time for this to happen. You also need to allow time for bidders to complete their internal authorisation processes. On small contracts, you can expect the bid team to have complete authority to bid and complete the contract, but mispriced mega-projects are potential company-killers, so bid teams will have to go through an internal governance process before they are permitted to submit the bid.

The law of diminishing returns applies here as anywhere else. Too long a time can be as unhelpful as too short a time: it pushes up the bid costs without much improvement in the bids.

> *Too long a time can be as unhelpful as too short a time: it pushes up the bid costs without much improvement in the bids.*

Tender validity period

This time, you will be asking the bidders to fix their price. It may be a fixed price in the sense of being a specified amount of currency for the entire delivery, it may be fixed rates for particular tasks or activities or it may be a fixed process for determining what payments should be made. However it is calculated, the price is fixed by the bid. Your conditions of tender must specify how long the fixed price must be kept fixed while you decide whether or not to accept it.

It is not reasonable to expect bidders to keep an offer open indefinitely. The longer the time period for acceptance of the bid, the more time you have to complete the evaluation and settle the contract, but generosity is not a virtue in this context. The longer the time period for acceptance of the bid, the greater the risk of adverse changes in a bidder's cost of delivery. That risk will be priced into their bid. Don't take more time than you need. (Be very sceptical of evaluators who claim they need more time to assess a bid than it took the bidder to prepare it.) To reduce cost, or to make a longer acceptance period viable, your conditions of tender can provide for some of the risk to be transferred to Government, such as exchange rate risk on foreign currencies. If prices of steel or other required commodities are particularly volatile, you could ask bidders to identify the commodity cost in their bids and agree to adjust that element of the price on the basis of an appropriate commodities index.

Variant bids

Tenderers delight in producing bids at variance with your request. You don't want to be forced to exclude the tenderer on that ground and you may want to give other bidders the opportunity to price the same variant. In the Portcullis House case the Agency was held in breach of an implied duty to treat all bidders fairly and equally because they considered an alternative design without allowing any other bidder an opportunity to compete with it on its terms. Make provision for variant bids in the conditions of tender: this may give you wider discretion to deal with the unexpected.

Forward programme

Although the only firm date you will commit to is the return date for the bids, you should give bidders a forward view of the programme to award of contract. (Don't forget to agree this with your Minister: contract award will have a prominent place in the media calendar.) Bidders also have stakeholders who need to be kept informed.

> *If you once get into a mindset that urgency trumps every other consideration, disaster will follow.*

A contract for a mega-project is probably worth billions and may last for 30 years. Try to remember this when someone says you do not have time to take a week longer on the procurement process. If you once get into a mindset that urgency trumps every other consideration, disaster will follow. The amount of time you lose by doing something stupid exceeds the time you appear to save by doing it. In the Air Traffic Control System case, a procurement consultant was engaged to comment on the process before the Civil Aviation Authority went to market. He advised the 12-month timetable was 'extremely tight if not impossible'. The advice was not only ignored, the process was subsequently revised to reduce the timetable even further. A contract was not signed until almost two years after the original target date and the Authority was still unsuccessfully defending its actions before the Federal Court three years later.

If your forward programme is plausible, the burning question for bidders will be the number of rounds of bidding expected before the contract is awarded. If there are three bidders, will you eliminate one and then ask for updated bids from the remaining two, or will you go straight to a preferred bidder? Once you have completed the initial evaluation, will there be an opportunity for a

BAFO (Best and Final Offer), or will the first bid they submit determine the final outcome? You do not necessarily have to commit to any of this before you have seen and evaluated the bids, but consider the impact of both your decision and its timing. For instance, if bidders believe there will be a second round, they will likely hold something in reserve in the first round, which is not helpful if you then have only one round. Your target date for award of contract will be a factor in forming the bidders' views on their best tactics, as will your track record on sticking to the procurement timetable.

Whatever programme you go with at the time of issue of the Request for Tenders, the conditions of tender should make it clear you have the necessary discretion to change your mind later: bidding may not go as you expect.

CONTRACT DOCUMENTS

If your stakeholders have not yet signed in blood that the specification is complete, now is the time to bring out the syringe and fill the fountain pen. Post-contract variations to the specification destroy projects, as witness Canada's purchase of 28 CH-148 Cyclone helicopters, dubbed 'the worst procurement in the history of Canada' by the Foreign Minister. The $1.8 billion acquisition contract signed in 2004 was amended to include additional electronics and armaments. The weight of this equipment triggered the need for design and development of more powerful engines, which then required a re-engineering of the entire helicopter. Delivery was put back from 2008 to 2010; no, make that 2012; no, make that 2013; no, make that 2018.

Your contract should also be as complete as you can make it without the final input from the successful bidder. The prices you are offered will be meaningless if you don't set out the contract terms in full. If you are still trying to sort out key commercial terms with your stakeholders, you are not ready to go out with a call for tenders.

If you are still trying to sort out key commercial terms with your stakeholders, you are not ready to go out with a call for tenders.

If you absolutely have to put out the call before you can secure a decision on some aspect of the project, ring-fence the uncertainty to the extent possible. On one New South Wales contract, there was an issue about which of two standards the contractor would be required to comply with in relation to one aspect of the works, which could only be determined after undertaking an initial study. Ideally the study would have been carried out by the Agency before any Request for Tenders was issued, but the amount of time involved was incompatible with a politically-acceptable procurement timetable. The contract instead provided for the study to be carried out by the contractor;

a price for the works on the assumption that the less onerous standard would be required; and a variation provision that would be triggered if additional works were required under the more onerous standard. This was less than ideal because of the schedule risk involved, but it did at least allow the bidders to come up with a firm price.

RETURNABLE SCHEDULES

The final thing you need to do in the Request for Tenders is to tell the bidders what it is you want them to provide. Just because you ask bidders to provide something doesn't mean they will do so, but if you fail to ask you can't complain if they don't provide it.

> *One of the difficulties faced by tenderers who understand the risks of a project is that their price is likely to be undercut by someone who doesn't.*

One of the difficulties faced by tenderers who understand the risks of a project is that their price is likely to be undercut by someone who doesn't. One of the difficulties faced by Government is how to get a good price *and* someone who knows what they are doing. A contractor losing a bit of money is not a cause for tears, although it can make contract management difficult. A contractor losing a lot of money is a court case waiting to happen. The material in the returnable schedules may be your only evidence of whether a bidder knows what it takes to deliver the project successfully. Don't waste the opportunity.

When you ask bidders to provide information, there is one simple rule: if you do not know what you are going to do with it, do not ask for it. Do not accept vague answers from the project team on this one. On one public sector project, the team came up with about 100 returnable schedules of things they wanted the bidders to tell them. They were then asked to provide, for each schedule, a single side of A4 paper explaining what the schedule was, the benefits of having the information and how the schedule would be incorporated into the contract. After this single intervention, the number of returnable schedules was down 30 per cent within a week.

Technical experts are particularly prone to ask for unnecessary information. Their commendable interest in their subject leads them to want to know in minute detail what the tenderer plans to do, whether they are going to use the latest experimental widget and whether they favour technique A over technique B. Sometimes you need to know. Quite often you don't. It is one thing to ask tenderers to spend millions providing you with information to enable you to award a contract. It is quite another to ask them to spend millions satisfying the professional curiosity of your engineers and technical advisers.

One useful question to ask is what the Agency would have to do differently if it didn't have the information: if the impact is trivial, collecting the information is a waste of everybody's time.

The problem with a mega-project is that you only get one go.

The decisions are often not as simple as this would suggest. The problem with a mega-project is that you only get one go. If the bidder makes an error in the tunnel geometry for a 16-kilometre tunnel and you don't find out until the tunnel is complete, you are probably going to have to adjust the road or railway to match the tunnel rather than the other way round. On the other hand, competent tunnelling contractors do not make significant errors in geometry and the contract may give you a later opportunity to review the design if you think you need to: are you making use of the current information to select a competent contractor or approve a tunnel design? Think about where the risks really lie and direct your efforts accordingly.

The information you ask for will be used in two contexts: making a choice between the bidders and, in the case of the successful bidder, forming part of the contract. Ask for the information to be presented in a way that facilitates these ends. Fitting into the contract takes priority. Making life more difficult for your evaluators may take up a bit of time now. Making the contract less comprehensible may land you in court later.

Are They Listening?

I am all in favour of listening to bidders. They tell you things you need to know. I'm even more in favour of bidders listening to the project director. The phrase you particularly want them to listen to is, 'Read the words.' I always say this to bidders at every possible opportunity. You have not invested all this time and effort into producing the contract and the specifications and the invitation to tender in order to have bidders respond on the basis of what they thought you might want rather than what you explicitly told them you did want.

Some bidders may have previous bad experience of Government agencies putting out ambiguous or even incomprehensible invitations to tender. Make it clear your standards are higher and tell the bidders to read the words. If they do identify any ambiguity that has slipped through your checks, you want them to ask about it, not guess.

Waiting for Submissions

The first thing any right-minded project director does after issuing the Request for Tenders is take a holiday. You will need the break. Just make sure somebody reliable is covering for you. Even on a small procurement, bidders will come back with questions. On a big one, however good the information you provide, they will come back with lots of questions. You need to provide a secure communications channel. Data room software generally comes with a Q&A facility, which you will probably find it convenient to use. Set it up so nothing is visible to the bidders without your sign off and everything is readily retrievable if you need evidence of who has looked at what. You can pull reports showing how many questions are open and how long bidders have been waiting for responses, which is a useful check.

Sometimes you can see the questions coming and deal with them in advance. When the Waratah train procurement commenced, new railway safety legislation had just been introduced. The bidders were bound to bombard the rail safety regulator with irritating demands for interpretations. (Never irritate your industry regulators, they have ways of making your life miserable.) The regulator agreed to refer all enquiries to the project team, and the launch event included a joint presentation that made clear both the approach the regulator would take to the legislation and the uselessness of any attempt to play the Agency off against the regulator.

Leaving questions unanswered frustrates the bidders and does nothing for bid quality.

Any question raised by a bidder prior to submissions should be dealt with promptly. Leaving questions unanswered frustrates the bidders and does nothing for bid quality. Take particular care in dealing with requests for extensions of time for bid submissions. Bidders are just as aware as you that extensions of time have different impacts on different bidders. The request may be an attempt to gain an advantage rather than redress a disadvantage and may even be an attempt to set you up for a later challenge. Being fair doesn't mean you aren't allowed to say no. It does mean you have to give reasonable consideration to such requests.

A request for an extension of time must be dealt with as a matter of urgency, even if the request comes in well before submissions are due. A week's extension granted early will have a very different impact from a week's extension granted the day before the period expires. Bidders plan the preparation of their bids in some detail. If they know at the beginning there is an extra week available, they may decide to produce a more detailed design or develop something else to add value to their bid. But most of their bid material will be finalised several days before the end of the submission period to allow for packaging and final checks and authorisations. If you grant an extension at the last moment, it is difficult for bidders to do anything with the extra time except clean up typos, which adds very little value.

Although you need to keep alert, the period before bids come in is normally relatively quiet. This is your opportunity to make sure all your project records and registers are up to date and to do detailed planning for the next phase. Crunch time is coming. You are about to have to select your preferred bidder.

Chapter 15
Evaluating the Tenders

> *The time to get the criteria right is the date you publish them.*

It is alarming how seldom Government agencies give much time or effort to planning evaluations. Agencies are aware they have to publish the evaluation criteria. The concept that it is a really good idea to work out if they are the right criteria *before* you publish them doesn't seem to have achieved quite the same currency. Perhaps people find it difficult to focus because it will be weeks or even months before the bids come back and the evaluation starts. That's just too bad. The time to get the criteria right is the date you publish them. If you have chosen the wrong criteria you will either end up with the wrong contractor or tie yourself in potentially actionable knots in order to come up with the right one.

Choosing Evaluation Criteria

You need different criteria at the shortlisting stage from the selection stage. In particular, price is not normally relevant to the shortlisting decision. The idea is to whittle down the number of bidders without imposing too much cost on the market or on your Agency. For bidders to produce a price, you have to give them the full commercial terms and conditions and the bidders have to process that information and also engage with their supply chains. A price given on the basis of indicative terms and conditions is meaningless at best, misleading at worst. Producing a firm price is a burden on the industry and is unnecessary to select a sensible shortlist.

How do you choose your evaluation criteria? There are no magic ones that will be unimpeachably fair and deliver the best candidate. The right criteria depend on the particular circumstances of the particular procurement. Don't pull out the criteria the Agency used last time and assume all will be well. Get some knowledgeable people around a table and think through the ways different criteria might play out in the current marketplace. A market leader in terms of product capability might be reported in the press as being in financial difficulty: how bad does their financial position need to be before it puts them out of the running (bearing in mind that the financial position of a supplier before winning a billion dollar contract is significantly different from the financial position after winning one)? If an unacceptable financial risk could be covered off effectively by some sort of third party guarantee, would that meet the relevant criterion and how would you communicate that to bidders?

Put the work into polishing your evaluation criteria up front.

Put the work into polishing your evaluation criteria up front. It is very difficult to change them during the process without laying the whole procurement open to challenge, so get them right in the first place.

You will know if you have selected good criteria because if you have:

- The criteria will allow you to achieve your objectives for the procurement. If you have an objective of knowledge transfer to local industry, for instance, you need a criterion associated with that or bidders won't offer it.

- Tenderers who meet the criteria will be capable of doing the entire job, not just bits of it. If the contract can be won by an incompetent, you have the wrong criteria. There are no prizes for selecting a technology provider who can deliver a system but can't make it work in the client environment.

- The criteria will enable you to distinguish between tenderers. That does not necessarily apply to every individual criterion: some may be there just to confirm a standard is met. But if all the scores are equal, you are no further forward.

- The criteria will not favour or exclude a bidder unfairly. Somebody has to win, but if you set criteria only one bidder can match, the 'competition' is a farce. Unethical to do it deliberately, stupid to do it by accident.

- The criteria will be capable of evaluation. Sounds obvious, but this is often overlooked. Will you have the information and expertise necessary to make a reasonable assessment of the bidders against each criterion?

Make a distinction between an evaluation criterion and the things you will take into account in evaluating the bids against the criterion. For instance, you will undoubtedly regard it as a plus if a tenderer has successfully completed similar projects. Rather than make that a criterion, you should instead call for the information and use it to evaluate against a more general criterion that the tenderer should demonstrate the appropriate capability. Being too specific can be a trap. If one company has successfully completed three projects, but another one has poached its entire project team, the 'experienced' company may be left with no actual expertise.

If your contract is long term, partnering and conflict management skills should not be overlooked even if they do not appear directly relevant to the substantive obligations of the contractor. Binding the Agency for 30 years to someone without relationship management skills may end in an expensive divorce.

Be very wary of making any criterion a pass/fail, that is, a mandatory exclusion if the bidder doesn't pass. Mega-projects are so complex there is rarely any one factor so overwhelming as to rule out a bid entirely if it is the only thing wrong. An exception would be the existence of legal sanctions against dealing with certain counterparties. If there is no illegality involved, and sometimes even if there is, there will be something you could negotiate to solve the problem. Whether you would want to go to so much trouble would depend on how all the other factors stacked up, but if you have made a pass on that criterion mandatory, you will not have the option.

Mega-projects are so complex there is rarely any one factor so overwhelming as to rule out a bid entirely if it is the only thing wrong.

Evaluation Methodology

The first rule of an evaluation methodology is that you should know what it is before you start evaluating the bids. If you make it up as you go along the methodology is less likely to be fair and it is harder to demonstrate any fairness it has. The whole purpose of your evaluation methodology is to select one bidder over another. If you wait until you have seen the bids before you choose the methodology, people will believe you have made your choice of methodology in order to be able to select one particular bidder. Write your methodology down and have it approved through your governance system before you allow the bids to be evaluated.

THRESHOLD QUESTIONS

Before bids are released to the evaluators, there will be a check to ensure bidders either complied with the submission requirements or any non-compliances are so minor as to make it unfair to exclude them on that basis. This is a threshold that must be crossed before any further evaluation of a bid becomes necessary or indeed appropriate.

If you have adopted any mandatory criteria, these could also be dealt with as threshold questions: that is, you do not evaluate any other aspect of the bid until it has been established the mandatory criteria have been satisfied. In practice, it is usual to evaluate the whole bid anyway. It is unlikely a bidder will fail – few bidders are going to spend millions putting together a bid and then miss ticking the critical box – so you are merely delaying the process if you evaluate the mandatory criteria before allowing the other evaluation teams to begin. It is also useful in risk management terms to be able to demonstrate to the bidder at the de-brief that they would not have been selected in any event (any bidder foolish enough to fail a mandatory criterion is unlikely to come out in front). It shows the bidder that a successful challenge to your decision on the mandatory criteria would achieve nothing.

A different type of threshold question is also possible. For instance, if you are at the shortlisting stage and you have a number of bidders offering technology A and a number of bidders offering technology B, you might decide to choose your shortlist from the bidders overall, or you might structure the evaluation with a threshold: that is, you first decide whether to choose technology A or technology B and then select your shortlist from only those bidders who offered the technology you chose. This apparently simple choice is disguising a much more serious issue.

Bidders invest in making bids to win contracts, not to subsidise Government's strategic decision-making process.

If the question whether technology A is better than technology B is so important you wouldn't shortlist anyone offering the wrong technology, the choice of technology is a strategic decision that should have been made before you put out the call. Bidders invest in making bids to win contracts, not to subsidise Government's strategic decision-making process. Governments being Governments, it may not be within your power to get the strategic decision made any other way, in which case you will need to put a threshold question into your evaluation methodology. If you make it clear to bidders that this is how you will be doing the evaluation, there should be no grounds for challenge. But it is very poor practice.

STRUCTURING THE EVALUATION

The essence of a good decision is relevant expertise plus sound judgment. In the case of a mega-project, the decision-maker will be a politician, who will almost certainly have no relevant expertise. Judgment is sometimes also a bit dodgy. The essence of a good evaluation methodology is that it provides a way for expertise and sound judgment to be brought to bear on the selection decision regardless of whether your Minister has any of either.

Selection is a single decision, but because of the complexity of a mega-project, to make a recommendation to the Minister on this one issue you need to make decisions on many smaller matters. How you group and integrate these is an important part of the evaluation methodology. All of these smaller decisions build the foundations on which the selection decision rests.

Think about the different types of decision that need to be made in an evaluation. Some are as simple as item X is better than item A. That kind of decision needs to be made by someone who has the relevant expertise. One competent subject matter expert is more likely to make the correct decision than a committee of the ignorant. It is a useful check to get a second opinion from another subject matter expert if one is available: it can protect the first from allegations of bias, and if the choice is very finely balanced, expert debate (as distinct from uninformed chit-chat) may lead to a better result. Generally you should ask the experts to form a view independently before you allow them to start debating the issue, otherwise the personalities of the evaluators may have greater weight than their expertise.

One competent subject matter expert is more likely to make the correct decision than a committee of the ignorant.

Most decisions are more complex: is X + Y + Z better than A + B + C? This is where things start going beyond the expertise of a single subject matter expert, so you need to allocate the evaluation of different parts of the bid to different teams. A typical structure is shown in Figure 15.1. The Evaluation Committee is supported by three specialist subcommittees, one for financial evaluation, one for looking at the contract and commercial terms, and one for technical issues. There may need to be further teams of evaluators dealing with highly specialised technical matters.

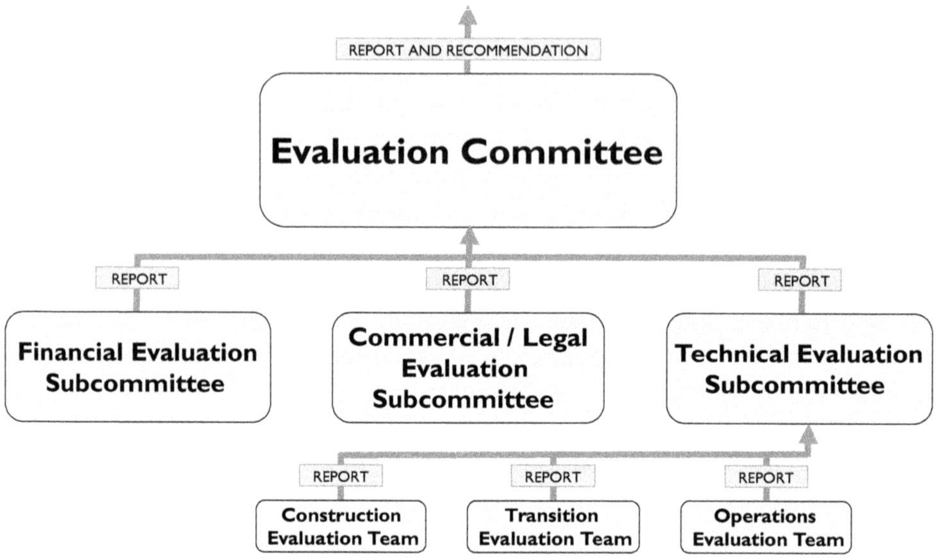

Figure 15.1 Typical evaluation structure

An alternative to the lowest layer may be to split the Technical Committee itself, giving four or even five reports feeding into the Evaluation Committee, but this may give undue emphasis to technical factors. Beware of burdening the Evaluation Committee with reports whose weight in kilograms is disproportionate to their weight in the scoring system. It will depend on the particular project whether you need the additional layer for the technical evaluation, and the composition of that layer if you do. Avoid adding further layers beyond that. Technical experts love delving into the detail, but you aren't setting this up so your technical experts can have fun. Go as deep as you need to – and no deeper.

COMMITTEE COMPOSITION – EVALUATION COMMITTEE

The Evaluation Committee is less about expertise and more about judgment. It reaches its conclusions by reading the subcommittee reports and exercising discretion and judgment rather than by direct analysis of the bids. This makes it possible to use senior people, who normally do not have the time to dedicate to direct analysis. Which is good, because you want the most senior people available. Partly because most of them achieved seniority by demonstrating their discretion and judgment and partly because it is not fair to junior people to expose them to cross-examination at the public inquiry if the Evaluation Committee gets it badly wrong.

I would be disappointed in a committee member who didn't review at least some of the raw bid material, but your evaluation methodology should make it clear this is not a requirement. For people used to small procurements, it may seem bizarre to have recommendations made by people who haven't read all of the bid submissions. In fact, raw bid material can be positively misleading to people without the relevant expertise, and on a mega-project no one can have all the relevant expertise.

Raw bid material can be positively misleading to people without the relevant expertise, and on a mega-project no one can have all the relevant expertise.

You should chair the Evaluation Committee, not least to ensure that no report will be issued without your sign off. The designated contract manager should be a member: they will be stuck with managing the selected contractor and will do it better if they are publicly fixed as having personally supported the selection. There should be one senior person – as senior as you can get – from each of the three subcommittee areas of expertise. Your Agency's chief financial officer is normally your best choice as the finance person, for instance. (In larger Government agencies, the chief financial officer may have a senior direct report who is designated to be on these Evaluation Committees.) Even if your personal expertise would qualify you to be one of the senior people, you need someone else. You as chair should be impartial and display and facilitate a balanced approach across the different disciplines.

Consider including a complete independent on the Evaluation Committee, particularly if it would otherwise be light on seniority or expertise. Experience really does help in spotting potential problems and finding ways to overcome them. The mere presence on the Evaluation Committee of a respected person from outside the Agency will give comfort to those asked to approve its recommendations and give pause to those who might wish to challenge them.

The attitude of Treasury varies, partly according to whether private finance is involved and partly according to the nature of the most recent mega-project fiasco. Sometimes they insist on having a representative as member (to satisfy themselves that Treasury's interests are being protected) and sometimes they insist on not being represented (so they can't be blamed for any subsequent catastrophe). In my experience, a senior Treasury representative brings an intelligent scepticism and doesn't tolerate any crap: invaluable qualities for this sort of exercise. They also help smooth the way at the end of the process if the Treasurer is called upon as signatory to approvals and guarantees. If the Treasury pendulum has swung towards

A senior Treasury representative brings an intelligent scepticism and doesn't tolerate any crap: invaluable qualities for this sort of exercise.

if-we're-not-represented-we-can't-be-blamed, invite them to nominate an observer rather than a member. Even without full participation, they normally add value.

Treasury apart, do not clutter your Evaluation Committee with stakeholder representatives: that is what your governance structure is for. The job of the Evaluation Committee is to make recommendations, and to make them strictly in accordance with the evaluation methodology. Let people with axes to grind do their grinding somewhere else.

Although the Evaluation Committee itself is best kept small, you will wish to have other people in attendance at various times and the methodology should permit you to invite them. I would normally have a representative of each of the key advisers present, for instance. Where a subcommittee's area is under discussion, the chair of the relevant subcommittee (if not a member of the Evaluation Committee anyway) should be invited to attend, both to explain the work of the subcommittee and to carry ungarbled guidance back to it. If you have a process auditor on the job, they will need to attend at least some of the Evaluation Committee meetings.

COMMITTEE COMPOSITION – SUBCOMMITTEES

No one person will read every word of all the bids, but every word of every bid must be read by someone, and preferably at least two someones. The basis of the subcommittee structure is that scoring for each criterion should be the responsibility of a particular subcommittee. The members of that subcommittee should have both sufficient expertise and also sufficient time to read and evaluate the relevant parts of the bids. If the Agency has its own experts they will already have day jobs and you may need to make special arrangements to free them up for the evaluation, perhaps by funding the backfilling of their positions for the necessary weeks. It is not enough to have people who can turn up to meetings, you need people who have time to process the raw bids.

Do not panic if there is not sufficient expertise within the Agency itself. This can be dealt with either by arranging for externals to sit on the subcommittees or by procuring an external firm to review the bids and prepare a report: the subcommittee then needs only to have sufficient time and expertise to read and understand the report and ask searching questions of the external firm.

> *Few people combine technical expertise and commercial astuteness with the ability to explain technical matters to the uninitiated.*

I normally prefer to structure the technical evaluation as a single technical subcommittee with a number of specialist teams reporting to it in respect of individual technical criteria, rather than having multiple technical subcommittees. This is because few people combine technical expertise and commercial astuteness with the ability to explain technical matters to the uninitiated. Concentrate these people into a single subcommittee, where they can apply their professional judgment and editing skills to the reports put forward by the technical teams. This greatly simplifies the task of the Evaluation Committee and reduces the risk it will do something stupid because the technical reports were beyond its comprehension.

Although the idea is that each criterion should be wholly considered by a single subcommittee which takes responsibility for the applicable score, there will be areas where subcommittees need to review matters jointly. Problems can arise, for instance, where an apparently minor mark-up to a technical specification changes the commercial effect of the agreement in a way that cannot be identified by looking at the mark-up of the terms and conditions alone. Experienced evaluators are usually attuned to such risks, but a bit of overlap in subcommittee membership is very helpful in making sure these things are picked up. It also helps if your evaluators are the same people you had helping you during the development stage, so the technical people are familiar with the contract structure and the legal and commercial people are familiar with the specification.

It is usually advisable to keep most of the technical team away from financial information: the dollars may colour their view of the technology. Also, the fewer people with pricing information, the less chance it will leak. The chair of the technical subcommittee and possibly one or two others will probably need to know something in order to contribute to some of the commercial and financial debates, but do not allow financial matters to be discussed at technical meetings.

Give yourself the right to attend meetings of the subcommittees. You won't have time for them all, but a random sampling encourages the troops and gives you some assurance the methodology really is being implemented as planned.

COMMITTEE ADMINISTRATION

Make sure each group in the evaluation structure has written terms of reference and that between them they cover the whole ground. The number of members should be greater than the number required for a quorum (someone is bound to go on holiday, fall ill or fall under a bus) but ensure group reports are signed off by all group members whether they attended the final meeting or not. Give yourself rights to appoint replacements for people who become unavailable.

Ensure group reports are signed off by all group members whether they attended the final meeting or not.

The Evaluation Committee should keep minutes. Subcommittees and technical teams also need records, but it is counter-productive to do anything other than keep these to a minimum.

In all cases, ensure the reasons for the scores are captured at the time a score is given or changed, even if only in a few words. You may never have to disclose the reasons to a court, but if you do, you will need evidence you had some. They will also come in handy when you script your de-briefing of the losing bidders at the end of the process: while you won't be giving them all the details of the evaluation down to this level, some of the items may turn out to be significant. Since you don't yet know which, record the lot.

FURTHER INFORMATION

However expertly you crafted the returnable schedules to be submitted by the bidders, and however faithfully they followed the instructions for completing them, there will always be more things you need to know in order to complete the evaluation. Bids for major contracts usually comprise a large and complex volume of documentation, which has been produced under high pressure in a short period of time. Inevitably, the bids will contain errors and inconsistencies and they may have been prepared on the basis of assumptions that are wrong, or invisible to Government. To ensure bids are fairly evaluated, the evaluation methodology needs to include arrangements for Government to seek clarification from bidders. As with the earlier arrangements for bidders to clarify the Request for Tenders, the data room software provided by the lawyers will offer a more secure and easily trackable facility than using an email-based approach.

You will also need some face time with the bidders. Video conferencing is an option if bringing people together in the same city is a problem. Always conduct meetings in a very structured way, to ensure consistency of approach across the bids. Your published process should allow you to make a recording of every meeting you have with a bidder (otherwise you may not be able to do it without their specific consent).

> *Be particularly careful where tenderers are also existing suppliers to the business. That role may bring them into contact when you are not expecting it.*

Do not discuss the evaluation with bidders outside a programmed session. Be particularly careful where tenderers are also existing suppliers to the business. That role may bring them into contact when you are not expecting it. The project director on the New South Wales Integrated Ticketing case was asked to provide an update on the tender process to another part of the business. When he turned up, he discovered one of the tenderers had been invited to attend. Since the update contained no more information than had already been provided to tenderers, he gave it anyway. A mistake. There was no process auditor or independent adviser present and no minutes were taken. The tenderer later sued, alleging things had been said by the project director that showed Government improperly influenced the recommendation of the Evaluation Committee.

If you want to be able to take into account anything other than material actually submitted by a bidder – such as references from previous customers, evidence of reputation in media reports, or past performance on projects for your Agency – make it clear you are entitled but not obliged to do so. Keep a record of anything you do take into account. Check references using structured interviews rather than random phone calls: this facilitates both the information-gathering and the record-keeping. Don't rely on anything damaging you found in the media or through a web search engine without offering the bidder a chance to explain.

Selecting a Shortlist

The shortlisting stage is less nerve-racking than the selection stage, but no less important. You will never manage to select the best bidder if they didn't make it onto the shortlist in the first place. And the selection stage will not be a tough competition that drives down prices if the shortlist has the wrong people on it.

How long is short? The ideal shortlist has only two bidders, both of whom are keen and capable. With only one rival to beat, each will be willing to invest in producing a really well-developed tender, and because both are capable, competition will keep the prices sharp.

If the market is weak, you may need a third player. The risk with two is that one drops out, leaving you negotiating with a single supplier: never a reliable way to get a good deal. The downside of having three is the 50 per cent increase in workload for your evaluators, which may prolong the competition or reduce the level of scrutiny given to individual bids. Four or more players is nearly always a bad idea: bidders will be less convinced of their chance to win and may hold something back in expectation of another elimination round, so you won't get the best they can offer.

Not only does it put up the cost to industry unnecessarily, it merely postpones the problem.

One reason for a long shortlist is that Government can't make up its mind. This is a truly terrible reason. Not only does it put up the cost to industry unnecessarily, it merely postpones the problem. Make sure your evaluation criteria and methodology allow sufficient differentiation between responses at the shortlisting stage: if everyone gets exactly the same score you will have no defensible grounds for eliminating anyone.

An equally terrible reason is that the Minister can't bear the screams from the eliminated bidders. If it happens to you, you haven't been managing expectations properly. In a contract competition, somebody loses. You need to warn the Minister it could be the one with its head office in the Minister's constituency. That way, when the bidder calls in protest, the Minister will have rehearsed a speech about all the bids being very high quality, such a shame you missed out, and will give the speech instead of being hustled into promising to reinstate the bidder.

One reason you might include an extra bidder on a shortlist is if the market or the general public is likely to attribute their elimination to unfair prejudice. The perception of an unfair process can be just as harmful as the reality. Not only may the eliminated bidder be encouraged to bring an action, the ultimate losing bidder from the shortlist may also be more likely to regard their loss as due to an unfair process. If there is a risk of perception of unfair prejudice – and still more if there is a real risk of actual unfair prejudice – be wary of eliminating someone at the shortlisting stage if the margin of difference is small.

> *Do not include a bidder on the shortlist because they are big and ugly and threaten to sue you.*

Do not include a bidder on the shortlist because they are big and ugly and threaten to sue you. They won't get any less big or ugly or threatening at the award of contract stage, and by then they will have invested millions and be that much keener to sue. If you have been following your process correctly, you will be able to demonstrate incontrovertibly why they were eliminated, and it will be a lot less complicated than demonstrating the same thing later.

Scoring and Weighting

The selection stage is the crunch. You know you want the best tenderer, you know the criteria you want to evaluate against, but how do you tell which tenderer is best?

There is no right answer to the question of how to score tenders on a mega-project. You will need to use more than one scoring system, because financial, commercial and technical issues are never amenable to a single scale. This gives you two issues: how to produce scores for the individual criteria and how to integrate them to make a selection.

FINANCIAL SCORE

Financial scores are almost invariably measured in your local currency. The lower the price, the better. The problem is working out what the 'price' is. What you are interested in is the total cost to Government. This is not the same thing as the amount received by the bidder. For instance, Government often contributes land that may be contaminated: if one bidder includes remediation in its price and the other requires Government to remediate the land before it is handed over, the price paid to the first bidder would be higher but the total cost to Government might be lower. Typical issues include:

- Part of the work is unquantified and covered by a schedule of rates: what cost should you attribute to that?

- One bidder says it will deliver the project six months before the other: how do you value that benefit?

- Government is taking exchange rate risk and the two bidders are operating in different currencies: how do you value the risk differential?

- The low price is driven by excessive debt: if Government insists on the bidder retaining more equity, what will that do to the price?

- The bidder has produced its own demand forecasts which differ from those used by Government: what account should be taken of this?

The financial advisers (internal or external) will build a financial model into which all these factors can be incorporated. Depending on the complexity of the transaction, this may be a simple spreadsheet or a risk-based model with Monte Carlo simulation capability. Financial models have one thing in common: they produce estimates, not actual costs. Increased complexity is not a guarantee of increased accuracy. All models used should be audited, because simple errors can deliver very misleading outputs (the inflation error in the InterCity West Coast franchise case shifted the loan facility amounts by about 50 per cent, for instance).

On the scale of a mega-project ... it is not unlikely that an apparent 'lead' of millions should be interpreted as a dead heat.

A model without errors is still only a model. On the scale of a mega-project, the margin of uncertainty can be large in absolute terms even if small in percentage terms: it is not unlikely that an apparent 'lead' of millions should be interpreted as a dead heat. Model outputs are often more fairly expressed as a range rather than a point estimate. Run some scenarios with different assumptions, including some extreme assumptions, to develop a feel for the spread of possible outcomes.

Avoid producing documents containing numbers with more significant figures than the accuracy of the model supports. It is misleading to tell your approving body the cost will be £7,368,457,246.03, even if that is the figure generated by the model. It may well be that three significant figures (£7.37 billion) or even two (£7.4 billion) will be the maximum you can justify. If two bidders differ by only one in the last significant figure, review the rounding to check whether the difference is meaningful.

LEGAL/COMMERCIAL SCORE

What you are assessing here is the mark-up of the commercial terms you issued with the call for tenders. Occasionally you get a bidder who will only do business on the precise wording of their standard terms, regardless of whether the legal effect of your draft contract is similar, and produces a mark-up with more red ink than black. This is extremely painful to review and gives no confidence in the bidder's ability to develop a good working relationship with the Agency. Fortunately, this approach is now rare. In the absence of such an onerous mark-up, the standard technique is for the lawyers to create a table showing, for each clause amended, the amendment made by each bidder. This presentation allows you to see which clauses are contentious and whether there are significant differences in approach between the bidders. It is also extremely useful to support negotiations when the time comes.

It doesn't give you a score. A score can seem a bit irrelevant when you have issued a fully drafted contract that was developed either after or concurrently with meaningful engagement with the market. The bidders will try to differentiate themselves on the quality of their technical solutions and services and also on price, but they are not trying to come up with new and exciting commercial terms that you will think are more impressive than anybody else's commercial terms. They know precisely what you want and your proposed terms are (or should be) fair and reasonable. Nonetheless, there will be differences in the contract mark-ups and you do need to evaluate that.

Amendments to a contract are as lines of code to software: the issue is not how many there are but what they do.

Do not award a score according to the number of amendments. Amendments to a contract are as lines of code to software: the issue is not how many there are but what they do. I would also recommend against trying to put a monetary value against each amendment and treating the total as a 'score' that combines with the finance 'score'. Some changes do need to be taken account of by the finance team: a transfer of geotechnical risk to Government, for instance, could have a significant financial impact and you need to have that incorporated in the cost to Government. But the impact of many contract amendments will be virtually impossible to quantify. Often the amended clauses will never be triggered except in a situation so dire neither you nor the bidder would sign the contract at all if either of you thought there was any real chance of it coming to pass.

A traffic light approach is simple and usually effective. It offers only three potential 'scores' and therefore may not allow much differentiation between bidders: whether this is important depends on how you intend to integrate the scores. Green means nothing you can't live with, although there may be some clauses you would try to improve before entering a contract. Amber means there are some significant issues, but no showstoppers, and the position can probably be made acceptable through negotiation. Red means the commercial terms are unacceptable and there is a risk the showstoppers are not negotiable.

TECHNICAL SCORE

Technical scoring is commonly done as a mark, often out of a hundred. There will normally be more than one technical criterion: each will be scored separately and a weighting applied to give the combined score. In some cases each criterion may be evaluated by dividing it into sub-criteria, scoring and weighting the sub-criteria and combining them to form the criterion score. Arrange for someone to audit the calculations.

This is not a competition to see who can come up with the most complicated evaluation spreadsheet. The more sub-criteria and sub-sub-criteria you have, the harder it will be to distinguish between the bids, because even a large difference in a sub-sub-criterion may only contribute 0.01 to the overall mark. On the other hand, there is value in having a system that demonstrates you have considered every aspect of the bids.

This is not a competition to see who can come up with the most complicated evaluation spreadsheet.

Bring your technical evaluation committee together before anyone starts drafting a technical evaluation methodology. Talk through what you are really looking for from the tenderers and what are the important differentiators. If the scoring system does not allow the differentiators to make a difference, you can spend a lot of time evaluating the bids and still come up with virtually identical scores, which is seriously unhelpful.

What do you do if a bidder comes up with something innovative that you did not anticipate? The 'wow' factor may deserve more than the 0.01 contribution to the overall mark prescribed by a rigid scoring and weighting system. If the innovation is central to the bid, a scoring system intended to compare apples with apples may have to be applied to a banana, which probably won't work very well. One way to deal with this is for your methodology to treat the scores generated by the system as indicative rather than definitive and allow the technical evaluation committee to make alternative recommendations where the scores do not fairly represent the true value for money to the Agency of the technical offerings.

Make sure the technical evaluators capture the reasons for every score as they go. When the committee prepares its report, it will need to say not only what the scores are, but what it is that differentiates the bidders in qualitative terms. If you have chosen to treat the scores as indicative and there is a recommendation for a ranking of the bidders different from the ranking generated by the scoring system, be particularly careful to ensure that the reasons are both adequate and adequately documented. Good documentation also makes it easier to have an independent check of the technical evaluation.

INTEGRATING THE SCORES

When you integrate scores to determine which bidder is in front overall, you effectively put all the scores into the same 'currency'.

When you integrate scores to determine which bidder is in front overall, you effectively put all the scores into the same 'currency'. In deciding whether a cost of \$3.6 billion plus a technical score of 72 is better than a cost of \$3.9 billion plus a technical score of 82, you are deciding the dollar value of the 10 point differential or the points value of the \$300 million differential, even if that is not how you phrase the decision inside your head.

It is possible to set the 'conversion rate' in advance of the evaluation. Some Agencies have a standard form procurement spreadsheet to make the selection for you when you have entered the technical scores and the price, allowing you to choose the weighting between the two. Do not use this standard form to make your decision, not least because it probably has no provision for taking into account differences in commercial terms. (The absence of provision for scoring commercial terms reflects an assumption you are doing business under the Agency standard contract. You aren't.)

You could instead come up with a project-specific formula that allows you to weight and integrate the three different currencies of financial, commercial and technical scores. You feed in the scores, the formula determines who is selected.

If you are utterly satisfied you understand how it works and have checked and are satisfied with the outcomes it would give in a wide range of scenarios, this is a potentially viable option. It certainly has advantages in terms of the risk of challenge. If your evaluation methodology involves a set formula that is adequately disclosed to the bidders and is followed precisely, bullets will just bounce off it even if the outcome is poor. Unfortunately, mega-projects are capable of throwing up more complications than you are capable of foreseeing: a fixed formula applied to unforeseen phenomena may give rise to other words beginning with the 'F' sound. 'Failure' is the most printable.

My preference is for the Evaluation Committee to recommend its preferred tenderer on the basis of the scores in the three different areas, but to do so by the exercise of judgment rather than the application of a pre-agreed formula. To reassure bidders, you can provide that if a bidder comes first in all three categories it must be selected. Where judgment becomes necessary is where no bidder is ahead in all categories. This can be a bit scary for the Evaluation Committee, because it is a big call. But if your Evaluation Committee does not have on it people who are capable of making such a judgment, you have the wrong people on your Evaluation Committee.

When the Evaluation Committee makes its recommendation based on judgment, there is one thing you need above all in order to prevent both challenge and poor outcomes: reasons for the decision. Good reasons that are based on evidence, not on prejudice. Reasons: have them, ask your advisers and independents to review them, write them down, disclose them.

The reasons will always be specific to your particular procurement, but never doubt one thing: if an outcome would be manifestly perverse and stupid, that is a really good reason for doing something else.

> *If an outcome would be manifestly perverse and stupid, that is a really good reason for doing something else.*

Picking a Winner

Keep an absolutely open mind on the selection for as long as you possibly can. The human brain is designed for confirmation bias. Once you have formed a view one way or the other, everything supporting that view will leap out at you and seem significant. Everything not supporting that view will be overlooked or downgraded. This has nothing to do with how intelligent you are, it is just the way brains work.

One of the reasons the Macphee Review recommended the Civil Aviation Authority do a partial rerun of the tender process in the Air Traffic Control

System case was that at an early stage the Board was given the false impression that one bidder represented a much higher software development risk than another: 'An unfair scepticism about [the] proposal coloured the evaluation process from this point onwards.' Another bidder was recommended on the basis of perceived differences in risk that were not supported by an objective view of the evidence.

Evaluation across all the different areas will take weeks. The negatives and positives about each bidder will not emerge evenly: keep reminding your evaluators that no one can be sure about the selection until the evaluation is complete.

Even when it is complete, you will not always have an obvious outright winner. Sometimes it will be really difficult to choose between two almost-equal bidders. More information is unlikely to make the selection easier. You put a lot of thought into your request to the bidders. Before you go back and ask for yet more material to review, consider whether it is really necessary, or whether you are just putting off making a difficult decision.

Select or Negotiate Further?

Sometimes what you need is not more information, but more certainty. Consider the scenario shown in Figure 15.2. Bidder 1 is clearly ahead of Bidder 2. Bidder 2 potentially offers better value for money, but there is no guarantee they would be ahead of where Bidder 1 is now when the contract is finalised: which should you select?

The best answer in these circumstances is probably not to select either bidder – yet.

When the decision is close, you will not be certain you are making the correct selection until you have reached the point where you have a contract you can sign. That means you cannot complete the evaluation without first negotiating the contract.

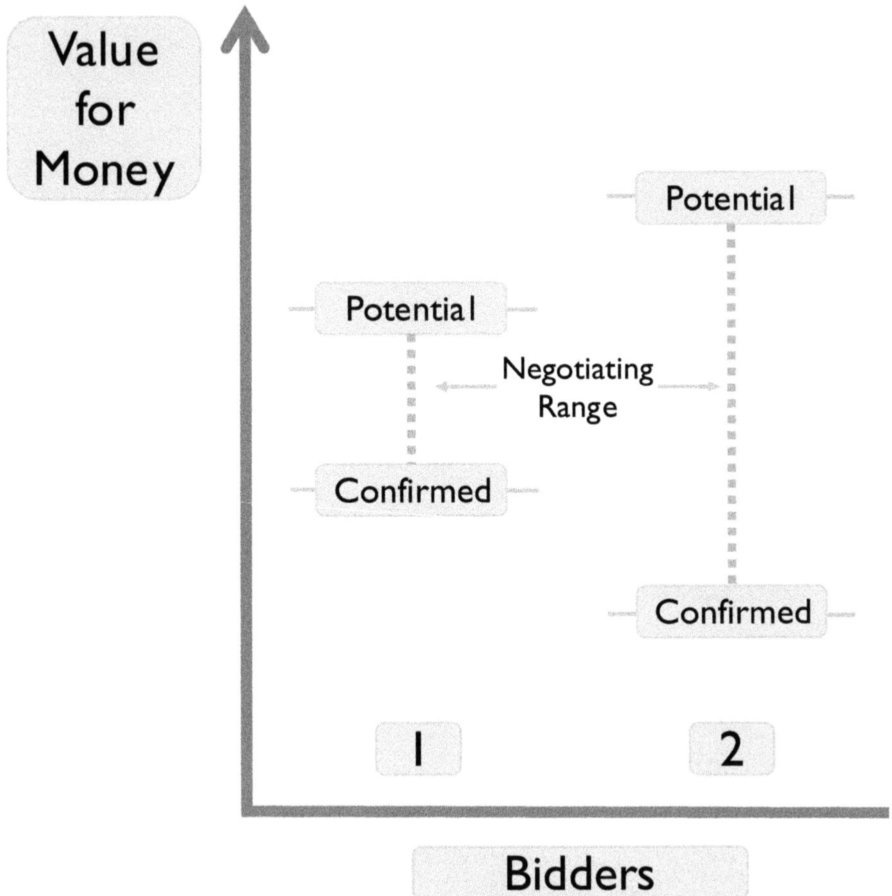

Figure 15.2 **Evaluation scenario**

Chapter 16

Negotiating the Contract

The procurement guidelines used by some Government agencies advise that the winning bid should be accepted without negotiation. This is one of those things that is fine when applied to small value procurements, but a total disaster when applied to a mega-project.

The rationale for the prohibition on negotiation is an ethical one. Government has a huge amount of purchasing power. When a business has won a tender in a competitive bidding process, the presumption is that the price is the best available. That is what the competitive process delivers. Screwing the price down further by taking advantage of Government's superior negotiating position is not nice. Government is not there to drive people out of business by standover negotiation tactics: hence the direction to accept the best bid and move on.

For the really big contracts, it doesn't work like that. The economic activity of some of the largest contractors rivals that of small countries, and the balance of power in a negotiation does not automatically rest with Government. Moreover, bidding for a contract to deliver a mega-project is not comparable to bidding for a contract to supply stationery. No matter how much thought goes into drafting the Request for Tenders, the reality is that for any project of such size and complexity, no bid will be capable of simple acceptance. Bridging the gap between tender and contract requires negotiation.

For any project of such size and complexity, no bid will be capable of simple acceptance.

Don't try to pretend you aren't doing it because the guidelines say you shouldn't. Accept the necessity and make your plans accordingly.

Where Do You Start?

Negotiation is not just the interaction with another party across a meeting table. If you give no thought to the negotiation until the bids have been evaluated, you have wasted your best opportunity to get the optimum deal for Government. In a tender process, negotiation starts before you begin.

What you need above all else is to generate true competition. If you have at least two competent bidders who are keen to win the contract and genuinely competing with one another, the chances of a good outcome are much better than if there is only one reluctant supplier in the marketplace. Even if your personal across-the-table negotiating skills are poor, competition can deliver really good outcomes for you by driving bidders to offer you the best they can.

If you have been paying attention to the earlier chapters in this book, by the time you issue the Request for Tenders you will already have set things up to maximise competition:

- you will have consulted with the market to ensure your deal structure will be attractive;
- you will not have eliminated potential competitors by including unnecessary 'requirements';
- you will have established a reputation as someone who manages a fair and streamlined tender process that will not deter bidders by generating unnecessary costs;
- your shortlisting process will have selected no more than two or perhaps three tenderers, so those remaining can feel their chances of winning the contract are high enough to justify the effort required to produce a really good bid.

The draft contract you issue with the Request for Tenders is the foundation of your negotiating position. In any negotiation, the starting point acts as an anchor that it is difficult to move very far away from. The choice of where to start is entirely down to you. Don't waste that by issuing a poorly-developed contract.

In any negotiation, the starting point acts as an anchor that it is difficult to move very far away from.

The contract you issue can never be entirely complete, because at the time you issue it you don't know the content of the winning bid. Nonetheless, you have a choice about how well developed the contract is. You are entitled to put forward a contract with a performance regime provision that consists of a heading and a statement to the effect that an appropriate performance regime will be negotiated with the preferred bidder. This is unlikely to deliver value for money. If the regime is to have enough teeth to impact performance, the bidders should take it into account in structuring their bids. If you leave it for later negotiation, a preferred bidder will not only resist all but the most toothless of performance regimes but also claim they need to adjust their pricing to allow for an increase in risk. The better developed the contract you send out, the lower the risk to you in the final negotiation.

The better developed the contract you send out, the lower the risk to you in the final negotiation.

Positioning the Contract

The contract issued with the Request for Tenders is your starting position in the negotiations. If you were bartering in a street market, the vendor would in the first instance ask for more than the price they would be willing to accept and you would offer less than you would be willing to pay. Both of you would expect the eventual price to end up somewhere in the middle: the opening offers merely indicate the bargaining has begun. Should you be making the contract much tougher than you really need, to give yourself something to concede?

In case you have forgotten, you are setting up a mega-project, not haggling over a bunch of bananas. Putting out a contract that is unreasonably skewed towards Government will not make you a hot-shot negotiator, it will make you look a prat. Government is not supposed to be capricious or vicious or brutal. Contract provisions at that end of the spectrum will be indefensible in the negotiation: if your only answer when asked why the provision was included is, 'Oh, we needed something to give away,' your 'concession' will be treated as worthless – which indeed it will be.

Your ideal positioning is not one where the contract is so much in your favour that you have a lot you can give away in a negotiation, it is one where there is little or no need to negotiate at all. All of the contract provisions should fall within the range that can be described as fair and reasonable, skewed towards Government so the bidder is pushing the edge of their comfort zone, but not so much skewed that they aren't willing to live with it.

Contracts that establish mega-projects are inevitably complex. It is in the interests of both parties that the contract should be well-structured and consistently drafted, with all of the pieces fitting together correctly. When you see a contract that is a complete dog's breakfast, the lawyer will always say by way of apology, 'It was very heavily negotiated.' While this may occasionally be an excuse for something that was poorly drafted in the first place, it is usually all too true. The more a contract is subject to

The more a contract is subject to negotiation, the more incoherent it becomes.

negotiation, the more incoherent it becomes. Inconsistencies slip in. Links from one clause to another are broken. Clauses added 'for the avoidance of doubt' create more doubt than they avoid.

It is also true that the more a contract is subject to negotiation, the more expensive it is to produce. Commercial negotiation is labour-intensive, and the labour in question is mostly the labour of people who charge a lot for their time. This puts up your costs and also increases costs for the bidders. Bid costs may not be charged to Government directly, but that doesn't mean Government doesn't end up paying. The more you push up industry overheads, the higher the prices industry will charge.

Prolonged negotiation increases cost and decreases quality. Don't go there. While some negotiation on a major contract is inevitable, don't increase it by making unreasonable demands in the first place. This means you should issue a contract that Government would be willing to sign and also one the preferred bidder would be willing to sign. Don't depart from industry standard clauses without a specific and defensible reason.

Maintaining Competitive Tension

The level of competition is not static through the tender process. Once shortlisting has taken place, competition is at its height. There may have been more competitors prior to that point, but it is only after shortlisting that things really get serious. Once a preferred bidder has been announced, competition is effectively gone: even if the runner-up is still in the wings and theoretically able to step in if negotiations with the preferred bidder are unsuccessful, this doesn't create much tension and what little there is will dissipate quickly, since the practicality of the alternative diminishes as time passes. The longer negotiations continue after appointment of a preferred bidder, the worse off Government will be.

There are other hazards. Signing the contract for a mega-project changes the world, but the world doesn't change unless the contract is signed. Unexpected things can happen between the appointment of a preferred bidder and the intended date for signing the contract. Among many other things, one of the losing bidders may bring an action for judicial review.

This is not to say unexpected events can't happen before a preferred bidder is announced – they can and they do and they will. But in the period between announcement of a preferred bidder and execution of the contract, Government is particularly vulnerable to a challenge to the procurement process. The losing bidders know they have lost unless something changes, but the risks associated with making a challenge – either formally or through a media campaign – are relatively low because there is as yet no contract to overturn.

The shorter the period between the announcement of a preferred bidder and the signing of the contract, the lower the risk to Government. The less there is left to negotiate at that time, the shorter the period will be. And if there is nothing left to negotiate, you don't have to announce a preferred bidder at all – you can sign the contract and announce that instead.

The shorter the period between the announcement of a preferred bidder and the signing of the contract, the lower the risk to Government.

Negotiation by Clarification

The first step is to do as much of the negotiation as practicable before coming face to face with the bidder in a formal negotiation. If you have issued a fair and reasonable draft contract then in theory there shouldn't be a great deal to negotiate, but it is unlikely you will unilaterally manage to come up with contractual terms that are 100 per cent acceptable.

If any terms in the draft contract are not acceptable to the bidders, they have to indicate their bid is conditional on those terms being changed. To take advantage of this, your Request for Tenders should require the tenderers to submit a full mark-up of the contract, so they not only indicate clauses that are unacceptable, but also provide drafting for a way of dealing with the subject matter of the clause that would be acceptable to them. Without such a requirement (and sometimes even with it), bidders may simply mark clauses as needing 'discussion', hoping to put off disclosing the extent of the changes they seek until they have secured preferred bidder status.

Some of the mark-up may be acceptable to you – great, no need to negotiate further. Some of it won't be, but depending on the complexity of the issues, you may be able to move the contract a long way forward through the clarification process that forms part of the evaluation.

You may observe, for instance, that one particular clause has been amended heavily by all bidders, suggesting you have misjudged the market on the issue. You can craft an alternative clause that is potentially acceptable to everyone, and send it out as a clarification question: 'Would your price or other terms of your bid change if clause X was amended as follows?' With a bit of luck everyone will find your amendment acceptable, and that is one more clause where you won't have to evaluate a mark-up and won't have to negotiate later. Even if they don't, you have sent a clear signal that you are willing to consider

Being out of step with everyone else doesn't necessarily mean you are wrong, but quite often it does mean precisely that.

alternative formulations, which will give you a place to start when formal negotiations begin. If you aren't willing to consider alternative formulations, do not use this approach – but do be sure your attachment to the original version is justified. Being out of step with everyone else doesn't necessarily mean you are wrong, but quite often it does mean precisely that.

Two things to be careful of if you use the clarification process to negotiate the contract: don't give away a bidder's confidential information to the other bidders, and don't give one bidder an unfair advantage. Generally, if two bidders mark-up the same clause, you should be willing to offer the same amendment to both. You should also consider offering the same amendment to bidders who have not requested a change. This is not always appropriate, because you are effectively conveying the information that another bidder has challenged the clause: it will depend on the circumstances whether fairness trumps confidentiality or vice versa.

Two or One?

The clarification process is unlikely to take you all the way to a completed contract. When the evaluation is complete, there will still be a need to negotiate to conclude a contract you can sign. The question you have to consider is whether you complete that negotiation with only one bidder, or with two.

If you negotiate with only one bidder, you effectively have a preferred bidder, even if you do not announce the fact. The lack of an announcement gives you a slightly better negotiating position – but only slightly. However confidential you try to keep the situation, it is almost inevitable that the bidder will become aware you are not negotiating with anyone else. As soon as they realise the competition has fallen away – and if it takes them longer than 24 hours you can count yourself lucky – they will be able to take a much harder line in the negotiation.

Where you have two bidders neck and neck, I would always recommend negotiating with both if you can. Where they are really close, the choice between them will come down to how much is conceded in the negotiation, so you will not be sure you have the best bid until the deal is fully negotiated. It is also exhilarating for the negotiator: it is not often you have the opportunity to negotiate from a position of such strength.

However, if you want to negotiate with two bidders rather than one you need to ask yourself whether the second bidder is a genuine alternative. If you would not be willing to do a deal with the second bidder if negotiations with the first are unsuccessful, or if the two bidders are so far apart it is inconceivable that further negotiation could put the second bidder in front of the first, back off. It is not fair to make the second bidder incur significant negotiating costs just because you want to give the first bidder a false impression of their position. Being unfair is not what Government is supposed to be about. Doing this sort of thing probably won't give any grounds for overturning the award of contract, but if you get found out you could well find the second bidder knocking on your door asking for costs. You may also find a shorter queue of bidders lining up for the next contract Government wants to put to tender.

The other thing you need to ask is whether you have the time and resource to negotiate with more than one bidder. Finalising two sets of complex documentation is no small task. It also requires considerable discipline to ensure you don't breach confidentiality: it is alarmingly easy to send documents to the wrong party or forget which bidder requested which amendment. On the other hand, the knowledge that a competitor is still in the race discourages a bidder from raising all but the genuinely important issues. Negotiating with two bidders often takes less time than negotiating with one. Talk it through with your lawyers and any necessary subject matter experts, and get an estimate of costs before you decide to go ahead.

Negotiating with two bidders often takes less time than negotiating with one.

Face-to-Face Negotiation

However much can be done through written exchange in the clarification process, there will come a point where you need to negotiate with a bidder face to face. This is a good time to remember that the bidder across the table today is going to be the contractor across the table tomorrow.

The tender process is the first step in building a relationship with the successful contractor. Even though there will be personnel changes on both sides over the life of the contract, and you personally may not be planning on continuing involvement after the contract has been established, the way you conduct the negotiations will be remembered and will colour the way the parties do business. The openness and trust that allow people to resolve issues without going to court don't appear out of nowhere. Start now. You are negotiating a relationship, not just a contract.

If you are conducting negotiations with two bidders, one of them will not become the contractor, but this shouldn't change your approach, even when you've reached the stage of being pretty sure which one it is. You may not be having a relationship with the losing bidder over many years, but it is the losing bidder who will think hard about whether to challenge the award of contract. Your professionalism in the negotiation will be one of the factors influencing that decision.

How should you conduct the negotiation? Three simple ground rules:

1. *Be prepared.* Remember, the longer negotiations continue, the worse off you will be. You have the mark-up from the bidders, so you know what the issues are before you start. Don't waste that knowledge. If you developed the contract properly, you should already know why each clause in the contract is there. If the clause is going to be contested, think of other ways you might achieve the same outcome. Think of other ways to achieve the outcome the bidder wants: win–win is always better than win–lose. Canvas the options with your stakeholders in advance so you don't have to hold up negotiations while you seek authority to agree changes.

2. *Be courteous.* You're not here to score points, you're here to reach agreement. Even if the strength of your negotiating position gives you the freedom to be a bastard, don't do it. Goodwill is an asset in any negotiation. Listen when other people are talking. Listening to what the other party has to say is the essence of courtesy and has the added advantage that you learn things you need to know. Plus, if your mouth is closed you can't put your foot in it.

3. *Be confident.* Speak calmly, breathe normally, don't constantly fiddle with your pen or some other prop. Many negotiators will see weakness as an invitation to go for the jugular, so don't announce your vulnerability. If you are not confident in your own negotiating skills, you can leave most of the talking to the lawyers – follow their lead. Confidence comes from practice and preparation. Do both.

Setting a Timetable for Negotiation

One of the problems with negotiation is that amendments breed amendments. When any matter is open to negotiation, other matters will sneak in. Bidders asked to discuss one issue will take the opportunity to raise another. A lawyer who focuses on a clause for the purpose of amending just one element will almost certainly notice other ways in which the clause could be improved, even if they were the lawyer who drafted it in the first place. Too much of this sort of thing and it feels as if you are stuffing cats in a bag: every time you open the bag to put in a cat, one of the others escapes again. At some point you have to pull the drawstring tight and stop chasing cats.

One of the ways to deal with this is to set a clear timetable for the negotiation. For example: 'We will set aside three afternoons for negotiation next week between 2pm and 6pm on Tuesday, Wednesday and Thursday. Session one will cover technical issues, session two will cover the performance and default regimes, session three will deal with everything else. The revised contract will be reissued on Friday afternoon and you will have until close the following Monday to send through any corrections (no new issues will be considered). The lawyers will then print up the contract for signature on the Friday.'

The timetable needs to be tight but realistic, so your ability to compress matters into a few days will depend on the number of issues outstanding. If the issues are about finalising drafting, it can save a lot of time to have the contract projected on a screen and amend it as you go. If the issues are ones of principle, you are better off focusing on the principle and letting the lawyers go away afterwards to draft up the appropriate clause with time enough to think the drafting through.

To make such a timetable work, both parties need to have sufficient authority to negotiate. You will make no progress if you or the other party has to go away to seek instructions every time a minor change is suggested. It is inevitable that formal approvals on either side will not be able to be given until the documentation is complete, but the people sitting around the negotiating table need to be confident that what they agree in the meeting will be formally ratified without amendment.

If you behave as if the timetable is unimportant, so will the bidder, and negotiations will drag on and on.

Once you have issued a timetable, do everything you can to stick to it – if you behave as if the timetable is unimportant, so will the bidder, and negotiations will drag on and on. Turn up at each meeting on time and fully prepared, with any necessary subject matter experts on hand. Do not allow people to ramble and waste time. Once an issue is settled, stop discussing it and don't revisit it. If the bidder concedes the point after your first sentence, there is no need to deliver the whole of your brilliantly persuasive speech, even if you did spend half the previous evening preparing it. If opposing technical experts embark on a long discussion that no one else understands, send them off to a separate room to sort the matter out, with a lawyer to help them capture the words for the contract and, if required, prevent them from throttling one another in their professional enthusiasm.

Sometimes you may need several teams of negotiators dealing with different areas. This can save a lot of time, but introduces the risk that the documentation may not be properly aligned. Make sure the teams each have a clear remit and sit down with them after each session to make sure you both understand the commercial implications of agreed changes.

The World's Greatest Negotiating Tactic

Many books have been written on the art of negotiation. Negotiators use a wide range of different tactics, not all of which are appropriate for a Government to adopt in the context of commercial negotiations. If you do a lot of negotiation, you will over time be subjected to just about every negotiating tactic ever invented (although hopefully not ones involving threats of physical harm). The more tactics you know, the better prepared you will be to cope when someone else uses them on you, but in my experience you can be remarkably successful knowing just one.

> *The single most effective phrase you can ever use in a negotiation is, 'Let me play that back to you.'*

The single most effective phrase you can ever use in a negotiation is, 'Let me play that back to you.' Use it. Use it every time the other party asks something of you or states a position.

Do not fear this could make you sound like a broken record. Even if it does, it is too important to set aside for that reason. If you don't want to sound quite so repetitive, come up with variant phrases. 'Let me check I heard that correctly.' 'So what you are saying is …' 'May I just see if I have understood you?' 'So your position is …' 'I think I know where you're coming from, but let me check.'

This simple approach has amazing benefits:

- If you know you are going to summarise the other person's words back to them, you are more likely to listen carefully to what they say. This will generate goodwill that you are bound to need sooner or later.

- If you are listening carefully, you are more likely to understand what they have said, which is critical to achieving the genuine 'meeting of minds' that a good contract represents.

- If you have not understood, you will find out immediately, eliminating the fruitless and acrimonious contests generated between parties taking aggressive stances about things the other party never said in the first place.

- If you have understood, but need to negotiate a different position, the other party will know you are disagreeing with them because your position is genuinely different, rather than assuming it was because you didn't understand what they said. This saves time and makes them much more likely to listen to you.

Regular use of that one simple tactic will make you one of the most effective negotiators in the business.

Hold Your 'No's

The other benefit of using the playback technique is that you never have to respond with an immediate 'no'. If you are not capable of saying 'no' you will make a terrible negotiator, but if you say it all the time you are probably not much better.

What you are trying to do is to persuade the other party to agree to your preferred position, or something acceptably close to it. Sometimes people will agree to things manifestly against their own interests because their negotiating position is so poor they think they have no choice, but you don't want either party to feel that way if you can avoid it. Your contract is so big the parties will be in an ongoing relationship for years: burdening the relationship with resentments will do no one any favours. The objective is not for you to say 'no', but for them to say 'yes'.

The objective is not for you to say 'no', but for them to say 'yes'.

One question I find useful when faced with a demand for a completely unacceptable clause is: 'What is the evil you are trying to address?' This helps you gauge how important the clause is to them: if they struggle to answer at all, the clause is probably there simply because the bidder's lawyers have it in their standard form – you can help them discover they are less attached to it than they first thought. If they do have a legitimate concern, you can then say, 'Okay, that's pretty evil,' which acknowledges their problem without accepting their solution, then follow up with, 'Can we deal with it some other way?' or, if applicable, 'I think you are already covered off against that risk in another clause.'

If the bidder has prepared their bid on the basis of a change in the contract that you will not agree to, they have a problem. If they stick to their position, so do you. Since the bid was predicated on you making the change, you can't accept the bid, which may leave you nowhere to go. Solving your problem means solving theirs as well. Sometimes the difficulty is simply that your explanation of your refusal doesn't give the person in front of you enough to satisfy their boss back in the office. Think up a better explanation. So long as they have a problem, you do too. A flat 'no' rarely solves it. Find a solution and the deal is done.

Negotiation by Media Release

Politicians can make or break a commercial negotiation for Government.

Politicians can make or break a commercial negotiation for Government. Usually they do neither. Allegations of corruption are politically damaging, so the better politicians stay out of the way of Government contracts lest they be seen to favour one bidder over another. In the case of a mega-project, they can't stay out of the way altogether. The amount of money involved is such that no Government agency has the delegation to award the contract without the authorisation of at least a Minister, and quite likely not without the authorisation of the entire Cabinet.

On the whole, it is simplest for you and safest for them if Ministers keep out of things until there is a recommendation on which they can base their decision. (Photo opportunities unaccompanied by controversial statements are normally harmless.) Occasionally, however, politicians can be helpful in setting a climate for negotiations. Statements to the effect that they are pleased to have two bidders of such excellent quality may encourage tenderers to be more reasonable in the negotiation than if they thought they were a clear front runner. Statements about being determined there should be no delay may encourage tenderers to believe that compliance with your timetable is genuinely important. If you have good relations with the Minister's Office, you can feed the Minister with lines that would be useful to you, or encourage them to keep out of the way.

Unfortunately, statements from politicians will not always work in your favour, particularly when you have no input into their content. On one negotiation I led, the politicians chose to announce the procurement as a done deal even though we had barely started negotiating a contract with the only supplier in the market. The supplier gleefully realised it was now politically impossible for Government to walk away from the deal and demanded concession after concession. Luckily for me, they became so carried away they demanded Government should indemnify the contractor against the possibility of the contractor's own employees committing fraud against the Government.

This was so manifestly unreasonable I was able to display shock and horror and throw them out of the meeting before they could retract it. They ever afterwards referred to this as my 'McEnroe moment'. ('You can NOT be serious!') With the assistance of the Government's lawyers, I immediately drafted a letter from my chief executive to the contractor, complaining they were not approaching the negotiations in a proper spirit, then dashed off to get the letter signed and delivered before the contractor's negotiating team could react. We were able to resume negotiations within a couple of days, with matters proceeding on a much more reasonable basis, and the contract was ultimately very successful. But the statement from the politicians was no help at all.

Deal Fever – the Dark Side of Competition

Deal fever is a dangerous illness.

Deal fever is a dangerous illness. It is very easy to get carried away in a negotiation. Have you ever wondered why auctioneers don't just announce what the reserve price is before people start bidding? Deal fever. Start people bidding down in their comfort zone, and the excitement of competition will push the price up and up and up. If you tell them what the reserve is while they are still calm enough to notice the price is too high, they won't bid at all.

When you are auctioning a work of art, it's only the bidders who have to worry about deal fever. When you are letting a major contract, you participate in the competition, so you have to worry about it too. Twice.

Once is because you may be the one infected. Keep on your guard. Just because the tenderer asks for a concession, that doesn't mean you have to give it. Just because a single concession is small, that doesn't mean the cumulative effect of a number of concessions can't be large. The best inoculation against deal fever is preparation. Think beforehand what you are and are not prepared to concede and don't go beyond the parameters you have set without calling for a break first. Make a habit of stepping back at regular intervals to review whether things are still on track.

Twice is because bidders infected by deal fever can cause even more damage than you can. You have not invested all the time and effort that goes into setting up a mega-project in order to have the contractor go bust before you have time to sneeze. Don't think it can't happen. For the Olympics, Sydney built the Airport Link, a new railway line between the airport and the city, with the stations constructed under a Public Private Partnership. In their enthusiasm, Government and contractor were carried away by optimistic demand forecasts, allowing the contractor to promise returns it could not possibly deliver.

The stations opened in May 2000 and the contractor was in receivership by Christmas. Happy New Year. Not.

If the risk is greater than the contractor can bear, it will come bouncing straight back to Government.

It may go against the grain to ask a bidder whether they have taken into account the cost of some factor that does not appear on the face of their bid, since they will inevitably seek to adjust their price upwards if it turns out they haven't. But the alternative is worse. If you sign up to a contract that is undeliverable from day one, pain and suffering will follow. The bigger the contract, the greater the pain and suffering. Government's pain and suffering. Never mind that the contract allocates the risk to the contractor: if the risk is greater than the contractor can bear, it will come bouncing straight back to Government.

You achieve the best outcomes in a negotiation when you can maintain a healthy competition between the bidders. Healthy, not feverish. Inoculate yourself against deal fever by preparing thoroughly. Protect the bidders against it by challenging anything you don't understand. A fair contract is one where the contractor can make a profit if they perform well. An unfair contract is a swine to manage and is likely to be riddled with disputes – that holds true even if the deal-fevered bidder brought the unfairness on themselves by offering more than they could afford to give.

Doing the Deal

Whether or not you have managed to stick to your timetable, there will come a point where it is more important to pull the drawstring and settle the contract than it is to stuff the last cat into the bag. No contract on this scale can be perfect. Once you have done enough to get value for money, the law of diminishing returns kicks in and there is a limit to how much benefit you can derive from polishing the stone. Worse, the longer the negotiation goes on, the more concessions you will make.

Recognise, too, that your mega-project is not the only game in town. As a young negotiator in the private sector, I was once very annoyed with a chief executive who insisted I close a deal with Government when there was still around £20 million on the table. It was only later I realised he had another deal with Government going on that was worth billions: the share of the £20 million I might have been able to negotiate was worthless when set against the goodwill generated by closing my deal on relatively generous terms. Government's responsibilities are vast – however big your mega-project, you cannot hold centre stage forever. Get on with it and get the deal done.

But before you pull the drawstring, pause. Think. Hold one final meeting with your advisers and check again that the essentials are all in place. Confirm with the executives who will be responsible for delivering Government's obligations that you have not inadvertently promised something they could not deliver. Once the contract has been signed, it is too late to discover you can't live without that last cat.

Chapter 17

Bullet-Proofing the Selection Decision

Remember the Swiss cheese model from Figure 5.2 in Chapter 5? The defensive walls to stop the bullets, walls with holes that grow when neglected, until finally the holes line up and the bullet with your name on it zaps all the way through? You have a selection decision to protect. It's time to go round filling in the holes.

Selection decisions on a mega-project are made at the political level, by a Minister or Cabinet or Cabinet Committee, or sometimes by a local Government body. Decisions are normally made on the basis of a report and recommendations from the Agency. The governance arrangements may include a requirement for the report and recommendations to be endorsed by a third party.

Although you end up with only one contractor, more than one decision will be required during the procurement. The number will depend on your process, but it would be common to need approval for the selection of the shortlist, approval to commence negotiations with one or more preferred bidders, and approval to enter into the contract. Approvals may also be necessary when you wish to do something permitted but not required by the original process, perhaps if you wish to recommend that bidders be given the opportunity to revise their pricing (often called a BAFO – Best and Final Offer). Depending on the applicable delegated authority and governance requirements, all these decisions may need to go to the political level, or one or more may be able to be made within the Agency, usually by the Board.

A selection decision can be considered bullet-proof if there exists no ground on which it can be successfully challenged. Whether it relates to the final award of contract or to an intermediate stage, a bullet-proof selection decision has the following characteristics:

> *A selection decision can be considered bullet-proof if there exists no ground on which it can be successfully challenged.*

- the evaluation report itself is bullet-proof;
- the recommendations are supported by the report;
- the endorsements are unqualified;
- the decision is made in accordance with the recommendations.

The bullet-proof evaluation report is only the first step: while it will be the step over which you have the most control, it is not enough to write a good report and hope for the best. As project director, there are levers available to you. Use them.

Bullet-Proofing the Evaluation Report

In Chapter 15 we looked at an evaluation structure involving an Evaluation Committee of senior and experienced people relying on detailed reports from experts in various fields, generally split into three areas, financial, legal/commercial and technical. The report structure should follow the evaluation structure, as shown in Figure 17.1: this ensures there are no gaps and also allows a clear view of what evidence supports the conclusions in the report.

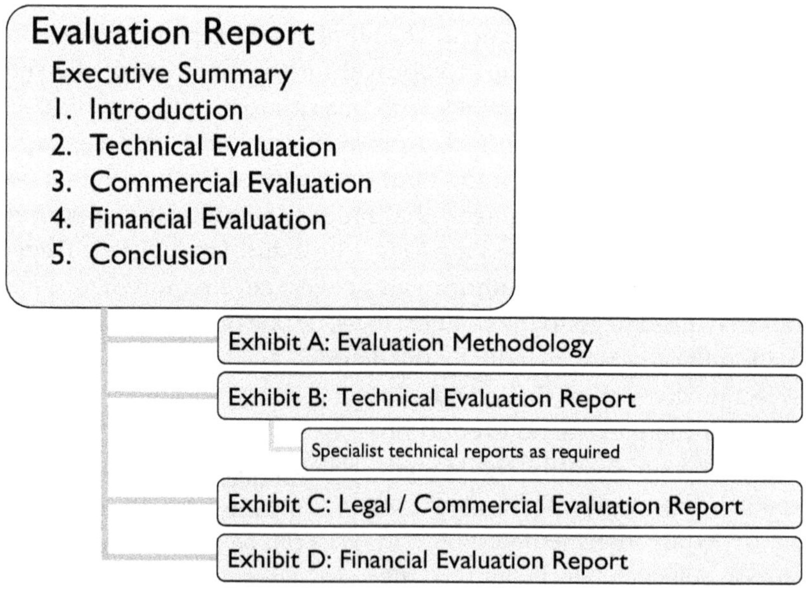

Figure 17.1 Evaluation report structure

Using this structure, each subcommittee that supports the Evaluation Committee produces its own report for submission to and acceptance by the Evaluation Committee. Set the report formats in advance and give yourself a break. If you plan it well, the executive summaries of the various subcommittee reports can be dragged and dropped into the relevant sections of the evaluation report almost without amendment: consistency beats originality, even if it does feel like cheating.

READ REPORTS IN DRAFT

As with advice from consultants, these reports should always be submitted first in draft form. People close to the raw bid material can't always step back and see the inconsistencies within their own area and may not have the opportunity to see cross-disciplinary inconsistencies. Why is a bidder who claims a product failure rate of one per hundred thousand accepting a performance regime demanding a failure rate of one per million? Spot this kind of thing while a report is still in draft.

People close to the raw bid material can't always step back and see the inconsistencies.

The Minister may only ever read the executive summary of the evaluation report, but if a decision is called into question every building block in the evaluation structure will be examined. Do not put yourself in the position of having relied upon a manifestly sub-standard report from your experts. Send poor drafts back for a re-write, but make it clear whether you are challenging the conclusions or merely the drafting. An Evaluation Committee full of senior people can be unintentionally intimidating. A chief financial officer who asks, 'When scoring against this criterion, did you take account of the fact that Bidder A has more of factor X than Bidder B?' may simply want to know. An evaluator hearing the question is quite likely to interpret it to mean the CFO wants them to adjust the scores to give greater weight to factor X: A 'helpful' evaluator may adjust the score when no change is justified and a belligerent evaluator may claim they are being bullied. Take care: you are supposed to be rendering the report bullet-proof, not manufacturing ammunition.

If something comes up after one of the reports has already been signed off, do not add a supplementary report. Have the additional material considered in its proper context by the original evaluators, keep a minute recording this has been done, and reissue the original report with any necessary amendments. As before, issue it in draft first. This is more trouble than a supplementary report, but normally well worth doing. Considering new material in isolation gives it a prominence it may not deserve.

RELIANCE ON EVALUATORS

The Evaluation Committee relies on the reports presented to it. That means it is also relying on the people who sign off on those reports. Check with individual evaluators to confirm they have had enough time and access to documents to complete their evaluation and aren't feeling unfairly pressured.

Their remarks will get back to the losing bidders long before the expiry of any statute of limitations relating to the procurement process.

Evaluators are conscious of confidentiality issues and will normally not say anything about the bids. Their personal experience of the evaluation process does not strike them as similarly confidential and as soon as the contract is awarded they will feel free to talk about it. Their remarks will get back to the losing bidders long before the expiry of any statute of limitations relating to the procurement process. The evaluators may say, 'The Agency was really concerned to do things right, the project director asked me personally whether I was satisfied with the report.' Or they may say, 'They pressured me to sign off the report without giving me a chance to look at the material properly, I felt really uncomfortable about it.' Your choice.

CODE NAMES

The code names you used for the bidders during the evaluation should also be used for the evaluation reports. This is to maintain confidentiality rather than as a protection against bias: many copies will be made of an evaluation report that goes to a Board or to Cabinet and even Cabinet security is not absolute. There may also be some protection against bias in the final decision-making: those carrying out the evaluation will either have known from the beginning or will have worked out who is who, but the identities matching the code names may not be known to those in the approvals chain.

EXHIBITS V. ATTACHMENTS

The evaluation report should include a statement that the report has been prepared in accordance with the evaluation methodology, and it should acknowledge that the Evaluation Committee has relied upon the various other reports. Practice varies as to whether the methodology and the other reports are considered to form part of the evaluation report or not. I prefer the evaluation report to stand alone, which is why Figure 17.1 refers to the other items as 'exhibits' rather than 'annexes' or 'appendices' or 'schedules'. (All these words are sometimes used interchangeably, which is unhelpful.)

The politically correct reason to exclude the additional material is that if the methodology and reports are considered to form part of the evaluation report, they must be attached to it and included in the approval submission. If the report is going all the way to a full Cabinet meeting, this represents an ecologically unsound quantity of dead trees.

The politically incorrect reason is that it is a rare approvals chain that does not contain at least one dangerous lunatic. Even normally sane persons have been known to take on lunatic tendencies when confronted with an evaluation report for a mega-project. The selection decision is a heavy and often unaccustomed responsibility. When a nervous approvals body is presented with more information than is strictly necessary, a minor matter of no particular consequence can assume grotesque proportions.

Part of the job of the evaluation report is to filter out what is irrelevant or misleading or unimportant so the decision can be made on proper grounds. The more information you include, the less effective the filter.

The Air Traffic Control System case, far from demonstrating how to deflect bullets, offered a staggering variety of ways to shoot yourself in the foot, including an example of the provision of inappropriate information. The Board was provided with a table showing the relative numbers of source lines of code in competing software development proposals: it became, quite unjustifiably, the single factor determining the selection of a preferred bidder. In that instance the directors were let down by those presenting the information, who claimed the numbers were comparable and the differences significant, despite the existence (unknown to the directors) of an expert's report saying this was not necessarily the case. But directors not being misled by someone else are more than capable of misleading themselves if presented with information beyond their expertise. Keep the evaluation report clean and clear. You are disclosing the existence of the other reports, so if anyone does want to see them, they can ask.

Directors not being misled by someone else are more than capable of misleading themselves.

MODELS AND SPREADSHEETS

All financial models and scoring spreadsheets used in the evaluation should be checked by an independent third party. For the spreadsheets, a simple check that the numbers are correctly calculated is probably sufficient. For financial models you may need more. In the InterCity West Coast franchise case for instance, the model used to calculate the subordinated loan facility contained a number of flaws: the outputs were mistakenly assumed not to have been adjusted for inflation and the inflation assumptions did not match the contract. These flaws could have been picked up by a third party review. However, a simple check of the calculations would not have dealt with the more fundamental issue, which was that the model was not fit for purpose.

The extent of the checks and audits you need will depend on the reliance you are placing on the models and spreadsheets. But you will seriously embarrass yourself and others if you recommend the wrong bidder because of an arithmetical error.

THE BIDDER'S EYE

As a final check, pretend you are the losing bidder and look at the draft evaluation report from their point of view. Even better, pretend you are the losing bidder's lawyer. Why was the other bidder preferred? Does this gap in the chain of logic indicate an evaluation error? How could someone with our terrific score for widget quality possibly fail to win the contract? Why is there no mention of the key features of our proposal? What evidence is there for saying our bid is more risky? Are the evaluation criteria exactly as they were published to the bidders?

> *If it doesn't contain an explanation you would feel comfortable presenting to the losing bidder, the evaluation report is not adequate.*

Although the bidders won't normally see the evaluation report, you will have to de-brief the losers and explain why they lost. If it doesn't contain an explanation you would feel comfortable presenting to the losing bidder, the evaluation report is not adequate. Bid teams are the sales division of contracting firms and if there is one thing the best sales professionals are good at it is reading body language. If you aren't convinced by the explanation, they won't be either.

Making the Right Recommendations

At the final point in the process, the recommendation is unequivocal: approve the entry into *this* contract with *this* bidder. Recommendations at intermediate stages normally involve not only a selection decision (eliminate Bidder A) but also a process decision (conduct negotiations or perhaps design development with Bidders B and C, then seek final pricing). All recommendations should be reasonable having regard to the evaluation report.

While you should always ensure the report supports the recommendation you want to make, it is pointless and potentially dangerous to do so by making the report itself misleading. At the first shortlisting stage in the Air Traffic

Control System case, a recommendation was made to retain three rather than two bidders, possibly influenced by prices which had been requested at this initial stage notwithstanding the absence of defined commercial terms. A table showing the relative ratings of the bidders in specific areas would have shown clearly that the third bidder had no chance, but this was omitted from the report. The recommendation was accepted, further submissions were requested from the three bidders, and ten wasted weeks later the third bidder was eliminated. If a properly prepared report does not support your recommendation, change the recommendation.

If a properly prepared report does not support your recommendation, change the recommendation.

The recommendations will often be contained within the evaluation report itself, but not necessarily. Sometimes an approving body will want to form its own view without benefit of recommendations from the Evaluation Committee, perhaps on the basis they are afraid the committee will recommend something they don't want. There are two situations where this may happen. One is where the Agency Board wants the recommendation to the Minister to be seen to come from them rather than the Evaluation Committee. This is straightforward: you present the completed evaluation report to the Board for approval. If you don't trust the Board to come up with the right recommendations, and even if you do, prepare some helpful drafts for the chair or chief executive to offer the Board. The other situation is where the choice of bidder also involves a threshold strategic decision of some kind such as a choice of technology, where a bid evaluation committee is really not the appropriate body to be making the recommendation. Ideally you would have managed to separate out the strategic decision from the bidder selection decision before calling for tenders. If you haven't, you have a very tricky bit of drafting ahead of you. Crafting a report to support a recommendation is relatively straightforward. Crafting a report capable of being relied upon to support either of two separate but opposing outcomes is a challenge.

Securing Unqualified Endorsements

There are three separate categories of endorsement that may be required by an approving body:

1. *Process endorsement*: independent sign off that the procurement process has been properly conducted.

2. *Stakeholder endorsement*: sign off from key stakeholders such as Treasury that they support the recommendation.

3. *Approver endorsement*: sign off from another approving body (such as the Agency Board) further down the approvals chain.

In all cases, the way to secure unqualified endorsement is to lay the groundwork well in advance. This has to be balanced against the need to keep the evaluation confidential. The longer the approvals process goes on, the harder it is to maintain confidentiality. You will need to demonstrate some impressive scheduling capability to line up meetings and signatories to move the paperwork from one end of the chain to the other in the minimum time frame.

PROCESS ENDORSEMENT

As a matter of good governance, an approving body should seek assurance that proper process has been followed before giving an approval.

As a matter of good governance, an approving body should seek assurance that proper process has been followed before giving an approval. The extent of the assurance required depends on local custom and practice and whether there have been any embarrassing process fiascos recently. Establish the requirements early so you can arrange for the assurance to be in place. The minimum is a statement in the evaluation report that proper process has been followed. This hardly constitutes independent assurance, but in the UK is often regarded as sufficient. The presence of an independent person on the Evaluation Committee who signs off on the report can give additional comfort, as can endorsement from a steering committee which has been monitoring the process.

An additional measure, usually required in Australian jurisdictions, is to appoint an independent person or firm to carry out an audit (in Australia referred to as a probity audit) to confirm the established process has been followed. This could have saved the procurement process in the InterCity West Coast franchise case, where the UK Department for Transport failed to comply with the process notified to bidders for the calculation of the amount of a subordinated loan facility. The lawyers had raised a concern about the process, which, because in their view the decision had already been made, they thought it would be 'unhelpful' to pursue. Had they or a third party been asked for a certificate to evidence the process had been followed, the certificate could not have been provided and the problem would have been dealt with.

If a process audit is required, it is essential to appoint the auditor early in the procurement process, so all steps are verified as you go along. Any process deviations or conflicts of interest can be picked up and 'cured' before they become serious enough to require the audit report to be qualified. This approach enables a clean and full audit report to be produced within 24 hours when the moment arrives.

STAKEHOLDER ENDORSEMENT

Stakeholder endorsement is usually more problematic than process endorsement. A process auditor is a professional doing a job. Follow the process and they will certify you have done so. A stakeholder is a lobbyist with a cause.

Establish as early as you can which stakeholders are the ones whose endorsement will be required. The fewer the better, but mega-projects tend to have impacts right across Government so it is virtually impossible to escape without any at all. If you have adopted a governance structure along the lines of the one described in Chapter 12 (see Figure 12.2), the best approach is usually to corral all your stakeholders onto either the internal or external steering committee: the internal steering committee endorses the report to the Board and the external steering committee endorses it to the politicians. Obtaining stakeholder endorsement then becomes largely a matter of committee management.

Be clear on the nature of the endorsement required. The stakeholders on your steering committee may only be providing assurance of process, or they may also be required to endorse the merits of the recommendation. The latter requires you to give them much more confidential information. This is an issue because all steering committees leak.

Sometimes 'leaks' take the form of legitimate confidential briefings. The Treasury representative will brief the Treasurer on progress, the Minister's representative will brief the Minister. So long as your committee members are persons of experience and discretion, this will do no harm and will smooth your way when it comes to the time for approvals. Indiscreet leaks are dangerous. Assume your steering committee is indiscreet, although don't be so crass as to accuse anyone. (If there is a particular issue, raise it off line with the chair of the committee and let them handle it.) Manage the risk by limiting the amount of sensitive information that is provided. You can often have a very useful discussion around purely hypothetical questions, for instance. Even where endorsement of the merits of a recommendation will be required, it is generally helpful to keep most of the

Assume your steering committee is indiscreet, although don't be so crass as to accuse anyone.

focus on process until the day comes for the endorsement. This is, after all, the public sector, where following a process is considered inherently meritorious. A committee that over a series of meetings has become comfortable about the process followed to arrive at a recommendation is more likely to feel comfortable with the recommendation itself.

Your key objective is to secure unanimous endorsement. Any dissent offers a potential avenue for challenge. While you should never embrace stupidity to secure consensus, consensus is valuable. There is usually at least some vestige of merit in a dissenter's view: acknowledge and accept the merit and the dissenter may cease to dissent.

APPROVER ENDORSEMENT

The usual intermediate approving body is the Agency Board, although in some circumstances there may be others. The key difference between securing approval from the Board and securing endorsement from a steering committee is that the steering committee exists only for the purpose of your project. The Board has other things on its mind. One of the difficulties faced by the project team in the InterCity West Coast franchise case was that it was 2012. Their franchise may have been worth £5.5 billion, but the Department for Transport was also dealing with the Aviation and Road Strategy, High Speed 2, Thameslink and Crossrail. Plus the London Olympics. The contract award decision that was eventually overturned by the Secretary of State was not even considered by the full Board, but only by a committee that did not have properly constituted terms of reference.

Never spring a surprise on the chair at a Board meeting: you will antagonise your best ally.

Negotiate with your chief executive and the chair as required to give you sufficient air time with the Board and agree with them what you will say. Never spring a surprise on the chair at a Board meeting: you will antagonise your best ally. A good chair knows the strengths and weaknesses of the Board: what will reassure them, what will spook them, what will send them off on a tangent. Take their advice on how to proceed.

It is usually a good idea to take a warm-up slot on the agenda at the Board meeting before the one at which the Board will have to approve the recommendations. Directors are subject to onerous duties and responsibilities under company law. Even in those cases where the statutory constitution of a Government agency excludes or exempts directors from liability under company law, there is still a huge loss of face involved in having given your blessing to a fiasco in the making. Unless your Agency considers mega-projects routine, you are facing up to a bunch of people in states ranging from mildly agitated to starkly terrified by the potential personal liability and loss of face associated with bungling a multi-billion dollar decision.

Your role is to provide reassurance. Explain to the Board the process you have followed, emphasising any elements of independent review. Explain the nature of the decision that will be facing them at the next meeting and, if this is an intermediate stage, where the decision fits in the overall process. Tell them when they can expect to receive the Board papers and the nature of the information they will receive. If this is the final award decision, the papers should include confirmation from the executives who will be responsible for delivering the Government obligations under the contract that they are able to deliver those obligations. If the evaluation report will be based on other reports you do not intend to include with the Board papers, reassure them that a copy of each report will be available at the meeting and that the key advisers and evaluators will be available if the Board want to question them. Listen to any specific issues they may raise: at this point the evaluation report is not yet complete, so you have the opportunity to ensure any areas the Board are particularly concerned about will be adequately covered in the report.

With this level of warm-up, there is a good chance the Board will approve the report and recommendations at the next meeting without too much drama. Just be careful how you present the papers to the Board. In the Air Traffic Control System case, the evaluation report with the initial preferred bidder recommendation was accompanied by a note with comments from the chief executive. Although the note did support the recommendation, it drew attention to the risks of the proposal from the recommended bidder but failed to point out that the risks had already been taken account of in the evaluation report and recommendation. The recommendation was rejected and the undue focus on the risks of that proposal so coloured the subsequent process that the eventual decision recommending a different bidder was overturned after the Minister directed an inquiry. The procurement process had to be rerun with only the two remaining shortlisted bidders participating.

With this level of warm-up, there is a good chance the Board will approve the report and recommendations at the next meeting without too much drama.

Recommendations Accepted

Your personal participation may or may not be required for the final step. Cabinet sometimes prefers to do everything behind closed doors and sometimes wants to grill the project director on every detail. When the 27 councillors of Brisbane City Council determined the award of the contract for the $3 billion CLEM7 tollway project, everyone went into sequestration for about three days while the evaluation findings were presented and debated.

If you have managed to line up a bullet-proof evaluation report with your recommendations supported by all required endorsements and subsidiary approvals, the final step is usually a doddle. If there are loose ends that are not expected to be problematic, such as completion of the last details of the contract, Cabinet will normally delegate responsibility for final approval to the Minister, or perhaps to Minister and Treasurer if private finance is involved: unless something goes wrong, this will be a purely administrative matter.

A doddle is not guaranteed. Rejection of recommendations is by no means unknown. It may just mean further information will be required or it may mean Cabinet really has decided to do something different. This is not necessarily fatal to the procurement process, although you will no doubt feel a trifle annoyed. Suppress your annoyance. You are not the decision-maker. The decision-maker must have adequate reasons for doing something different from your recommendations, but if they have, they can.

The decision may be more vulnerable to challenge, since it will not be tenderly wrapped in a carefully documented consensus stretching from the evaluators all the way to the decision-maker, but it is not automatically doomed. There will still be things you can do to protect the decision. Being bullet-proof is good. Not being shot at is even better.

Being bullet-proof is good. Not being shot at is even better.

Pacifying the Losing Bidders

The losing bidders are never going to be happy with the selection decision. There are only so many mega-project contracts available, they have just missed out on one of them and they are millions out of pocket. Happiness doesn't enter into it.

That does not mean they will challenge the decision. Provided you and your Minister have not given them reason to expect that you will pay them to go away regardless of the merits of the case, they are only likely to challenge it if:

- they think the reasons for the decision are not plausible;
- they believe they have real grounds for challenge; or

- they are so thoroughly outraged by the decision that they will challenge it regardless.

Since you will have set things up to allow no valid ground for challenge, whether or not you are taken to court anyway will depend on how well you communicate the decision to the losing bidders.

COMMUNICATING THE DECISION

Communicating the decision should be done in three stages. The first is a telephone call from you to the bid manager, made as close as possible to the public announcement. This is a simple courtesy call, to make sure they are not embarrassed by missing the announcement. Give them the result, but do not offer any explanation. Thank them for their participation and advise them you will email the media release immediately and be in touch shortly to set up a full de-brief. Then get off the phone. The losing bid managers have other people to notify as a matter of urgency and may also have tears to shed or furniture to smash. Give them space to deal with that.

> *The losing bid managers have other people to notify as a matter of urgency and may also have tears to shed or furniture to smash.*

The second stage is the media release. The announcement will normally come from the office of the Minister or the Prime Minister, which means you may or may not be offered any say in its drafting. Releases are often mostly puffery so the content may not matter too much. One possible flashpoint is the statement of the value of the contract (on a mega-project this is a huge and highly announceable number so there is no way it will be omitted from the media release). Depending on how the value is calculated, it may appear to the losing bidder that their price was significantly lower, which will immediately pre-dispose them towards a challenge. If the headline number is likely to have this effect, be prepared to move to the full de-brief very quickly, so the bidder has their explanation before they have had a chance to work themselves up into a state of indignation.

It is helpful if at least some of the things the media release praises the winning bidder for are things where they clearly scored better than the losing bidders. To accept the decision without challenge, particularly if they didn't see it coming, the losers need an explanation of it that makes sense to them. They will not make sense of a decision that appears to be based on factors where they know they are better than the opposition.

The third and most important stage is the full de-brief of the losing bidders. Set this up as soon as possible: the longer you delay telling them why they lost, the more suspicious they will be of the decision, particularly if the media release didn't offer them anything plausible. The de-brief should be done as a meeting, not a phone call. Do not under any circumstances go alone. Have a third party present – a process auditor or lawyer – and record the meeting.

Be prepared. This is not just a matter of reading from a script: the bidders will ask questions. You need to give good answers. That doesn't mean bidders have to be told everything they want to know, but you need to communicate to them your absolute confidence in the decision. If you are not confident, they will notice. In the InterCity West Coast franchise case, the project team had decided not to release to bidders the model used for calculation of the subordinated loan facility because they were concerned it could be challenged. That was not, of course, what they told the bidders, but the message got across anyway. The Laidlaw Inquiry quoted a note made by the losing bidder of a meeting with the project director: 'Eventually, after MUCH more debate and probing, I believe I got to the heart of the matter. Whilst it was presented less obviously, he was effectively telling me that they COULD NOT contemplate releasing their stress-test model because it is very basic and would be open to challenge.'

Anticipate their questions and have good answers ready. Do not lie.

You need not and should not allow 'debate and probing'. The decision has been made, it is not up for debate. Nonetheless, the losing bidder is entitled to know the reasons for the decision and it is very much in Government's interests that they should find the reasons convincing. Anticipate their questions and have good answers ready. Do not lie. In the Portcullis House case an official gave the losing bidder false reasons for the decision, achieving nothing except to add the tort of misfeasance in public office to the defendant's list of transgressions.

This is also your last opportunity to put final touches to the bullet-proofing by adding to your trail of evidence that you followed the process. Ask the bidder if they have any complaints or concerns: hope they say no and deal with the complaints or concerns if they say yes.

If a challenge is made, your evidence trail is the fastest way to shoot the legs out from under it. On one New South Wales tender, the chief executive of the losing bidder sought an audience with the Minister to complain the process had been unfair. The project director, invited and forewarned by the Minister, reviewed his collection of evidence and brought along a recording of the de-briefing meeting held with the losing bid team. At the psychological moment he played an extract, an exchange with the tenderer's bid manager which went roughly as follows. Question: 'Do you understand why we decided to award the contract to the other party?' Answer: 'Yes we do.' Question: 'Are you satisfied the process was properly conducted?' Answer: 'Yes, we are.' Question: 'Do you have any complaints about the process?' Answer: 'No, we don't.' End of meeting. History does not record what the chief executive later said to his bid manager, but the challenge died in the Minister's office.

Publication of the Contract

These days it is customary to post copies of all major Government contracts on the internet for public scrutiny. Check out the regulations or guidelines applicable to your Agency to find out when the contract must be posted, whether a contract summary document is also required and what information may or must be redacted from the contract before publication.

By the time the contract goes up, the losing bidders have normally moved on to the next tender process and may not bother to look at it. But if they are still feeling edgy, they will scrutinise it for evidence of unfairness: did you offer the winning bidder terms you didn't offer to them? If you have carried out the evaluation and negotiation properly, this should not be an issue. Just stay on the alert and be prepared to squash any sign of trouble in the days after the contract is published.

Don't Forget Your Team

The people most likely to persuade a losing bidder to challenge an award are your own team.

The people most likely to persuade a losing bidder to challenge an award are your own team. If they are unhappy with the decision, if they feel they were pressured into signing off something they didn't really support, if they don't feel confident that right was done, then their feelings will, one way or another, be communicated to the losing bidders. Any sign of unease in Government ranks will feed the will to challenge. Conversely, if your team is enthusiastic about the chosen contractor, proud of their own contribution and confident in the process and in their colleagues, potential challenges will wither for want of encouragement.

In case you hadn't noticed, your team have worked their socks off for months to get this contract awarded. When the announcement is made, bring them all together, recognise their efforts and celebrate the achievement. Prise the chief executive out of the corner office: let the team see their contribution is appreciated at the highest level. They deserve the most recognition you can win for them.

And don't forget the advisers. 'Thank you' is the most under-utilised phrase in the client's vocabulary.

Contract Completion

The winning bidder, who can at least be relied on not to sue you in relation to the procurement process, is at signing transformed into the contractor who may sue you in relation to the contract. Try not to create an instant cause of action by making a mess of completion.

For most mega-projects, signing the contract will not be quite enough to finish the deal: there will be financing to put in place or other conditions precedent to be met. Don't fall at this last hurdle. Everyone has been working long hours to make it as far as exchange of contracts and won't have much in reserve. I know of one completion that had to be put off for two days because a critical member of the bidder's finance team collapsed with exhaustion. There are no prizes for killing people. Take the time you need to get it right.

Completion completed. Congratulations. Completion of the contract marks completion of the set-up phase. From here on, the job is not contract establishment but contract management. For many project directors, this is the time to walk away and hand the contract management to someone else. Do everyone a favour. Make your handover as professional as the set-up itself.

PART V
Finishing in Style

Chapter 18

Handover to Contract Management

With the contract safely signed and the last losing bidder safely de-briefed you are probably feeling pretty satisfied with life. After the rigours of the last months, you may even be able to *have* a life, if you haven't forgotten how.

As always, don't relax entirely. This is a critical time. The project does not yet have any momentum behind it, and three months lost from the schedule now is three months lost. Contingency was put into the schedule for the things that will go wrong later, not to give everyone a chance to put their feet up at the start. There are six key tasks:

Contingency was put into the schedule for the things that will go wrong later, not to give everyone a chance to put their feet up at the start.

1. Transition the administration from the procurement phase.
2. Establish the internal project governance arrangements.
3. Conduct a risk review.
4. Explain the contract to everyone who needs to know.
5. Lay the foundations of the relationship with the contractor.
6. Start building momentum on the project.

I do not claim these to be in order of importance and they certainly are not in order of interest, but any one of them can de-rail the project if neglected.

If you are intending to manage the contract yourself, these tasks will be yours. If you aren't, and if everything has gone according to plan, your successor has been on the team from an early stage, knows it all and is now hoping you will push off as soon as possible so they can have the project director title and a pay rise. But things don't always go according to plan and you may need to hold things together for a while until a contract manager is recruited.

Administration

While you were setting up the contract, your project existed in a little bubble of its own. This was necessary to protect the confidentiality of the tender process, but that process is over. Unless the project has been separately established as its own corporation, and possibly even if it has, you now have to participate fully in the Agency administrative systems. This is either an opportunity to connect with an expanded support system or a descent into mindless bureaucracy.

This is either an opportunity to connect with an expanded support system or a descent into mindless bureaucracy.

ACCOUNTS PAYABLE

The priority task is to sort out invoicing and payments under the contract. Nothing generates ill will faster than failure to pay invoices on time. Even if the first payment to the contractor is some distance off, put the arrangements in place early. You may need to seek the intervention of the chief financial officer, as the payment terms are unlikely to be the Agency standard. Any requirement for sign-offs from Treasury for milestone payments, for instance, may completely paralyse an Agency accounts payable department which depends for its routine functioning on procedures that do not recognise Treasury's existence.

HUMAN RESOURCES

Be less quick to surrender the project team to the jurisdiction of the human resources department. For some things you will have no choice: you will get no plaudits from your team for shielding them from irritating bureaucracy if they are also shielded from such useful things as training programmes and pay rises. But if you have been able to secure any special privileges on the recruitment front, hang onto them. If you need to take on people who are capable of inspecting a new frigate or helicopter during construction and confirming milestone payments have been earned, the recruitment timing needs to be driven by the construction schedule, not by the latest public sector hiring freeze.

TRANSACTION BIBLE

> *You may not be able to avoid arguments about what the words mean, but there is no need to have arguments about what the words* are.

Arrange for your lawyers to produce a 'bible' of the transaction: the definitive version of what everyone signed up to, including a true copy of every single document forming part of the contract. This is essential to ward off future disputes. You may not be able to avoid arguments about what the words mean, but there is no need to have arguments about what the words *are*.

It will also give you some peace of mind. If you are like me you will spend at least six months after the transaction waking up in the middle of the night thinking, 'What about the risk of X? Did we remember to cover that off?' Normally I remember that we did and go straight back to sleep, but sometimes I have to make a note to check it in the morning. Having a definitive version of all of the contract documents, preferably one that is electronically searchable, enables you and your lawyers to track down the answers to such questions very quickly.

FILING

> *Parliaments have wide powers to demand information from Government agencies.*

The National Audit Office will soon be knocking on the door wanting to report on the project and requests under freedom of information legislation will come in about the outrageous sums you spent on consultants. Parliaments have wide powers to demand information from Government agencies. If things get a bit political on the Select Committees there may be little consideration given to the amount of time people from the Agency will have to spend collecting the information, which will be particularly irritating as there is no onus on any member of a Select Committee to read a single document of the van-loads that an indiscriminate request may generate.

The part of your paperwork that related to the bid process itself was, of course, brought fully up to date at the time of obtaining the approvals for award of contract. Your conflict of interests register has no gaps, your evaluation reports and adviser opinions are all safely on file, your minute books are up to date. The rest of it may need a bit of attention. Sort it out before the team scatters to other projects and everyone loses interest entirely.

A project on this scale usually lasts for at least five years and may last for 30. Demands for information about the conduct of the procurement phase may come in immediately, triggered by the award of the contract, or they may arrive much later. Even if the project is going well, a fiasco on a different project may trigger a request for comparative information. Now is the time to make sure all the information likely to be requested can be found quickly, even by someone who wasn't there at the time.

Regulation of Government record-keeping means you will need to retain and archive most of your files. Confirm with your General Counsel what documents you are entitled to destroy, usually drafts and copies, then lead a mission to destroy them. It will be hard enough for someone to find anything in the files five years from now without cluttering the archives with this stuff. It also protects the contract management team against reliance on material that was superseded by the contract.

Clean up the electronic files as well as the paper ones. Close the secure drive you used to store all the evaluation material and archive it away from casual access. Review the access privileges on any ongoing systems being used by the contract management team. You no longer need to be quite so paranoid about people having access to project information, but contract signature triggers changes in personnel and activity that mean your access arrangements from the procurement phase are out of date.

DELEGATIONS

The transition to the contract management phase will change the organisation structure for the project team. If your Agency does not do projects on this scale regularly, the standard delegations framework may not be adequate for the day-to-day running of the project. Check that the contract manager role has enough authority to be able to manage the contract effectively. This does not mean they have to have the delegated authority to do everything the contract manager has the power to do under the contract. For instance, there may be a provision that a notice to the contractor terminating the contract must be signed by the contract manager. There is no way the Agency Board would delegate to a contract manager the authority to make that decision: it will be reserved to the Board or possibly even the Minister. The contract manager signing the notice will merely be the mechanism by which termination is effected.

> *There is no way the Agency Board would delegate to a contract manager the authority to make that decision.*

If the delegations given to the contract manager or other members of the project team are greater than the Agency is accustomed to allow its employees, the governance framework may need to be adjusted to give the appropriate comfort to the Board.

Governance Framework

The governance framework you had in place for the procurement phase may not be appropriate once the contract has been established. You have both an internal and an external steering committee that may or may not be surplus to requirements. The balance will depend on a number of factors.

The first is whether the committee is still needed for the purposes of supporting delegated authority in relation to the project. On something of this scale, the contract manager will not be allowed total control and even the Agency Board's authority may be restricted. It is reasonably likely, for instance, that the Minister will reserve the right to approve any contract variation above a certain threshold. (Variations are the kiss of death to budgets and schedules but it would be foolish to assume you will always be able to avoid them.) The Minister may be willing to accept submissions direct from the Agency, or may require any submission to be endorsed by the external steering committee: if the latter, the external steering committee needs to continue.

Variations are the kiss of death to budgets and schedules.

Another factor is the extent to which there exist other channels of communication for the contract manager to connect with the stakeholders. There may, for instance, be a standing committee of similar composition to monitor the progress of all major projects: once the contract has been signed, the contract manager may be better off delivering project updates through the same channel. If the other projects have significant interfaces with yours, it may be actively counter-productive to maintain a separate committee.

Also important is the amount of attention the project will need from the stakeholders. Part of the reason for establishing the original governance framework was to ensure that you as project director had the access you needed to people critical to the success of the project. Depending on the nature of the project, it may continue to need more attention from those stakeholders than can be achieved through a committee which is dealing with a dozen other major projects as well. Retaining the same committee gives you some assurance that its members have the necessary understanding of a complex contract.

The choice to retain or cull the steering committees will not be yours to make, although you should have significant influence. A steering committee may be torn between reluctance to schedule yet more meetings and reluctance to admit its own irrelevance. If your own view is that the committee is now surplus to requirements, say so tactfully but don't push too hard, lest you arouse suspicion that you are trying to conceal things from the stakeholders. Suggest meetings be held quarterly instead of monthly. If the committee withers away, the contract manager can kill it off later.

The contract manager may well find it more useful to have regular one-on-one meetings with a few of the key stakeholders. Encourage them to put these into the diary while everyone still thinks the project is the most important thing in the universe. It is then up to the contract manager to make the meetings sufficiently useful to both parties to retain that level of access.

Risk Review

Now is a good time to have a thorough review of the risk register and the risk management plan for the project. Signing the contract will have changed the status of your procurement process risks and risk controls. Some should be able to be dispensed with altogether. Ongoing risks may have changed if final negotiations resulted in late changes to the contract. Check that these are adequately reflected in your risk assessments.

Although you will have tried to plan ahead for the contract management phase, things develop a whole new focus when the deed is done. You now have, not a hypothetical contractor with generic characteristics, but a specific contractor bringing with them specific risks. Generic risks of manufacture in a foreign country are now specific risks of manufacture in the country selected by your contractor. The generic risk of communications failures between the Agency and the contractor may be augmented by the location of the contractor's main team in a different city. Generic construction risks are now the specific risks of the design and methods of construction adopted by the contractor.

The hypothetical is now actual. Conduct a full review and make sure the updated risk management plan really is being implemented.

Explaining the Contract

You have lived and breathed this contract for months. You, your contract manager and your lead lawyer not only know every provision in it, you also know why the provisions that aren't in it were left out. Everybody else is, to a greater or lesser extent, dangerously ignorant.

It is very easy to assume people know more than they do.

That includes the project team. It is very easy to assume people know more than they do. Yes, they have been working on the project for months, but the hours the technical team spent discussing the specification were also hours they spent not discussing the commercial terms. Promises the contractor made in the original bid documentation may not have survived through to contract signature, but the people who evaluated the bid are not necessarily aware of that. When you realise the project team doesn't know everything, it will occur to you that the ignorance of the rest of the organisation is probably abysmal.

This can be a major issue if other parts of the organisation are responsible for delivering some of Government's obligations under the contract. Before the Agency entered into the contract, you sought assurances from the relevant executives that their teams were able to deliver those obligations, but the people doing the work may not have appreciated the implications and the executives may have moved on. It is one thing to put the demolition of a building into a work schedule, for instance, but schedules are easily rearranged, especially when the relevant project manager is unaware of the scale of the damages your contractor could seek for delays caused by being given late access to a cleared site. For a privately-financed mega-project, delay costs could amount to a million dollars a day.

For a privately-financed mega-project, delay costs could amount to a million dollars a day.

Ignorance is dangerous. Do not bother to hand out copies of the transaction bible except to the in-house lawyer and the contract manager. Few people will expend the energy required to read it and many people wouldn't understand it even if they did read it. Put together a mini roadshow explaining the contract and take it round the Agency and other stakeholders, including the surviving steering committees. Make sure people understand where their contribution fits into the project and what the contractual implications are if they fail to deliver. Let the contract manager lead the roadshows. If the contract is to be managed successfully, it is critical that the person in charge of managing it understands it very thoroughly. Explaining things to other people really fixes it in your mind, so let the contract manager do the explaining.

The other benefit of explaining to other people how the contract works right up front is that, if a mistake has been made, you will find out at a time when it may still be possible to do something about it. On one contract where cost overruns were to be shared between the parties, I prepared a presentation on how the sharing mechanism operated, using a number of worked examples. I was appalled to discover an error in the formula that had been missed by everyone (including me), which had the effect that the more defects in the final deliverable, the more the contractor would be paid. Needless to say, this was the reverse of what was intended. My discovery was made within days of concluding the contract, so it was not difficult to persuade the contractor to acknowledge the error and sign an amending agreement. If the error had gone undetected until the original negotiators had moved on, it could have been a different story, particularly if the parties had been in dispute at the time.

Do not lose the slide pack from the roadshow after the initial presentation. Natural staff turnover on the project and within the Agency will mean an ongoing need to educate people about the contract and there will probably be another Government along shortly, with a new Minister to brief.

The Contractor Relationship

Behaviours driven by a desire to win the contract may not survive contract award.

The team that won the bid is not the team that delivers the contract. This may be literally true: key personnel restrictions in the contract can give only limited comfort about team stability and quality. But it is also true in another sense: even if the individuals don't change, the management of them does. Behaviours driven by a desire to win the contract may not survive contract award, as the contractor's project manager becomes subject to the relentless private sector pressure to meet the monthly budget. A specification that was originally examined to see how the tenderer could deliver something attractive to the customer is now examined to see how it can be delivered more cheaply.

Efficiency is desirable. Cutting corners indiscriminately is not. If the Agency is to receive the deliverables it is paying for, the contractor needs to know from the start that you are paying attention and will hold them to the contract.

CONTRACT GOVERNANCE

The contract contains provision for the governance of the relationship between the Agency and the contractor. Where regular meetings are called for, start the groups running as soon as you can. You need to establish the ground rules early on. If the contract is an alliance contract, for instance, and that model is not familiar both to the parties and the individuals on the teams, it will not work the way it is supposed to unless you take active steps to promote and nurture alliance contract behaviours. (It may come as a surprise to many people with a public sector background, who are used to contractors making a profit at Government's expense, that it is possible to structure a cost sharing arrangement so the more profit the contractor makes, the lower the total cost to Government.) Conversely, people used to alliance contracts may have difficulty coming to terms with the rigid structure of a privately-financed project. Some joint workshops may help both parties develop a shared understanding of how they will operate.

That shared understanding is really important, but don't get too carried away with the touchy-feely stuff, even in an alliance contract. This is a competitively-awarded contract, not a negotiated partnership or joint venture. (A so-called Public Private Partnership is not a partnership at all.) The idea is to achieve mutually beneficial collaboration within the framework of a contract that has fixed consequences for defined outcomes. Collaboration, not blurring or changing the obligations of the parties.

Matching lightweights against heavyweights gives one-sided outcomes in business as in boxing.

You also need to give some thought to structuring the one-on-one communications channels between the parties. Their project director and your contract manager are an obvious pairing, but others may need more thought. Depending on the type of project, for instance, their design manager and your design review manager may be necessary counterparts. An important factor in the choice of individuals to take on the various roles in the contract management team is whether they have the expertise, experience and emotional intelligence to deal with their opposite number at the contractor. Matching lightweights against heavyweights gives one-sided outcomes in business as in boxing. If individuals are over-matched, build support for them into the governance and communications arrangements. Stick strictly to contract protocols requiring contract amendments to be formally confirmed in writing. Consider having a senior adviser present at key meetings to assist an inexperienced manager.

UNDERSTANDING CONTRACTUAL INCENTIVES

Remember that the contractor's organisation and project team will be as ignorant as yours. You worked hard in structuring the contract to ensure the incentives would drive the right behaviour. If the people on the contractor's project team are not sufficiently familiar with the contract, they may not realise the implications. In the Waratah train procurement, the contractor started to receive the payments for the daily availability of each train when the train was delivered but was also subject to incentives for the reliable performance of the trains in service. The contractor needed to balance the opportunity to receive availability payments, which pushed them to deliver early, with the need to meet reliability targets, which pushed them to run the trains in testing for longer before putting them into service. In such situations, any failure of the contractor to understand the incentive structure will lead to the 'wrong' behaviour, which does neither party any good.

If the contract includes provision for a Dispute Resolution Board, the need to explain the contract to the Board, who come in with no previous understanding of it, can provide useful cover for explaining the contract to the contractor's representatives, who may otherwise insist they need no explanation even if they do. A joint presentation at the first meeting, normally within one month of contract award, will aid the understanding of the parties as well as the Board.

KEY PERSONNEL

It often seems the first thing to happen after contract award is that the contractor turns up with changes to the key personnel listed in the contract. This is deeply irritating, since the quality of these people was part of the reason you selected the contractor in the first place. If the list has more than a handful of people on it, however, it is probably inevitable that at least one person will have had a better offer and moved on. It is difficult for a bidder to build a committed team when they haven't yet won the contract. There is no point in complaining if someone is no longer employed by the contractor, but some righteous indignation is called for if the person is being transferred elsewhere in the contractor's organisation. Bidding with the A Team and building with the B Team is not acceptable. Regrettably, that doesn't mean it doesn't happen.

Bidding with the A Team and building with the B Team is not acceptable.

Changes are not automatically bad. The failure of the other bidders to win the contract may free up good people – perhaps better people – to join the contractor. But the quality of the people on the contractor's project team may be the difference between success and failure of the project. The contract will have given the Agency rights to approve or review changes to the key personnel list, so make use of those rights: at the very least insist on seeing CVs and checking you are being offered equivalent or better qualifications and experience.

REDUCING FRICTION

Many projects will involve critical interactions between the Agency and the contractor that will be repeated many times: submission of a design by the contractor for review by the Agency; the Agency granting access to a site for the contractor to start work; the contractor presenting a completed unit for inspection and acceptance testing by the Agency. One of the best things you and the contractor can do in the early stages of the project is take the first instance of an interaction, plan it in detail and run it as a pilot. Follow up immediately to see how it can be done better. Then do the same thing with the next one. Some of these interactions may happen hundreds of times. If each one is a source of friction, that generates a lot of heat. A bit of effort up front can save an extraordinary amount of time and angst later.

Building Momentum

Every project manager knows that when a project is well advanced, you rarely need to look at the schedule to discover what is on the critical path. Some days it seems every person who calls is either complaining of being held up because of delays somewhere else or seeking assurance that they won't be. You have no need to generate a sense of urgency because everyone else is doing it for you.

In the early days, it is much more difficult. People rarely grasp that when something takes 12 months to do, and the delivery date is 12 months away, they have to start *now*. You are likely to have much more trouble in this regard with the people delivering the Government obligations under the contract than with the contractor. You probably put milestone payments into the contract, some capable of being achieved relatively quickly, to give the contractor an incentive to get on with it. Your public sector project managers have no such incentive.

There is a tendency for people to think everything is the contractor's problem and they don't have to worry about it until the project has been delivered. But not only does Government often have to make significant inputs during the delivery phase to enable the contractor to do the job, it is also the case that if the operational phase isn't being planned simultaneously with the delivery phase, the handover from delivery to operations will be a fiasco.

It can be hard for people to grasp the magnitude of what has happened. If you have just set up a billion dollar contract then, by definition, the business of the Agency is a billion dollars' worth of different. It just doesn't look much different on day one. It is up to you to share the vision and the schedule and get people moving.

It is up to you to share the vision and the schedule and get people moving.

Before You Go

Once you are satisfied your handover to the contract manager is a handover rather than a hospital pass, it is time to move on. Before you go, take the trouble to leave behind a 'lessons learned'. The art and science of setting up major Government contracts is constantly evolving and every project has its own subtleties and pitfalls. Hold one last workshop and capture the things everyone did well and the things that could have been done better. Learning from experience is good. Learning from other people's experience is so much less painful. Save the next project director from doing it the hard way.

Chapter 19
A Final Word

This book has been my own attempt at a 'lessons learned', not from a single project, but from 30 years in the public and private sectors. I was driven to it by the number of major Government projects in various countries that have ended in acrimonious dispute because of basic failures in the procurement process. Millions upon millions upon millions of pounds and dollars thrown away on fiascos that could have been avoided. Millions upon millions upon millions of pounds and dollars that could have been spent achieving something worthwhile. Governments do *not* have to go on making these mistakes. Failure is avoidable. Success is achievable.

I look back at the book now and wonder if the messages I really wanted to pass on have made it through. Have I generated yet another standard form that people will apply mindlessly and then wonder why everything has fallen round their ankles? I hope not. Let me offer some final precepts to take away with you. They should now be fully familiar, but in case you missed something along the way, here are my top ten.

1. **Be clear on the objectives**
   If you are not given clear objectives, help your muddled bosses to work out what they want. Keep the objectives in mind whenever you make a decision and put the objectives in front of other stakeholders whenever they have to do the same. If you don't know where you want to go you will end up somewhere else.

2. **Leave your brain switched on**
   Setting up a major project can take over your entire existence. There are so many things to be done, people to be consulted, information to be evaluated. Do not become so absorbed that you lose the plot. There needs to be a bit of your brain left over that can look on what is happening with sufficient detachment to assess where you are and whether you are still aiming at the right target.

3. **Find the best people**
Mega-projects come with mega-risks and mega-decisions. You won't get first-rate outcomes with third-rate people. Expensive good advice costs less than cheap bad advice. Mix public sector and private sector experience, employees and contractors, old hands and new faces, whichever way works to give you the full range of skill sets and an energising diversity of perspective. Plan ahead so the people are there when you need them. Have some reserve capacity to call on in a crisis.

4. **Identify the scope. All of it**
The scope for the contractor, the scope for Government, the scope for your team. Who does what and how everything fits together. If you define the scope correctly up front, you know the expertise you want from your contractor, the bidders will price the job you need them to do and the finished product will fit seamlessly into the operations of the Agency. And if you get the scope right in the first place, you won't be tempted into project-killing variations.

5. **Allocate risk to people who know what to do with it**
The primary job of the contract is to allocate risk to parties capable of managing it. A risk misallocated is a risk mispriced – and it is usually Government that picks up the bill. Align the contract risk incentives with the behaviours you want to encourage. Contractors follow the money, so make sure it leads them to the right place.

6. **Design the right procurement process**
The standard form of anything will never be appropriate for a mega-project. Having the right procurement process is essential because you may end up in court if you don't follow it. If the process doesn't work, fix the process. You don't have to fix the standard form itself, just its application to your project.

7. **Consult. Properly**
Consult the market, consult your stakeholders, consult your team. Other people know things you don't. Listen to what they tell you, even if it's not something you want to hear. Especially if it's not something you want to hear. Ignoring problems just gives them time to grow into bigger problems. Always make allowance in the schedule for the changes that will be necessary after a consultation.

8. **Insist on good governance**

   A mega-project is not your personal frolic. Tempting as it may be to evade the supervision of the ignorant fools who seek to fetter your genius, the right governance framework will both assist and protect you. People in the senior echelons of the public sector are rarely fools and it is your job to enlighten any ignorance you may encounter. Your reputation contributes to the success or failure of the project. Safeguard it with governance that demonstrates your integrity to others.

9. **Distinguish between price and value for money**

   A low price is a snare and a delusion. No contractor undertakes a mega-project as a loss leader. If you do not understand how the contractor can make money, do not sign the contract. Either the contractor will make money in ways you are not anticipating (such as delivering low quality work or claiming variations for things you mistakenly thought were included in the price) or they will lose money, with the attendant risk that the project will be delivered badly or not at all.

10. **Acknowledge your own fallibility**

    As a leader, you need to make decisions with confidence and competence. That doesn't mean they won't be wrong. Consider always the possibility of error. No one is perfect and you have a lot on your plate. Actively seek out diverse perspectives and make sure your team feels able to challenge your opinions. Before you make any significant decision, pause, reflect, consult. Solicit independent review of both process and substance.

I would love to be able to say that if you follow these precepts you can't go wrong, but my professional indemnity insurance couldn't take the hit. The world can always find new pathways to error and law courts will never go out of business.

But please, please, don't go out and make the same stupid mistakes Government made last time. Almost all failures are utterly unnecessary. Set up your project for success.

Appendix: Case Study References

This Appendix sets out brief highlights of the principal case studies identified in this book, together with the main references used. Projects referred to in the text but not included in this Appendix have been sourced from my own experience, interviews with participants, Government websites or media reports. I have generally avoided the use of material not already in the public domain.

Without exception, the cases were more complicated than I have made them appear. In selecting facts to make a point it is not practicable to acknowledge the full range of pressures the decision-makers were struggling with at the time. I am only too well aware from personal experience that one can in good faith and with the best of intentions make or acquiesce in decisions which hindsight would have dismissed as a thoroughly bad idea. My apologies to anyone who feels I have been unfairly critical.

Air Traffic Control System

The Australian Civil Aviation Authority commenced a tender process for the procurement of an air traffic control system in 1991. The aim was to sign a contract within 12 months, an extremely tight timetable given that significant negotiations with the preferred bidder would be required. In the event, a contract was not signed until almost two years after the original target date and the Authority was still unsuccessfully defending its actions before the Federal Court three years later.

The tender process was particularly notable for poor decisions made by the Board of the Civil Aviation Authority because of poor submissions made to them. Three bidders rather than two were shortlisted because a table of the relative ratings of the bidders in specific areas, which would have shown clearly the third bidder had no chance, was omitted from the report. A preferred bidder recommendation was rejected because an accompanying note from the chief executive misled the Board into thinking the recommended bid was very risky. The final preferred bidder recommendation was accepted on the basis of material suggesting a significant difference between the bidders, without the Board having the benefit of an expert report pointing out that the difference was not necessarily significant. That decision was set aside following the Macphee Review and the process was rerun with only the two remaining shortlisted bidders participating.

The later court case related to the rerun. Far from having learned its lesson, the Authority was found to have failed to evaluate the new tenders in accordance with the methodology in the Request for Tenders and to have accepted an out of time change from one bidder without informing the other – elementary process errors that could easily have been avoided.

SOURCES

The Honourable Ian Macphee AO, *Independent review of the Civil Aviation Authority's Tender Evaluation Process for The Australian Advanced Air Traffic System*, Australian Government Publications Service 1992.

Hughes Aircraft Systems International v. Air Services Australia (1997) 76 FCR 151. [Note: The action was brought against Air Services Australia as the successor body to the Civil Aviation Authority].

CH-148 Cyclone Helicopters

This case illustrates the dangers of post-contract variations to the specification. The contract for the $1.8 billion purchase of 28 CH-148 Cyclone helicopters by the Canadian Government was signed in 2004 but was amended soon after to include additional electronics and armaments. The weight of this equipment triggered the need for design and development of more powerful engines, which then required a re-engineering of the entire helicopter. Delivery was put back from 2008, first to 2010 then successively so that by the end of 2014 the anticipated delivery date was 2018 – a decade late.

SOURCES

2010 Fall Report of the Auditor General of Canada to the House of Commons, Minister of Public Works and Government Services Canada 2010.

'The Worst Procurement in the History of Canada': Solving the Maritime Helicopter Crisis, Michael Byers and Stewart Webb, Canadian Centre for Policy Alternatives, February 2013.

Holyrood Inquiry

The bill for the construction of a new Scottish Parliament building at Holyrood went from a January 1998 estimate of £90 million for completion in July 2001 to a final £431 million completing in August 2004. The inquiry by The Rt Hon Lord Fraser of Carmyllie QC found the major issue was the decision to adopt a 'construction management' approach, which left the design and construction risks with a client not well placed to manage them.

SOURCES

The Holyrood Inquiry: A Report by The Rt Hon Lord Fraser of Carmyllie QC on his Inquiry into the Holyrood Building Project, Scottish Parliamentary Corporate Body, September 2004.

Management of the Holyrood Building Project, The Auditor General for Scotland and Audit Scotland, June 2004.

The New Scottish Parliament Building: An Examination of the Management of the Holyrood Project, The Auditor General for Scotland and Audit Scotland, September 2000.

InterCity West Coast Franchise case

In 2012 the UK Department for Transport embarked on a tender process for the InterCity West Coast franchise, one of the largest passenger rail franchises in the country. A preferred bidder was selected, but the runner-up, Virgin Trains, brought an action for judicial review before the £5.5 billion contract could be signed. The Department then investigated and discovered a number of problems, principally relating to the use of a financial model that had originally been developed to calibrate a provision in the franchise contract for the sharing of GDP risk (GDP is highly correlated with rail passenger revenues). The same model was then extended to calculate the amount of a subordinated loan facility to be provided on behalf of the franchisee: it was not fit for this purpose. In addition to the problems inherent in the model, the Department had calculated the amounts of the facility in a way which was different from the process notified to the bidders. The competition was cancelled, meaning that Virgin Trains, as the incumbent, secured a two-year extension of its franchise to enable the competition to be re-run.

The inquiries into the failed competition were thorough and provide an unusually close and fascinating look at the workings of a Government tender process. Although various deficiencies were identified, the fundamental failure was of governance. The project team knew that if they released the financial model they were using to the bidders, their process would be challenged. They therefore chose not to release the model. No one was able to step far enough back to see that their efforts might be better directed at establishing a process that would not be challenged.

SOURCES

Report of the Laidlaw Inquiry, 6 December 2012 (HC 809).

Report by the Comptroller and Auditor General, 7 December 2012 (HC796).

The Brown Review of the Rail Franchising Programme, January 2013 (Cm 8526).

Transport Committee Eighth Report of Session 2012–13 (HC 537).

Jasper Inquiry

This Inquiry by the New South Wales Independent Commission Against Corruption serves as a reminder of the value of following due process in the prevention of corruption. The investigation was code-named 'Operation Jasper'. The NSW Government sought tenders for coal exploration licences. The Minister corruptly sought to favour associates, with conduct including improperly influencing the selection of the licence area, passing confidential information to associates, and extending the tender period after it had already closed in order to allow an associate to bid. The extension of the tender period, although clearly not in accordance with proper process, went unchallenged.

SOURCES

Investigation into the Conduct of Ian Macdonald, Edward Obeid Senior, Moses Obeid and Others, Independent Commission Against Corruption Report, July 2013.

Metronet PPP

In 1998 the UK Government decided to set up public private partnerships for the private sector to maintain and upgrade the London underground railway, which would continue to be operated in the public sector by London Underground. A consortium known as Metronet was awarded two of the three contracts, which were finally signed in 2003 notwithstanding the vigorous protests from Ken Livingstone, the Mayor of London.

Costs promptly escalated by many hundreds of millions of pounds, and an interim review by the PPP Arbiter indicated that Metronet would be able to pass only a small proportion of those costs to Government. In 2007, Metronet went into administration and Government had to pick up the pieces.

These public private partnerships could be used to provide a case study on practically anything, since they were complex and wide ranging in their obligations and highly controversial in their establishment. One key issue was the extraordinary inefficiencies generated by a 'tied supply chain': four of the five members of the Metronet consortium set up a separate 'special purpose vehicle' called Trans4m, through which they awarded themselves generous subcontracts. The contract with Trans4m gave Metronet very little in the way of enforcement levers and Metronet had little opportunity to contract work elsewhere on more reasonable terms.

SOURCES

Anthony King and Ivor Crewe, *The Blunders of Our Governments*, Oneworld Publications, 2013. (This is a splendid book, covering far more than the Metronet PPP. I recommend it.)

Louise Butcher, *London Underground PPP: Background*, Standard Note: SN1307, House of Commons Library, updated 16 January 2012.

House of Commons Transport Committee, *Update on the London Underground and the Public-Private (PPP) Partnership Agreements, Seventh Report of Session 2009–10*, 26 March 2010.

House of Commons Transport Committee, *The London Underground and the Public–Private Partnership Agreements, Second Report of Session 2007–08*, 25 January 2008.

House of Commons Committee of Public Accounts, *London Underground Public Private Partnerships, Seventeenth Report of Session 2004–05*, 31 March 2005.

House of Commons Transport Committee, *The Performance of the London Underground: Sixth Report of Session 2004–05*, 18 March 2005.

National Audit Office, *London Underground PPP: Were They Good Deals? Report by the Comptroller and Auditor General HC 645 Session 2003-2004*, 17 June 2004.

Christian Wolmar, *Down the Tube: The Battle for London's Underground*, Aurum Press, November 2002/Kemsing Publishing 2012.

House of Commons Transport, Local Government and the Regions Select Committee, *Second Report: London Underground*, 5 February 2002.

New South Wales Integrated Ticketing case

In 1999 the New South Wales Government commenced a procurement process for a ticketing system that would use a single software platform for tickets on all public transport. Two bidders were shortlisted. Following the announcement of a preferred bidder, a member of the losing consortium sought to prevent the award of contract. The plaintiff appears to have been the tenderer from hell. The court found 'lack of good faith' and 'gross breaches of their obligations of honesty' and also found that 'part of its strategic plan was, if possible, to prevent the [project] from going ahead at all if [the other party] was the successful contractor'.

Although the Government was ultimately successful in the litigation, the judge was scathing about the terms and conditions contained in the call for tenders: 'Aspirational statements may provide a warm inner glow but they are no substitute for unambiguous language targeted at actual risks with clearly stated consequences. Had such a call been issued in this case, this litigation may well not have ensued.' Attention to matters of process pays dividends.

SOURCE

Cubic Transportation Systems Inc & Anor v State of New South Wales & 2 ors [2002] NSWSC 656.

Portcullis House

Portcullis House was built for the UK House of Commons at Westminster in the late 1990s. Protections against terrorist attack meant the windows were 'probably the most expensive fenestration system ever'. The tender process for the fenestration contract underwent a number of revisions while in progress, affected by a lack of understanding of the law applying to the process and a wish to favour British firms. A key issue was that the tender documents for the fenestration contract failed to set out specific evaluation criteria. An official compounded the error by giving a losing bidder false reasons for the selection decision. The bidder had offered the lowest price and successfully sued the Corporate Officer of the House of Commons for failing to award them the contract.

SOURCES

Harmon CFEM Facades (UK) Ltd v. The Corporate Officer of the House of Commons [1999] EWHC Technology 199.

Queensland Health Payroll System Inquiry

The introduction of a new payroll system for Queensland Health in March 2010 was described by the subsequent Commission of Inquiry as a 'catastrophic failure'. Thousands of staff received the wrong amount, or nothing at all. It took months to develop a functioning payroll system, with more than 400 additional payroll staff engaged to enable Queensland Health to pay its employees.

The case can be used to draw many different lessons, since there were many different mistakes. Perhaps the most striking was the impact made by the man who was in effect the project director for Government, a contractor who was allowed to operate with 'exuberant indiscretion' and virtually no supervision or governance. He was appointed despite the express written refusal of his previous manager to provide any reference. The Executive Director to whom he reported received complaints about his exceeding his authority but, far from dealing with the matter, left him 'unchallenged and uncontrolled'. He was allowed to issue a Request for Proposals which took the form of a short email, with no suggestion that his manager realised how inappropriate this was for a contract for a prime contractor role on a project of this scale. No action was taken even in relation to an allegation (upheld by the Commission of Inquiry) that he had improperly interfered with the evaluation process.

Also notable was the complexity of the project requirements: the payroll system had to support 85,000 staff employed under two different pieces of legislation, covered by 12 industrial awards and impacted by six different industrial agreements, which between them created over 200 allowances and up to 24,000 combinations of pay. Government failed either to simplify the project requirements or to implement any effective management of the risks imported by such complexity.

SOURCES

The Hon Richard Chesterman AO RFD QC, *Queensland Health Payroll System Commission of Inquiry Report*, 31 July 2013.

KPMG, *Queensland Health: Review of the Queensland Health Payroll System*, 31 May 2012.

Auditor-General of Queensland, Report to Parliament No.7 for 2010, 'Information Systems Governance and Control, Iincluding the Queensland Health Implementation of Continuity Project', Finance and Compliance Audits, June 2010.

Railtrack Privatisation

Railtrack was created as part of the privatisation of British Rail in the mid-1990s. It was the owner and operator of all of the railway infrastructure (except trains) formerly owned by British Rail. Its privatisation was extremely controversial, pushed through in the dying days of a Conservative Government against virulent protest from a Labour Opposition that was correctly expected to win a landslide victory as soon as the Government could be forced to the polls. The privatisation process was unimpeachable: no action was brought under the prospectus even though the later abrupt descent into administration occurred within the applicable statute of limitations. That success had a price, measured in the compromises made to secure the flotation. The subsequent history of Railtrack was short and inglorious. The delivery of Stage 1 of the Channel Tunnel Rail Link on time and on budget, perhaps its one genuinely impressive achievement, was airbrushed out of history when its interests in the Link were divested as part of the 2002 settlement with Government following the administration.

SOURCES

The Flotation of Railtrack, Report by the Comptroller and Auditor General, HC 25 Session 1998-99, 16 December 1998.

Christian Wolmar, *On the Wrong Line: How Ideology and Incompetence Wrecked Britain's Railways*, Kernsing Publishing, 2012 or Aurum Press 2005, revised and updated from the original, *Broken Rails*, Aurum Press 2001.

DISCLAIMER

I was employed by Railtrack Limited, the network-owning subsidiary of Railtrack Group PLC, from May 1995 until December 2002. I joined the company, then Government owned, as Privatisation Legal Adviser. After the flotation in 1996 I remained with the company in various roles, mostly related to the establishment or re-negotiation of major contracts, until the conclusion of the settlement with Government after the company had been placed in administration in 2001. Any opinions expressed in relation to the company are my own, and should not be attributed to my former employer.

Royal Mail Privatisation

In October 2013, the UK Government sold 60 per cent of its shares in Royal Mail plc which was then listed on the London Stock Exchange. The shares, sold at 330 pence, closed on the first day of trading at 455 pence, a 38 per cent increase. Five months later the shares were trading 72 per cent above the sale price. The National Audit Office found the Government could have achieved better value, notwithstanding the market uncertainties associated with a strike ballot of employees and the possibility of the United States breaching its debt ceiling. Among other issues:

- The independent corporate financial adviser was only incentivised to achieve the sale, not to optimise value for the taxpayer.

- The inherent limitations of the standard book-building process adopted meant it was not effective at revealing demand for shares at prices above the high end of the published range and lacked flexibility for a price increase when demand exceeded expectations.

SOURCES

The Privatisation of Royal Mail, National Audit Office, HC (2013-14) 1182.

Royal Mail Privatisation, House of Commons Business, Innovation and Skills Committee, HC (2014-15) 539.

Waratah Train Procurement

The Waratah train procurement involved the procurement of 626 carriages of double-deck passenger rolling stock, 78 × eight-car trains plus two spare cars, by Rail Corporation New South Wales through a Public Private Partnership. The contractor also constructed a test track and maintenance facility and provided simulators for training purposes. The procurement was initiated in 2004, the contract was signed in 2006 with a net present value of $3.65 billion and the last train was delivered in 2014. The contractor will continue to maintain the trains and make them available to Sydney Trains, a successor to Rail Corporation New South Wales, for around 30 years.

Some areas of particular interest are:

- The procurement phase lasted around two and a half years. Public Private Partnerships do require a significant set-up period, but this one could have been concluded up to 12 months earlier had the Government not decided to use the procurement process to facilitate the strategic decision of whether to procure single-deck or double-deck rolling stock.

- The contract contained a range of obligations and incentives intended to smooth the introduction of the trains into service. Government also identified and carried out various enabling works and planning activities outside the scope of the contract for the same purpose. The introduction of the trains was remarkably successful, with on-time running of the network sustained throughout the delivery period.

- The trains were delivered later than planned in the original contract schedule. The first train was more than a year late, but the delay was pulled back over the delivery period so the final train was just less than nine months behind schedule. The delay significantly increased the cost to the contractor, not least because of the extended interest on the debt finance, but these costs were essentially passed on to the train manufacturer subcontractor through a liquidated damages provision in the subcontract. Since the new trains were primarily replacements for older trains which could be maintained in service, there was little additional cost to Government.

SOURCES

Rail Corporation New South Wales, *Rolling Stock Public Private Partnership Summary of Contracts,* December 2006 and *Updated Summary of Contracts,* March 2012.

DISCLAIMER

I was employed by Rail Corporation New South Wales from April 2004 as the Project Director for the establishment of the Public Private Partnership for the Waratah train procurement, handing over project responsibility to my successor, who had been working with me throughout, a few months after signature of the contracts. I remained with the Agency until January 2014. Any opinions expressed in relation to the project are my own, and should not be attributed to my former employer.

Index

For Product Safety Concerns and Information please contact our EU
representative GPSR@taylorandfrancis.com
Taylor & Francis Verlag GmbH, Kaufingerstraße 24, 80331 München, Germany

www.ingramcontent.com/pod-product-compliance
Ingram Content Group UK Ltd.
Pitfield, Milton Keynes, MK11 3LW, UK
UKHW050054200926
475702UK00019B/2824

* 9 7 8 1 0 3 2 8 3 7 2 4 6 *